RECONSTRUCTION
O P P O S I N G   V I E W P O I N T S®

Other Books in the American History Series:

RECONSTRUCTION

OPPOSING VIEWPOINTS®

David L. Bender, *Publisher*
Bruno Leone, *Executive Editor*

William Dudley, *Series Editor*
John C. Chalberg, Ph.D., professor of history,
Normandale Community College, *Consulting
Editor*

Brenda Stalcup, *Book Editor*

Greenhaven Press, Inc.
San Diego, California

Cover illustrations, clockwise from top: 1) 1868 *Harper's Weekly* illustration of disguised Ku Klux Klan members (Archive Photos); 2) photograph of ruins in Charleston, South Carolina (National Archives); 3) photograph of Andrew Johnson (Library of Congress); 1867 *Harper's Weekly* illustration of blacks voting (Stock Montage, Inc.)

Library of Congress Cataloging-in-Publication Data

Reconstruction : opposing viewpoints / Brenda Stalcup, book
    editor.
        p.   cm. — (American history series)
    Includes bibliographical references (p.   ) and index.
    ISBN 1-56510-227-4 (library) — ISBN 1-56510-226-6 (pbk.)
    1. Reconstruction. 2. Reconstruction—Sources.
    3. Reconstruction—Historiography. I. Stalcup, Brenda.
    II. Series: American history series (San Diego, Calif.)
    E668.R42   1995   94-28639
    973.8—dc20   CIP
                                                                          AC

© 1995 by Greenhaven Press, Inc., PO Box 289009,
San Diego, CA 92198-9009

Printed in the U.S.A.

"America was born of revolt, flourished in dissent, became great through experimentation."

Henry Steele Commager, American Historian, 1902-1984

Contents

Foreword

Aboard the *Arbella* as it lurched across the cold, gray Atlantic, John Winthrop was as calm as the waters surrounding him were wild. With the confidence of a leader, Winthrop gathered his Puritan companions around him. It was time to offer a sermon. England lay behind them, and years of strife and persecution for their religious beliefs were over, he said. But the Puritan abandonment of England, he reminded his followers, did not mean that England was beyond redemption. Winthrop wanted his followers to remember England even as they were leaving it behind. Their goal should be to create a new England, one far removed from the authority of the Anglican church and King Charles I. In Winthrop's words, their settlement in the New World ought to be "a city upon a hill," a just society for corrupt England to emulate.

A Chance to Start Over

One June 8, 1630, John Winthrop and his company of refugees had their first glimpse of what they came to call New England. High on the surrounding hills stood a welcoming band of fir trees whose fragrance drifted to the *Arbella* on a morning breeze. To Winthrop, the "smell off the shore [was] like the smell of a garden." This new world would, in fact, often be compared to the Garden of Eden. Here, John Winthrop would have his opportunity to start life over again. So would his family and his shipmates. So would all those who came after them. These victims of conflict in old England hoped to find peace in New England.

Winthrop, for one, had experienced much conflict in his life. As a Puritan, he was opposed to Catholicism and Anglicanism, both of which, he believed, were burdened by distracting rituals and distant hierarchies. A parliamentarian by conviction, he despised Charles I, who had spurned Parliament and created a private army to do his bidding. Winthrop believed in individual responsibility and fought against the loss of religious and political freedom. A gentleman landowner, he feared the rising economic power of a merchant class that seemed to value only money. Once Winthrop stepped aboard the *Arbella*, he hoped, these conflicts would not be a part of his American future.

Yet his Puritan religion told Winthrop that human beings are fallen creatures and that perfection, whether communal or individual, is unachievable on this earth. Therefore, he faced a paradox: On the one hand, his religion demanded that he attempt to live a perfect life in an imperfect world. On the other hand, it told him that he was destined to fail.

Soon after Winthrop disembarked from the *Arbella*, he came face-to-face with this maddening dilemma. He found himself presiding not over a utopia but over a colony caught up in disputes as troubling as any he had confronted in his English past. John Winthrop, it seems, was not the only Puritan with a dream of a heaven on earth. But others in the community saw the dream differently. They wanted greater political and religious freedom than their leader was prepared to grant. Often, Winthrop was able to handle this conflict diplomatically. For example, he expanded, participation in elections and allowed the voters of Massachusetts Bay greater power.

But religious conflict was another matter because it was grounded in competing visions of the Puritan utopia. In Roger Williams and Anne Hutchinson, two of his fellow colonists, John Winthrop faced rivals unprepared to accept his definition of the perfect community. To Williams, perfection demanded that he separate himself from the Puritan institutions in his community and create an even "purer" church. Winthrop, however, disagreed and exiled Williams to Rhode Island. Hutchinson presumed that she could interpret God's will without a minister. Again, Winthrop did not agree. Hutchinson was tried on charges of heresy, convicted, and banished from Massachusetts.

John Winthrop's Massachusetts colony was the first but far from the last American attempt to build a unified, peaceful community that, in the end, only provoked a discord. This glimpse at its history reveals what Winthrop confronted: the unavoidable presence of conflict in American life.

American Assumptions

From America's origins in the early seventeenth century, Americans have often held several interrelated assumptions about their country. First, people believe that to be American is to be free. Second, because Americans did not have to free themselves from feudal lords or an entrenched aristocracy, America has been seen as a perpetual haven from the troubles and disputes that are found in the Old World.

John Winthrop lived his life as though these assumptions were true. But the opposing viewpoints presented in the American History Series should reveal that for many Americans, these assumptions were and are myths. Indeed, for numerous Americans, liberty has not always been guaranteed, and disputes have been an integral, sometimes welcome part of their life.

The American landscape has been torn apart again and again by a great variety of clashes—theological, ideological, political, economic, geographical, and social. But such a landscape is not necessarily a hopelessly divided country. If the editors hope to prove anything during the course of this series, it is not that the United States has been destroyed by conflict but rather that it has been enlivened, enriched, and even strengthened by Americans who have disagreed with one another.

Thomas Jefferson was one of the least confrontational of Americans, but he boldly and irrevocably enriched American life with his individualistic views. Like John Winthrop before him, he had a notion of an American Eden. Like Winthrop, he offered a vision of a harmonious society. And like Winthrop, he not only became enmeshed in conflict but eventually presided over a people beset by it. But unlike Winthrop, Jefferson believed this Eden was not located in a specific community but in each individual American. His Declaration of Independence from Great Britain could also be read as a declaration of independence for each individual in American society.

Jefferson's Ideal

Jefferson's ideal world was composed of "yeoman farmers," each of whom was roughly equal to the others in society's eyes, each of whom was free from the restrictions of both government and fellow citizens. Throughout his life, Jefferson offered a continuing challenge to Americans: Advance individualism and equality or see the death of the American experiment. Jefferson believed that the strength of this experiment depended upon a society of autonomous individuals and a society without great gaps between rich and poor. His challenge to his fellow Americans to create—and sustain—such a society has itself produced both economic and political conflict.

A society whose guiding document is the Declaration of Independence is a society assured of the freedom to dream—and to disagree. We know that Jefferson hated conflict, both personal and political. His tendency was to avoid confrontations of any sort, to squirrel himself away and write rather than to stand up and speak his mind. It is only through his written words that we can grasp Jefferson's utopian dream of a society of independent farmers, all pursuing their private dreams and all leading lives of middling prosperity.

Jefferson, this man of wealth and intellect, lived an essentially happy private life. But his public life was much more troublesome. From the first rumblings of the American Revolution in the 1760s to the North-South skirmishes of the 1820s that ultimately produced the Civil War, Jefferson was at or near the center of American political history. The issues were almost too many—and too crucial—for one lifetime: Jefferson had to choose between sup-

11

porting or rejecting the path of revolution. During and after the ensuing war, he was at the forefront of the battle for religious liberty. After endorsing the Constitution, he opposed the economic plans of Alexander Hamilton. At the end of the century, he fought the infamous Alien and Sedition Acts, which limited civil liberties. As president, he opposed the Federalist court, conspiracies to divide the union, and calls for a new war against England. Throughout his life, Thomas Jefferson, slaveholder, pondered the conflict between American freedom and American slavery. And from retirement at his Monticello retreat, he frowned at the rising spirit of commercialism he feared was dividing Americans and destroying his dream of American harmony.

No matter the issue, however, Thomas Jefferson invariably supported the rights of the individual. Worried as he was about the excesses of commercialism, he accepted them because his main concern was to live in a society where liberty and individualism could flourish. To Jefferson, Americans had to be free to worship as they desired. They also deserved to be free from an over-reaching government. To Jefferson, Americans should also be free to possess slaves.

Harmony, an Elusive Goal

Before reading the articles in this anthology, the editors ask readers to ponder the lives of John Winthrop and Thomas Jefferson. Each held a utopian vision, one based upon the demands of community and the other on the autonomy of the individual. Each dreamed of a country of perpetual new beginnings. Each found himself thrust into a position of leadership and found that conflict could not be avoided. Harmony, whether communal or individual, was a forever elusive goal.

The opposing visions of Winthrop and Jefferson have been at the heart of many differences among Americans from many backgrounds through the whole of American history. Moreover, their visions have provoked important responses that have helped shape American society, the American character, and many an American battle.

The editors of the American History Series have done extensive research to find representative opinions on the issues included in these volumes. They have found numerous outstanding opposing viewpoints from people of all times, classes, and genders in American history. From those, they have selected commentaries that best fit the nature and flavor of the period and topic under consideration. Every attempt was made to include the most important and relevant viewpoints in each chapter. Obviously, not every notable viewpoint could be included. Therefore, a selective, annotated bibliography has been provided at the end of each book to aid readers in seeking additional information.

The editors are confident that as this series reveals past conflicts, it will help revitalize the reader's views of the American present. In that spirit, the American History Series is dedicated to the proposition that American history is more complicated, more fascinating, and more troubling than John Winthrop or Thomas Jefferson ever dared to imagine.

John C. Chalberg
Consulting Editor

Introduction

"Reconstruction policies that were originally devised to affect only the South ultimately resulted in the reconstruction of the entire nation."

Early in the morning of April 10, 1865, just before first light, the thunder of cannons woke the residents of Washington, D.C. In communities throughout the North, town bells loudly tolled as citizens went from house to house, pounding on doors to wake those inside. Startled from their peaceful sleep, families asked each other what possibly could be the reason for the alarm. Were Rebel forces approaching? Was the town on fire? As they rushed to the windows and hurried into the streets, the townspeople soon learned the answer: On the previous day, Robert E. Lee had surrendered to Ulysses S. Grant at Appomattox Court House. After four years of war, the Confederates had capitulated; the Union had won. Though there would be scattered fighting for the next few weeks, for all intents and purposes the Civil War was finally over.

The North immediately broke out in exuberant celebration. Union soldiers threw their hats in the air and embraced each other, laughing and crying. In Chicago, 100,000 people marched through the streets in a victory parade. At the nation's capital, an excited crowd gathered at the White House, calling for President Abraham Lincoln and demanding a speech. To the crowd's amusement, Lincoln responded by asking the band to play the Confederate battle song "Dixie." Lincoln explained, "I have always thought 'Dixie' one of the best tunes I have ever heard. Our adversaries over the way attempted to appropriate it, but I insisted yesterday that we fairly captured it." Secretary of the Navy Gideon Welles described the mood of the day in his diary: "The nation seems delirious with joy. Guns are firing, bells ringing, flags flying, men laughing, children cheering; all, all jubilant."

Exhilaration over the news of the surrender caused many Northerners to feel benevolent toward their former foes. In March 1865, in his second inaugural address, President Lincoln had called for "a just and a lasting peace," with "malice toward none; with charity for all." Now that peace had arrived, the American people were inclined to agree with him. At Appomattox, Union troops divided their rations among Lee's starving soldiers, while Grant instructed his officers, "The Rebels are our countrymen again." Two days after the surrender, an editorial in the *Boston Post* suggested:

15

It is natural that this final success should . . . beget expressions of true magnanimity and forgiveness toward the people of the rebellious states, which, three or six months ago, would have been thought impossible. It is but a token of that solid and lasting reunion which we have always insisted was so easy of accomplishment, if proposed in the right spirit.

An easily accomplished reunion was exactly what many Northerners expected. It was a widely held opinion in the North that the southern planter aristocracy had been the moving force behind secession: The majority of Southerners had not really wanted to secede or to fight and therefore would readily rejoin the Union. Nor could four years of warfare completely erase the shared history of the North and the South. The Civil War had not been fought between people who spoke different languages, who followed different religions, or who for centuries had considered each other an alien threat. Although differences in lifestyles and political beliefs had propelled Northerners and Southerners to war, ultimately these were people who spoke the same language, who were accustomed to the same form of government, and who, until very recently, had conducted themselves as one nation. Now that the divisive issue of secession and slavery had been settled by the outcome of the war, Northerners thought, surely the North and the South would fit back together again much as they always had. Writing shortly after Lee's surrender, Professor James Russell Lowell of Harvard University echoed the sentiments of most Northerners: "There is something magnificent in having a country to love. . . . I worry a little about reconstruction, but I am inclined to think that matters will very much settle themselves."

Unfortunately, reconstruction would never progress so smoothly, nor could the conciliatory mood of the North withstand the events of April 14, 1865. That night, while attending a performance at Ford's Theater in Washington, D.C., President Lincoln was shot in the head by John Wilkes Booth, an actor and Confederate sympathizer. Mortally wounded, Lincoln was carried to a nearby boardinghouse as cabinet members and congressmen rushed to the scene. Soon the shocking news came that another attack had occurred: An accomplice of Booth had stabbed Secretary of State William Seward repeatedly, though not fatally. Then a stash of weapons was found in the hotel where Vice President Andrew Johnson was staying—a third accomplice had been sent to kill Johnson but had lost his nerve and fled. It was quickly becoming apparent that there had been a conspiracy not just to kill the president but, by eliminating other high officials, to cripple—or even overthrow—the federal government. Perhaps, thought some of those gathered at Lincoln's bedside, the assassination plot was not the doing of a few deranged individuals; perhaps it was an act of war, devised by the Confederate government in a last desperate effort to save the South.

On the morning of April 15, only five days after Lee's surrender at Appomattox, Abraham Lincoln died. It was the first assassination of a United States president. The North, so recently immersed in celebration, mourned. Charitable feelings toward the South were replaced by distrust, fear, and an intense desire for retribution. George Templeton Strong of New York expressed the northern reaction: "There is a profound, awe-stricken feeling that we are, as it were, in immediate presence of a fearful, gigantic crime, such as has not been committed in our day and can hardly be matched in history. . . . Let us henceforth deal with rebels as they deserve." In his April 26 eulogy for Lincoln, Dr. George B. Loring warned against lenient treatment of the South:

> When those men who had undertaken to destroy the government, and had deluged this land in blood, came forward but half-penitent, . . . [Lincoln's] arms were ever open to receive them, and no bosom was broader than his. My friends, his clemency was his danger. And now that he has laid down his life, let us remember that danger and be warned by it. I insist upon it that the great end for which this war has been fought, the great business of his life, will never be accomplished by what is usually called clemency—mercy not directed by justice.

Secretary of War Edwin Stanton responded to cries for vengeance by organizing an extensive manhunt—not just for John Wilkes Booth and his accomplices, but also for Jefferson Davis, the former president of the Confederacy. Davis was still at large; he had refused to accept the finality of Lee's surrender and had fled into the Deep South, urging his people to continue fighting. Lincoln had been inclined to quietly allow Davis and other Confederate government officials to escape the country, stating that he would not "take any part in hanging or killing those men, even the worst of them." Now, though, Stanton was convinced that Davis was involved in the assassination plot. Andrew Johnson, who had succeeded Lincoln as president, talked loudly of hanging traitors and issued a proclamation that accused Davis of being the mastermind behind the conspiracy. The U.S. government put a $100,000 bounty on Davis's head. On April 25, Booth was cornered by federal troops and killed; four other conspirators were captured and, in the summer of 1865, were tried and hung. The 4th Michigan Cavalry surrounded Jefferson Davis in Georgia on May 10, 1865; Davis surrendered, half expecting to be executed immediately.

Davis, however, had not actually taken part in Booth's assassination conspiracy, and although he would spend two years in prison, he would never stand trial for treason and would be allowed to live out his old age undisturbed. Receiving even more lenient treatment, Robert E. Lee spent the Reconstruction years as president of

Washington College (which would be renamed Washington and Lee University in Lee's honor after his death in 1870). Rather than hanging traitors, tough-talking Andrew Johnson would spend most of his presidency pardoning Confederates by the hundreds. Only one Confederate war criminal would be convicted and executed: Captain Henry Wirz, the commander of the infamous Andersonville prison, where over 13,700 Union prisoners had died from disease, exposure, and starvation. The North might howl for blood and vengeance, but when it came to executing those who had been—and now again were—their own countrymen, most Northerners simply could not go through with it.

In many respects, this conflict between the desire to quickly return the South to its former place in the Union and the desire to take revenge on a defeated adversary is characteristic of the debates of the Reconstruction era. Many Americans felt an intense longing to restore the nation as it had been, or as nearly as possible, and to put the Civil War behind them as if it had never happened. At the same time, though, the outcome of the Civil War had ensured that the United States would be drastically different from what it was before. The main issues that had divided the country—slavery and states' rights—had not really been resolved by the war. True, slavery had been abolished, but there was no consensus on how to integrate the recently freed slaves into American society, and to what extent. True, the war had determined that the southern states would not be allowed to secede and that the federal government was paramount over the individual states, but the exact boundaries of the federal government's jurisdiction had yet to be defined. The America of 1865 was not the America of 1861, and no amount of goodwill could ever bring back "the nation as it was." Throughout Reconstruction, battle-weary Americans would be torn between the desire to ignore the immense changes brought on by the war and the formidable necessity of dealing with those changes.

In the case of the freed slaves, the hands-off approach to Reconstruction was intensified by the ethic of self-determination that was prevalent in nineteenth-century America. According to this theory, any hard-working individual who practiced frugality, self-reliance, and self-discipline would invariably gain wealth, position, and the respect of society. Conversely, those individuals who could not support themselves—who needed aid for food, shelter, and clothing—were considered lazy, lacking the initiative necessary to improve their condition. The northern states in particular adhered to the work ethic, and most Northerners approached the problems arising from emancipation with this belief firmly in mind. The slaves had been given their freedom, had been placed on equal footing with all other Americans, Northerners reasoned. From this point on, blacks should be fully capable of pulling themselves up by their bootstraps, the same way that many white Americans had done.

The difficulty with this theory, of course, was that it assumed the freed slaves *had* a bootstrap. The truth was that most freed slaves didn't even own the rags on their backs; much less did they possess the necessary "bootstraps" of a roof over their heads, a patch of land to grow their food, and a cursory education in reading and writing. Furthermore, many white Southerners had far different ideas about the importance of black self-sufficiency. Cotton was a labor-intensive crop: If the freed slaves settled on their own land and spent their time growing food crops, who would work the cotton fields? Cotton was the South's primary export: If the cotton crop failed, the effect on the South's economy, already shattered by war, would be devastating. Most of the planters were nearly destitute, their Confederate dollars now worthless: How could they be expected to pay cash wages to their black laborers, Southerners demanded, when they had no cash themselves?

For southern whites, the most common way to ensure that former slaves would go back to work in the cotton fields was to systematically deprive blacks of those bootstraps that would allow self-reliance. In many areas of the South, whites uniformly refused to sell land to former slaves or to hire them in any capacity except as field hands. Blacks who did acquire land were often forced off their farms by white intimidation or violence. Southerners replaced slave labor with a system of agriculture called sharecropping, in which black laborers worked not for wages but for a predetermined share of the crop when it was harvested. This system limited the ability of freed slaves to choose their own employers: If the crop failed, or if the laborers had already spent their share of the crop by purchasing goods on credit, they would be required to continue working for the same planter until their debt was paid off. By charging exorbitant prices and falsifying accounts, many white plantation owners made sure that none of their workers ever got out of debt. In this way, sharecropping often bound black workers to one plantation owner as securely as slavery had done.

Exactly what measures would enable the freed slaves to become self-sufficient and productive members of society was an important issue of debate during Reconstruction. Was it really enough to free the slaves and then leave them to their own devices? Or should the freed slaves be compensated, either in cash or in land, for their years of unpaid labor? Should the federal government provide food, clothing, and education for the freed slaves, or would such aid keep the freedmen in a state of dependency? Should government agencies such as the Freedmen's Bureau attempt to protect black workers by negotiating with plantation

19

owners on their behalf and regulating sharecropping contracts, or would this constitute too large a federal intrusion into private enterprise? Did freeing the slaves automatically grant them the rights of citizenship and suffrage, or did those rights need to be granted by federal law and constitutional amendments—and should those rights be granted so quickly to people who were largely uneducated and had never really experienced democratic rule?

Even some of the most progressive-thinking abolitionists believed that their work had reached fruition with the passage of the Thirteenth Amendment to the Constitution. At the May 1865 meeting of the American Anti-Slavery Society, long-time abolitionist William Lloyd Garrison argued that the organization had no further purpose now that slavery was abolished and introduced a resolution to disband the society. Garrison believed that prejudice towards blacks arose from their status as slaves, not because of their race. Now that slavery was abolished, Garrison reasoned, discrimination against blacks would rapidly disappear, placing blacks at an equal advantage with whites on the "dusty road of competition." Although he supported black suffrage, Garrison felt that the American Anti-Slavery Society's work was now over; further advancements should be achieved by the freed slaves themselves.

Other prominent abolitionists at the May 1865 meeting, including Wendell Phillips and Frederick Douglass, disagreed with Garrison's views. Himself a former slave, Douglass noted that in previous years the American Anti-Slavery Society had not only worked to abolish slavery in the South but had also fought against racial segregation and discrimination in the North. "That was good anti-slavery work twenty years ago," Douglass told the society's members. "I do not see why it is not good anti-slavery work now. . . . Slavery is not abolished until the black man has the ballot. While the Legislatures of the South retain the right to pass laws making any discrimination between black and white, slavery still lives." On this occasion, the majority of the American Anti-Slavery Society's delegates agreed with Douglass and rejected the proposal to disband. Nevertheless, the conflict between doing too much for the freed slaves and not doing enough would beleaguer each step of reconstruction policy.

Throughout Reconstruction, the unresolved question of the extent of states' rights was closely linked with that of the new role of blacks in America. While abolitionists such as Frederick Douglass argued in favor of black suffrage, many Democrats and white Southerners contested the right of the federal government to grant black citizenship and suffrage. Prior to the Civil War, there had never really been any concept of national citizenship; a person could not be a U.S. citizen if he or she was not first a citizen of an individual state. In June 1865, Wendell Phillips commented, "It is a singular fact that, unlike all other nations, this nation has yet a question as to what makes or constitutes a citizen." With the Civil Rights Act of 1866 and the Fourteenth Amendment, Radical Republicans set a precedent by establishing black citizenship on a federal level and requiring the states to comply. Many Democrats—from both the North and the South—were horrified by these and further civil rights measures, which they considered to be a blatant usurpation of states' rights.

This conflict between those Americans who felt that the federal government had primary power over the states and those who believed that the rights of the states were paramount stretched back to the Revolutionary War and the first debates over the founding of the nation. In fact, when the Confederate States of America fashioned their government, they drew upon the Articles of Confederation—the first constitution of the United States—which had provided for a weak central government that was dependent on the willingness of the individual states to comply with its measures. During the nineteenth century, the Democrats supported the idea that the federal government should be limited in scope and could be no greater than the states that had united to form it. Democrats were the predominant party in the South and had been the prevailing force behind the secession, while Democrats in the North had generally upheld the right of the southern states to secede peacefully from the Union. On the other hand, the Whigs and (after the dissolution of the Whig Party) the Republicans argued that a strong central government was a necessity and that the U.S. Constitution gave the federal government authority over the individual states. Southern Whigs opposed secession, and many former Whigs refused to fight for the Confederacy during the Civil War; some even aided the Union.

Although the Civil War resulted in the failure of southern secession, these divisions between Democrats and Republicans—between proponents of states' rights and advocates of a strong central government—would persist throughout Reconstruction. The issue of the right to secede had not been settled definitively; one reason Jefferson Davis never stood trial for treason was that his lawyers planned to argue that the states had a constitutional right to secede, and Salmon P. Chase, the chief justice of the Supreme Court, cautioned President Johnson that Davis was correct and would likely win a case fought on those grounds. Congressional measures that were formulated by Republicans to secure black citizenship, to give blacks national suffrage, and to protect freed slaves against southern violence were all attacked by Democrats as unconstitutional federal interference in areas that should be governed solely by the states. Up to this point the states had determined which citizens were eligible to vote, establishing criteria that varied from state to state, and Democrats insisted that any attempt of the national government to take this authority away from the states was unconstitutional. Laws that gave the president the power to protect the freed slaves by stationing federal troops in the South appeared to many Americans as being perilously similar to the "British tyranny" that had sparked the Revolutionary War almost a century earlier.

Because of these debates over states' rights and civil rights, reconstruction policies that were originally devised to affect only the South ultimately resulted in the reconstruction of the entire nation. The legislation and amendments passed during Reconstruction ushered in the era of a powerful central government, with a corresponding decline in the authority of the individual states. The Fourteenth and Fifteenth Amendments irrevocably changed the definition of U.S. citizenship to include all Americans, regardless of race. As the viewpoints in this volume reveal, these modifications in the fabric of American government and society were the focus of heated controversy between those who wanted to leave well enough alone and those who favored extensive change. The accomplishments of the Reconstruction era are still a volatile issue among historians: Did reconstruction go too far, or did it not go far enough? In the present day, Americans still struggle with questions of civil rights, racial equality, and centralized government, making it all the more important to consider the lessons of Reconstruction.

CHAPTER 1

Reconstructing a Nation: Opposing Plans

Chapter Preface

The Civil War was a devastating conflict, beyond anything that the United States had yet experienced. In sheer physical terms, the amount of death and carnage was overwhelming. Out of a total population of 35 million Americans, approximately 620,000 had been killed in the war; another 400,000 had been wounded, many of whom had sustained permanent debilitating injuries. Large swaths of the South, including some of its most important urban areas, lay in ruins. Miles of railroad had been destroyed, bridges burned, buildings reduced to rubble. In 1865, journalist Sidney Andrews described the scene in Columbia, South Carolina:

> [Columbia] is now a wilderness of ruins. Its heart is but a mass of blackened chimneys and crumbling walls. Two thirds of the buildings in the place were burned, including, without exception, everything in the business portion. Not a store, office, or shop escaped; and for a distance of three fourths of a mile on each of twelve streets there was not a building left. . . . Those ghostly and crumbling walls and those long-deserted and grass-grown streets show the prostration of a community,— such prostration as only war could bring.

Equally devastating was the emotional toll of the Civil War. The division of one nation into two warring opponents, the traumatic experience of "brother fighting brother," left deep scars in the national psyche. Mired in the despondent, apathetic mood common to a conquered people, Southerners faced the eradication of their old way of life. The upheaval of southern societal and economic systems caused by the emancipation of nearly 4,000,000 slaves affected not only the former Confederacy but also the four slave states (Delaware, Maryland, Kentucky, and Missouri) that had not seceded from the Union.

The nation had been ripped asunder by slavery, secession, and war. To resurrect the United States as it had been in 1860 was impossible, and there was no clear consensus on what new form the reconstructed country should take. The outcome of the Civil War had determined that no state could secede from the Union, but now Americans faced the dilemma of how best to readmit the rebellious states into the nation. The war had established the supremacy of nationalism over the theory of states' rights, but now the problem arose of redefining the limits of states' rights and federal power. Emancipation had solved the nation's predicament over slavery, but now both the North and the South were

24

confronted with new questions of how the freed slaves should be integrated into American society, and to what extent. To be successful, any plan for reconstruction would need to address these daunting issues.

Further complicating matters was the piecemeal nature of reconstruction prior to the end of the war. As sections of the South fell to Union troops, President Abraham Lincoln proclaimed martial law in those areas and appointed military governors in accordance with his powers as the commander in chief of the armed forces. In 1863, Lincoln did publish a Proclamation of Amnesty in which he presented an outline for reconstruction, but in this document and others that followed, Lincoln stressed his willingness to consider other options and adapt reconstruction policies as necessary. The Civil War ended in 1865 without a peace treaty or any terms of settlement that would establish a firm method for readmitting the southern states to the Union. Moreover, most of Congress believed that the authority to oversee reconstruction belonged to them or at least should revert to them once the war ended and Lincoln's wartime powers expired.

Perhaps the most haunting question concerning reconstruction is how the outcome might have differed had Lincoln not been assassinated. Would he have been able to successfully guide the country through the arduous and controversial process of reconstruction? His reluctance to abide by a single plan might not have proved harmful to reconstruction, as one of Lincoln's greatest strengths was his judicious flexibility. His successor, Andrew Johnson, was a very different man. According to historian Eric Foner:

> If in Lincoln, early poverty and the struggle for success somehow produced wit, political dexterity, and sensitivity to the views of others, Johnson's personality turned in upon itself. . . . No one could doubt Johnson's personal courage, yet early in his career other less commendable qualities had also become apparent, among them stubbornness, intolerance of the views of others, and an inability to compromise. . . . [Johnson] found himself, as President, thrust into a role that required tact, flexibility, and sensitivity to the nuances of public opinion—qualities Lincoln possessed in abundance, but that Johnson lacked.

Shortly after assuming office, President Johnson formulated a plan of reconstruction (one he believed had had Lincoln's approval) and then adhered firmly to it. He refused to make any concessions or consider other alternatives when his policy was criticized by members of Congress. Johnson and the most liberal members of the Republican Party (known as the Radical Republicans) found themselves on opposite sides of the question of reconstruction. Johnson's approach—largely supported by Democrats, conservative Republicans, and white Southerners—was to reunite the country very quickly with as little federal interference as possible. The Radical Republicans and the majority of the moderate Republicans preferred a more extensive approach to reconstruction that would involve reworking the economic, agricultural, and political systems of the South from the ground up. The Radicals, many of whom had been abolitionists, also wanted to extend citizenship and suffrage to the newly freed slaves, an idea that Johnson condemned. The result of this dissension would be a three-year struggle between Johnson and Congress over the control of reconstruction.

VIEWPOINT 1

"The President was thereby authorized at any time thereafter, by proclamation, to extend . . . pardon and amnesty."

Reconstruction Is an Executive Function

Abraham Lincoln (1809-1865)

Although the Civil War would not be officially over until 1865, by mid-1863 the Union Army already occupied Tennessee, Louisiana, and North Carolina. Accordingly, President Abraham Lincoln began to consider the work of reconstruction. Lincoln's official objective throughout the war was the preservation of the Union, and his plans for reconstruction would express the same goal. On December 8, 1863, Lincoln issued the following Proclamation of Amnesty, which established the conditions for a reconstruction that would be placed largely under the authority of the executive branch. In this document, Lincoln views the rebel southern states as being guilty of treason and cites the power given to the president by the Constitution to grant pardons in such cases.

Lincoln's intent to use this executive prerogative to reinstate the South into the Union as quickly and leniently as possible was roundly criticized by the Radical Republicans. A liberal faction within the Republican Party, the Radical Republicans favored a more comprehensive and severe restructuring of southern society, one that would ensure equal treatment of blacks and whites. Unlike the advocates of moderate reconstruction, the Radical

Abraham Lincoln, "Proclamation of Amnesty." In *A Compilation of the Messages and Papers of the Presidents, 1789-1897*, vol. 6, edited by James D. Richardson. Washington, DC: 1896-99.

Republicans believed that reconstruction fell under the authority of Congress rather than the president. Despite opposition from the Radicals, Lincoln began to implement his moderate reconstruction plan during his lifetime. After Lincoln's assassination, however, a Congress dominated by Radical Republicans reversed many of his policies.

Whereas in and by the Constitution of the United States it is provided that the President "shall have power to grant reprieves and pardons for offenses against the United States, except in cases of impeachment"; and

Whereas a rebellion now exists whereby the loyal state governments of several states have for a long time been subverted, and many persons have committed and are now guilty of treason against the United States; and

Whereas, with reference to said rebellion and treason, laws have been enacted by Congress declaring forfeitures and confiscation of property and liberation of slaves, all upon terms and conditions therein stated, and also declaring that the President was thereby authorized at any time thereafter, by proclamation, to extend to persons who may have participated in the existing rebellion in any state or part thereof pardon and amnesty, with such exceptions and at such times and on such conditions as he may deem expedient for the public welfare; and

Whereas the congressional declaration for limited and conditional pardon accords with well-established judicial exposition of the pardoning power; and

Whereas, with reference to said rebellion, the President of the United States has issued several proclamations with provisions in regard to the liberation of slaves; and

Whereas it is now desired by some persons heretofore engaged in said rebellion to resume their allegiance to the United States and to reinaugurate loyal state governments within and for their respective states:

A Full Pardon

Therefore, I, Abraham Lincoln, President of the United States, do proclaim, declare, and make known to all persons who have, directly or by implication, participated in the existing rebellion, except as hereinafter excepted, that a full pardon is hereby granted to them and each of them, with restoration of all rights of property, except as to slaves and in property cases where rights of third parties shall have intervened, and upon the condition that every such person shall take and subscribe an oath and thenceforward keep and maintain said oath inviolate, and which oath shall be registered for permanent preservation and shall be of the tenor and effect following, to wit:

I, — — —, do solemnly swear, in presence of Almighty God, that I will henceforth faithfully support, protect, and defend the

Loyalty Oaths and Pardons

On December 8, 1863, shortly after Abraham Lincoln announced his program for reconstruction, he presented his third State of the Union address to Congress. In the excerpts that follow, Lincoln explains some of his reasons for assigning the power of reconstruction to the executive branch. He also asserts that his actions are constitutionally sound.

With reference to a resumption of the national authority within the states wherein that authority has been suspended, I have thought fit to issue a proclamation, a copy of which is herewith transmitted. On examination of this proclamation it will appear, as is believed, that nothing will be attempted beyond what is amply justified by the Constitution. True, the form of an oath is given, but no man is coerced to take it. The man is only promised a pardon in case he voluntarily takes the oath. The Constitution authorizes the executive to grant or withhold the pardon at his own absolute discretion; and this includes the power to grant on terms, as is fully established by judicial and other authorities. . . .

I may add at this point, that while I remain in my present position I shall not attempt to retract or modify the Emancipation Proclamation; nor shall I return to slavery any person who is free by the terms of that proclamation or by any of the acts of Congress. For these and other reasons it is thought best that support of these measures shall be included in the oath; and it is believed the executive may lawfully claim it in return for pardon and restoration of forfeited rights, which he has clear constitutional power to withhold altogether, or grant upon terms which he shall deem wisest for the public interest. It should be observed, also, that this part of the oath is subject to the modifying and abrogating power of legislation and supreme judicial decision.

The proposed acquiescence of the national executive in any reasonable temporary state arrangement for the freed people is made with the view of possibly modifying the confusion and destitution which must, at best, attend all classes by a total revolution of labor throughout whole states. It is hoped that the already deeply afflicted people in those states may be somewhat more ready to give up the cause of their affliction, if to this extent this vital matter be left to themselves; while no power of the national executive to prevent an abuse is abridged by the proposition.

Constitution of the United States and the Union of the states thereunder; and that I will in like manner abide by and faithfully support all acts of Congress passed during the existing rebellion with reference to slaves, so long and so far as not repealed, modified, or held void by Congress or by decision of the Supreme Court; and that I will in like manner abide by and faithfully support all proclamations of the President made during the existing rebellion having reference to slaves, so long and so far as not modified or declared void by decision of the Supreme Court. So help me God.

The persons excepted from the benefits of the foregoing provisions are all who are or shall have been civil or diplomatic officers or agents of the so-called Confederate government; all who have left judicial stations under the United States to aid the rebellion; all who are or shall have been military or naval officers of said so-called Confederate government above the rank of colonel in the Army or of lieutenant in the Navy; all who left seats in the United States Congress to aid the rebellion; all who resigned commissions in the Army or Navy of the United States and afterward aided the rebellion; and all who have engaged in any way in treating colored persons, or white persons in charge of such, otherwise than lawfully as prisoners of war, and which persons may have been found in the United States service as soldiers, seamen, or in any other capacity.

And I do further proclaim, declare, and make known that whenever, in any of the states of Arkansas, Texas, Louisiana, Mississippi, Tennessee, Alabama, Georgia, Florida, South Carolina, and North Carolina, a number of persons, not less than one-tenth in number of the votes cast in such state at the presidential election of the year A.D. 1860, each having taken oath aforesaid, and not having since violated it, and being a qualified voter by the election law of the state existing immediately before the so-called act of secession, and excluding all others, shall reestablish a state government which shall be republican and in nowise contravening said oath, such shall be recognized as the true government of the state, and the state shall receive thereunder the benefits of the constitutional provision which declares that "the United States shall guarantee to every state in this Union a republican form of government and shall protect each of them against invasion, and, on application of the legislature, or the executive (when the legislature cannot be convened), against domestic violence."

And I do further proclaim, declare, and make known that any provision which may be adopted by such state government in relation to the freed people of such state which shall recognize and declare their permanent freedom, provide for their education, and which may yet be consistent as a temporary arrangement with their present condition as a laboring, landless, and homeless class will not be objected to by the national executive.

And it is suggested as not improper that in constructing a loyal state government in any state the name of the state, the boundary, the subdivisions, the constitution, and the general code of laws as before the rebellion be maintained, subject only to the modifications made necessary by the conditions hereinbefore stated, and such others, if any, not contravening said conditions and which may be deemed expedient by those framing the new state government.

To avoid misunderstanding, it may be proper to say that this proclamation, so far as it relates to state governments, has no reference to states wherein loyal state governments have all the while been maintained. And for the same reason it may be proper to further say that whether members sent to Congress from any state shall be admitted to seats constitutionally rests exclusively with the respective houses and not to any extent with the executive. And, still further, that this proclamation is intended to present the people of the states wherein the national authority has been suspended and loyal state governments have been subverted a mode in and by which the national authority and loyal state governments may be reestablished within said states or in any of them; and while the mode presented is the best the executive can suggest, with his present impressions, it must not be understood that no other possible mode would be acceptable.

"A more studied outrage on the legislative authority of the people has never been perpetrated."

Reconstruction Is a Legislative Function

Henry Winter Davis (1817-1865)

In 1863, President Abraham Lincoln proposed a reconstruction policy that kept under executive control the authority to readmit states to the Union and that established lenient terms for readmission. Responding to Lincoln's plan, Representative Henry Winter Davis and Senator Benjamin Wade (1800-1878) drafted a bill that outlined a reconstruction plan more in line with Radical Republican aims. The Wade-Davis Bill, which was passed by Congress in 1864, firmly placed the responsibility for reconstruction in the hands of Congress and set up stricter terms for the reentry of the southern states.

Lincoln pocket-vetoed the Wade-Davis Bill and, on July 8, 1864, issued a statement defending his action. Lincoln stated that he was unwilling to commit to any single plan of reconstruction and therefore would not sign the bill, but he *was* willing to implement parts of the vetoed bill that might be suitable in certain situations. Lincoln was also reticent to sign the Wade-Davis Bill because he had already declared Arkansas and Louisiana "reconstructed" under the terms of his 1863 plan, but neither state was able to meet the more rigorous conditions of the Wade-Davis plan.

Outraged by Lincoln's veto, Davis wrote the following document, which was co-signed by Wade and published in the *New York Daily Tribune* on August 5, 1864. In this manifesto, Davis charges Lincoln with overstepping his executive powers and declares that the authority to regulate reconstruction resides com-

Henry Winter Davis, "The Wade-Davis Manifesto," *The New York Daily Tribune*, August 5, 1864. Reprinted in *Years of Turmoil*, John Niven, ed., Addison-Wesley, 1969.

pletely with Congress.

A steadfast Unionist, Davis was first elected to Congress in 1855 and, though originally a strong supporter of Lincoln, became increasingly critical of Lincoln's Civil War and Reconstruction policies. Davis planned to run for the presidency himself but died before his aspirations could be realized.

To the Supporters of the Government:

We have read without surprise, but not without indignation the proclamation of the President of the 8th of July, 1864. The supporters of the administration are responsible to the country for its conduct, and it is their right and duty to check the encroachments of the executive on the authority of Congress, and to require it to confine itself to its proper sphere. . . .

The President did not sign the bill to "guarantee to certain States, whose governments have been usurped, a Republican form of government," passed by the supporters of his Administration in both houses of Congress, after mature deliberation. The bill did not therefore become a law, and it is therefore nothing. The proclamation is neither an approval nor a veto of the bill; it is therefore a document unknown to the laws and Constitution of the United States. So far as it contains an apology for not signing the bill, it is a political manifesto against the friends of the government. So far as it proposes to execute the bill, which is not a law, it is a grave executive usurpation. . . .

Had the proclamation stopped there, it would have been only one other defeat of the will of the people by an executive perversion of the Constitution. But it goes farther. The President says:

> And whereas the said bill contains, among other things, a plan for restoring the States in rebellion to their proper practical relations in the Union, which plan expresses the sense of Congress upon that subject, and which plan it is now thought fit to lay before the people for their consideration—

By what authority of the Constitution? In what forms? The result to be declared by whom? With what effect when ascertained? Is it to be a law by the approval of the people, without the approval of Congress, at the will of the President? Will the President, on his opinion of the popular approval, execute it as law? Or is this merely a device to avoid the serious responsibility of defeating a law on which so many loyal hearts reposed for security? But the reasons now assigned for not approving the bill are full of ominous significance. The President proceeds:

33

Now, therefore, I, Abraham Lincoln, President of the United States do proclaim, declare, and make known that, while I am (as I was in December last when by proclamation I propounded a plan for restoration) unprepared, by a formal approval of this bill, to be inflexibly committed to any single plan of restoration—

That is to say, the President is resolved that the people shall not, by law, take any securities from the rebel States against a renewal of the rebellion, before restoring their power to govern us. His wisdom and prudence are to be our sufficient guarantees! He farther says:

And while I am also unprepared to declare that the Free-state constitutions and governments already adopted and installed in Arkansas and Louisiana shall be set aside and held for naught, thereby repelling and discouraging the loyal citizens who have set up the same as to farther effort—

That is to say, the President persists in recognizing those shadows of governments in Arkansas and Louisiana which Congress formally declared should not be recognized; whose representatives and senators were repelled by formal votes of both houses of Congress, and which, it was formally declared, should have no electoral vote for President and Vice-President. They are mere creatures of his will. They can not live a day without his support. They are mere oligarchies imposed on the people by military orders, under the forms of elections, at which generals, provost-marshals, soldiers, and camp followers were the chief actors, assisted by a handful of resident citizens, and urged on to premature action by private letters from the President. In neither Louisiana nor Arkansas, before Banks's defeat, did the United States control half the territory or half the population. In Louisiana, General Banks's proclamation candidly declared, "*The fundamental law of the State is martial law.*" On that foundation of freedom he erected what the President calls "the free Constitution and government of Louisiana. . . ."

The President, by preventing this bill from becoming a law, holds the electoral votes of the rebel States at the dictation of his personal ambition. If these votes turn the balance in his favor, is it to be supposed that his competitor, defeated by such means will acquiesce? If the rebel majority assert their supremacy in those States, and send votes which elect an enemy of the government, will we not repel his claims? And is not that civil war for the presidency inaugurated by the voice of rebel States? Seriously impressed with these dangers, Congress, "the proper constitutional authority," formally declared that there are no governments in the rebel States, and provided for their erection at a proper time. . . . The President's proclamation "holds for naught" this judgment, and discards the authority of the Supreme Court, and strides headlong toward the anarchy his proclamation of the 8th of December inaugurated. If electors for President be allowed to be chosen in either of those States, a sinister light will be cast on the motives which induced the President to "hold for naught" the will of Congress rather than his government in Louisiana and Arkansas. . . .

The Powers of Congress

Even the President's proclamation of the 8th of December formally declares that "whether members sent to Congress from any State shall be admitted to seats constitutionally rests exclusively with the respective houses, and not to any extent with the executive." And that is not the less true, because wholly inconsistent with the President's assumption, in that proclamation, of a right to institute and recognize State governments in the rebel States, nor because the President is unable to perceive that his recognition is a nullity if it be not conclusive upon Congress.

Under the Constitution, the right to senators and representatives is inseparable from a State government. If there be a State government, the right is absolute. If there be no State government, there can be no senators or representatives chosen. The two houses of Congress are expressly declared to be the sole judges of their own members. When, therefore, senators and representatives are admitted, the State government under whose authority they were chosen is conclusively established; when they are rejected, its existence is as conclusively rejected and denied. And to this judgment the President is bound to submit. . . .

A more studied outrage on the legislative authority of the people has never been perpetrated. Congress passed a bill, the President refused to approve it; and then, by proclamation, puts as much of it in force as he sees fit, and proposes to execute those parts by officers unknown to the laws of the United States and not subject to the confirmation of the Senate. . . . The bill provided for the civil administration of the laws of the State till it should be in a fit temper to govern itself, repealing all laws recognizing slavery, and making all men equal before the law. These beneficent provisions the President has annulled. People will die, and marry, and transfer property, and buy and sell, and to these acts of civil life courts and officers of the law are necessary. Congress legislated for these necessary things, and the President deprives them of the protection of the law. The President's purpose to instruct his military governors to "proceed according to the bill"—a make-shift to calm the disappointment its defeat has occasioned—is not merely a grave usurpation, but a transparent delusion. He can not "proceed according to the bill" after preventing it from becoming a law. Whatever is done will be at his will and pleasure, by persons responsible to no law, and more interested

35

to secure the interests and execute the will of the President than of the people, and the will of Congress is to be "held for naught," unless "the loyal people of the rebel States choose to adopt it. . . ."

The Radical Reconstruction Plan

The Wade-Davis Bill, excerpts of which appear here, required a majority of a state's citizens to take an oath of loyalty to the Union before a state constitutional convention could be held (Lincoln's plan only required ten percent). It also prevented former Confederate leaders from voting or holding office and made some provisions for the protection of freed slaves.

Sec. 7. *And be it further enacted,* That the [state constitutional] convention shall declare on behalf of the people of the State their submission to the Constitution and laws of the United States, and shall adopt the following provisions, hereby prescribed by the United States in the execution of the constitutional duty to guarantee a republican form of government to every State, and incorporate them in the constitution of the State; that is to say:

First. No person who has held or exercised any office, civil or military (except offices merely ministerial and military offices below the grade of colonel), State or Confederate, under the usurping power, shall vote for or be a member of the legislature or governor.

Second. Involuntary servitude is forever prohibited, and the freedom of all persons is guaranteed in said State. . . .

Sec. 13. *And be it further enacted,* That if any person declared free . . . be restrained of liberty with intent to be held in or reduced to involuntary servitude or labor, the person convicted before a court of competent jurisdiction of such act shall be punished by fine of not less than $1,500 and be imprisoned not less than five nor more than twenty years.

Sec. 14. *And be it further enacted,* That every person who shall hereafter hold or exercise any office, civil or military (except offices merely ministerial and military offices below the grade of colonel), in the rebel service, State or Confederate, is hereby declared not to be a citizen of the United States.

It was the solemn resolve of Congress to protect the loyal men of the nation against three great dangers: (1) the return to power of the guilty leaders of the rebellion; (2) the continuance of slavery; and (3) the burden of the rebel debt. Congress required assent to those provisions of the Convention of the State and, if refused, it was to be dissolved. The President "holds for naught" that resolve of Congress, because he is unwilling "to be inflexibly committed to any one plan of restoration"; and the people of the United States are not to be allowed to protect themselves unless their enemies agree to it. The order to proceed according to the bill is therefore merely at the will of the rebel States, and they have the option to reject it and accept the proclamation of the 8th of December, and demand the President's recognition. Mark the contrast! The bill requires a majority, the proclamation is satisfied with one tenth; the bill requires one oath, the proclamation another; the bill ascertains votes by registering, the proclamation by guess; the bill extracts adherence to existing territorial limits, the proclamation admits of others; the bill governs the rebel States *by law*, equalizing all before it, the proclamation commits them to the lawless discretion of military governors and provost-marshals; the bill forbids electors for President, the proclamation and defeat of the bill threaten us with civil war for the admission or exclusion of such votes; the bill exacted exclusion of dangerous enemies from power, and the relief of the nation from the rebel debt, and the prohibition of slavery forever, so that the suppression of the rebellion will double our resources to bear or pay the national debt, free the masses from the old domination of the rebel leaders, and eradicate the cause of the war; the proclamation secures neither of these guarantees.

It is silent respecting the rebel debt and the political exclusion of rebel leaders, leaving slavery exactly where it was by law at the outbreak of the rebellion, and adds no guarantees even of the freedom of the slaves the President undertook to manumit. It is summed up in an illegal oath, without a sanction, and therefore void. The oath is to support all proclamations of the President during the rebellion having reference to slaves. Any government is to be accepted at the hands of one tenth of the people not contravening that oath. Now that oath neither secures the abolition of slavery, nor adds any security to the freedom of the slaves whom the President declared free. It does not secure the abolition of slavery, for the proclamation of freedom merely professed to free certain slaves, while it recognized the institution. Every Constitution of the rebel States at the outbreak of the rebellion may be adopted, without the change of a letter, for none of them contravene that proclamation, none of them *establish* slavery. . . .

The President has greatly presumed on the forbearance which the supporters of his administration have so long practiced, in view of the arduous conflict in which we are engaged, and the reckless ferocity of our political opponents.

But he must understand that our support is of a cause, and not of man; that the authority of Congress is paramount, and must be respected; that the whole body of the Union men of Congress will not submit to be impeached by him of rash and unconstitutional legislation; and if he wishes our support, he must confine himself to his executive duties—to obey and execute—not to make the laws; to suppress by arms armed rebellion, and leave political reorganization to the Congress.

VIEWPOINT 3

"They did, in fact, withdraw from the Union and made themselves subjects of another government of their own creation."

The South Is a Separate, Conquered Nation

The Joint Committee on Reconstruction

In December 1865, Congress established the Joint Committee on Reconstruction, instructing its fifteen members to investigate the condition of the South and to make recommendations for all bills concerning reconstruction. Two theories of reconstruction were being considered: a moderate plan that advocated rapid reinstatement of the South and a radical plan that called for a complete overhaul of southern society. An outspoken proponent of Radical Reconstruction, Senator Thaddeus Stevens set the agenda for the committee, which consisted primarily of Republicans; only three members were Democrats.

In the following excerpts from the committee's report to Congress of June 20, 1866, the majority members argue that the states of the former Confederacy had forfeited all rights previously held as states of the Union. The report contends that the South was in effect a conquered nation, separate from the Union, and therefore could not claim any constitutional guarantees or congressional representation. The implications of this argument were important: Without rights as states, the southern territories could be remolded as the Radical Republicans saw fit; without representation, the southern Democrats were barred from the U.S. Congress. Many of the resolutions of the Joint Committee on Reconstruction were later incorporated into the Fourteenth Amendment.

Excerpted from part 3 of the *Report of the Joint Committee on Reconstruction*, 39th Cong., 1st sess., 1866.

A claim for the immediate admission of Senators and Representatives from the so-called Confederate States has been urged, which seems to your committee not to be founded either in reason or in law, and which cannot be passed without comment. Stated in a few words, it amounts to this: That inasmuch as the lately insurgent States had no legal right to separate themselves from the Union, they still retain their positions as States, and consequently the people thereof have a right to immediate representation in Congress without the imposition of any conditions whatever; and further, that until such admission Congress has no right to tax them for the support of the Government. It has even been contended that until such admission all legislation affecting their interests is, if not unconstitutional, at least unjustifiable and oppressive.

It is believed by your committee that all these propositions are not only wholly untenable, but, if admitted, would tend to the destruction of the Government.

Insurrection

It must not be forgotten that the people of these States, without justification or excuse, rose in insurrection against the United States. They deliberately abolished their State governments so far as the same connected them politically with the Union as members thereof under the Constitution. They deliberately renounced their allegiance to the Federal Government, and proceeded to establish an independent government for themselves. In the prosecution of this enterprise they seized the national forts, arsenals, dockyards, and other public property within their borders, drove out from among them those who remained true to the Union, and heaped every imaginable insult and injury upon the United States and its citizens. Finally they opened hostilities, and levied war against the Government.

They continued this war for four years with the most determined and malignant spirit, killing in battle and otherwise large numbers of loyal people, destroying the property of loyal citizens on the sea and on the land, and entailing on the Government an enormous debt, incurred to sustain its rightful authority. Whether legally and constitutionally or not, they did, in fact, withdraw from the Union and made themselves subjects of another government of their own creation. And they only yielded when, after a long, bloody, and wasting war, they were compelled by utter exhaustion to lay down their arms; and this they did not willingly, but declaring that they yielded because they could no longer resist, affording no evidence whatever of repentance for their crime, and expressing no regret, except that they had no longer

A Territorial War

William Whiting served in President Lincoln's War Department as an expert in the international laws of war. In his July 28, 1863, open letter to the Philadelphia Union League, Whiting points out that, unlike many civil wars, the American Civil War did not involve a political faction attempting to overthrow the government. Rather, it was a civil war fought between two geographical blocs over territory. Therefore, according to Whiting, the international code of law applies to both sides of the Civil War just as if they were two separate warring nations.

The entire circle of the Southern States abandoned the Union, and carried with them all the Border States which they could influence or control.

Having set up a new government for themselves; having declared war against us; having sought foreign aid; having passed acts of non-intercourse; having seized public property, and made attempts to invade States which refused to serve their cause; having raised and maintained large armies and an incipient navy; assuming, in all respects, to act as an independent, hostile nation at war with the United States—claiming belligerent rights as an independent people alone could claim them, and offering to enter into treaties of alliance with foreign countries, and treaties of peace with ours—under these circumstances they were no longer merely insurgents and rebels, but became a belligerent public enemy. The war was no longer against "certain persons" in the rebellious States. It became a territorial war; that is to say, a war by all persons situated in the belligerent territory against the United States. . . .

A state of foreign war instantly annuls the most solemn treaties between nations. It terminates all obligations in the nature of compacts or contracts, at the option of the party obligated thereby. It destroys all claims of one belligerent upon the other, except those which may be sanctioned by a treaty of peace. A civil territorial war has the same effect, excepting only that the sovereign may treat the rebels as subjects as well as belligerents.

Hence civil war, in which the belligerents have become territorial enemies, instantly annuls all rights or claims of public enemies against the United States, under the Constitution or laws, whether than Constitution be called a compact, a treaty, or a covenant, and whether the parties to it were States, in their sovereign capacity, or the people of the United States as individuals.

the power to continue the desperate struggle.

It cannot, we think, be denied by any one, having a tolerable acquaintance with public law, that the war thus waged was a civil war of the greatest magnitude. The people waging it were necessarily subject to all the rules which, by the law of nations, control a contest of that character, and to all the legitimate consequences following it. One of those consequences was that, within the limits prescribed by humanity, the conquered rebels were at the mercy of the conquerors. That a government thus outraged had a most perfect right to exact indemnity for the injuries done and security against the recurrence of such outrages in the future would seem too clear for dispute. What the nature of that security should be, what proof should be required of a return to allegiance, what time should elapse before a people thus demoralized should be restored in full to the enjoyment of political rights and privileges, are questions for the law-making power to decide, and that decision must depend on grave considerations of the public safety and the general welfare.

It is moreover contended, and with apparent gravity, that, from the peculiar nature and character of our Government, no such right on the part of the conqueror can exist; that from the moment when rebellion lays down its arms and actual hostilities cease, all political rights of rebellious communities are at once restored; that, because the people of a State of the Union were once an organized community within the Union, they necessarily so remain, and their right to be represented in Congress at any and all times, and to participate in the government of the country under all circumstances, admits of neither question or dispute. If this is indeed true, then is the Government of the United States powerless for its own protection, and flagrant rebellion, carried to the extreme of civil war, is a pastime which any State may play at, not only certain that it can lose nothing in any event, but may even be the gainer by defeat. If rebellion succeeds, it accomplishes its purpose and destroys the government. If it fails, the war has been barren of results, and the battle may be still fought out in the legislative halls of the country. Treason, defeated in the field, has only to take possession of Congress and the cabinet. . . .

We now purpose to re-state, as briefly as possible, the general facts and principles applicable to all the States recently in rebellion.

A Hostile Act

First. The seats of the senators and representatives from the so-called Confederate States became vacant in the year 1861, during the second session of the Thirty-sixth Congress, by the voluntary withdrawal of their incumbents, with the sanction and by direction of the legislatures or conventions of their respective States. This was done as a hostile act against the Constitution and Government of the United States, with a declared intent to overthrow the same by forming a southern confederation. This act of declared hostility was speedily followed by an organization of the same States into a confederacy, which levied and waged war, by sea and land, against the United States. This war continued more

41

than four years, within which period the rebel armies besieged the national capital, invaded the loyal States, burned their towns and cities, robbed their citizens, destroyed more than 250,000 loyal soldiers, and imposed an increased national burden of not less than $3,500,000,000, of which seven or eight hundred millions have already been met and paid. From the time these confederated States thus withdrew their representation in Congress and levied war against the United States, the great mass of their people became and were insurgents, rebels, traitors, and all of them assumed and occupied the political, legal, and practical relation of enemies of the United States. This position is established by acts of Congress and judicial decisions, and is recognized repeatedly by the President in public proclamations, documents, and speeches.

Second. The States thus confederated prosecuted their war against the United States to final arbitrament, and did not cease until all their armies were captured, their military powers destroyed, their civil officers, State and confederate, taken prisoners or put to flight, every vestige of State and confederate government obliterated, their territory overrun and occupied by the federal armies, and their people reduced to the condition of enemies conquered in war, entitled only by public law to such rights, privileges, and conditions as might be vouchsafed by the conqueror. . . .

Sixth. The question before Congress is, then, whether conquered enemies have the right, and shall be permitted at their own pleasure and on their own terms, to participate in making laws for their conquerors; whether conquered rebels may change their theater of operations from the battle-field, where they were defeated and overthrown, to the halls of Congress, and, through their representatives, seize upon the Government which they fought to destroy; whether the national treasury, the army of the nation, its navy, its forts and arsenals, its whole civil administration, its credit, its pensioners, the widows and orphans of those who perished in the war, the public honor, peace and safety, shall all be turned over to the keeping of its recent enemies without delay, and without imposing such conditions as, in the opinion of Congress, the security of the country and its institutions may demand.

Seventh. The history of mankind exhibits no example of such madness and folly. The instinct of self-preservation protests against it.

VIEWPOINT 4

"It can not be that a successful war, waged for the preservation of the Union, had the legal effect of dissolving it."

The South Is Not a Separate, Conquered Nation

Andrew Johnson (1808-1875)

Andrew Johnson was the only southern senator to support the Union during the war, keeping his seat in the Senate after his fellow Southerners withdrew. Selected to be Abraham Lincoln's running mate for the 1864 presidential election, Johnson was propelled into the presidency by the assassination of Lincoln in April 1865. Although Johnson closely followed Lincoln's reconstruction policies, the speed at which he accelerated the pardoning of Confederates alarmed both moderate and radical Republicans.

By the time Johnson delivered the following address, he had spent almost two years enmeshed in a power struggle with Congress over reconstruction. One of the hotly debated points was the status of the former Confederate States. In his State of the Union address of December 1867, Johnson asserts that the southern states have never been separated from the Union. Supporting his argument with a strict interpretation of the Constitution, Johnson declares the Union indivisible. The Civil War, he argues, was fought not between two separate countries but between a rebellious faction and a loyal populace. Johnson also insists that, having never been separated from the Union, the southern states cannot be denied their basic constitutional rights and representation.

Excerpted from Andrew Johnson's "Third Annual Message," December 3, 1867. Reprinted in *The State of the Union Messages of the Presidents, 1790-1966*, vol. 2, Fred L. Israel, ed., Chelsea House/Robert Hector Publishers, 1966.

When a civil war has been brought to a close, it is manifestly the first interest and duty of the state to repair the injuries which the war has inflicted, and to secure the benefit of the lessons it teaches as fully and as speedily as possible. This duty was, upon the termination of the rebellion, promptly accepted, not only by the executive department, but by the insurrectionary States themselves, and restoration in the first moment of peace was believed to be as easy and certain as it was indispensable. The expectations, however, then so reasonably and confidently entertained were disappointed by legislation from which I felt constrained by my obligations to the Constitution to withhold my assent.

It is therefore a source of profound regret that in complying with the obligation imposed upon the President by the Constitution to give to Congress from time to time information of the state of the Union I am unable to communicate any definitive adjustment, satisfactory to the American people, of the questions which since the close of the rebellion have agitated the public mind. On the contrary, candor compels me to declare that at this time there is no Union as our fathers understood the term, and as they meant it to be understood by us. The Union which they established can exist only where all the States are represented in both Houses of Congress; where one State is as free as another to regulate its internal concerns according to its own will, and where the laws of the central Government, strictly confined to matters of national jurisdiction, apply with equal force to all the people of every section. That such is not the present "state of the Union" is a melancholy fact, and we must all acknowledge that the restoration of the States to their proper legal relations with the Federal Government and with one another, according to the terms of the original compact, would be the greatest temporal blessing which God, in His kindest providence, could bestow upon this nation. It becomes our imperative duty to consider whether or not it is impossible to effect this most desirable consummation.

The Union and the Constitution are inseparable. As long as one is obeyed by all parties, the other will be preserved; and if one is destroyed, both must perish together. The destruction of the Constitution will be followed by other and still greater calamities. It was ordained not only to form a more perfect union between the States, but to "establish justice, insure domestic tranquility, provide for the common defense, promote the general welfare, and secure the blessings of liberty to ourselves and our posterity." Nothing but implicit obedience to its requirements in all parts of the country will accomplish these great ends. Without that obedience we can look forward only to continual outrages upon individual rights, incessant breaches of the public peace, national weakness, financial dishonor, the total loss of our prosperity, the general corruption of morals, and the final extinction of popular freedom. To save our country from evils so appalling as these, we should renew our efforts again and again.

Andrew Johnson implemented Lincoln's reconstruction plan but lacked Lincoln's flexibility and tactfulness.

To me the process of restoration seems perfectly plain and simple. It consists merely in a faithful application of the Constitution and laws. The execution of the laws is not now obstructed or opposed by physical force. There is no military or other necessity, real or pretended, which can prevent obedience to the Constitution, either North or South. All the rights and all the obligations of States and individuals can be protected and enforced by means perfectly consistent with the fundamental law. The courts may be everywhere open, and if open their process would be unimpeded. Crimes against the United States can be prevented or punished by the proper judicial authorities in a manner entirely practicable and legal. There is therefore no reason why the Constitution should not be obeyed, unless those who exercise its powers have determined that it shall be disregarded and violated. The mere naked will of this Government, or of some one or more of its branches, is the only obstacle that can exist to a perfect union of all the States. . . .

It is clear to my apprehension that the States lately in rebellion are still members of the National Union. When did they cease to be so? The "ordinances of secession" adopted by a portion (in most of them a very small portion) of their citizens were mere nullities. If we admit now that they were valid and effectual for the purpose intended by their authors, we sweep from under our feet the whole ground upon which we justified the war. Were those States afterwards expelled from the Union by the war? The direct contrary was averred by this Government to be its purpose, and was so understood by all those who gave their blood and treasure to aid in its prosecution. It can not be that a successful war, waged for the preservation of the Union, had the legal effect of dissolving it. The victory of the nation's arms was not the disgrace of her policy; the defeat of secession on the battlefield was not the triumph of its lawless principle. Nor could Congress, with or without the consent of the Executive, do anything which would have the effect, directly or indirectly, of separating the States from each other. To dissolve the Union is to repeal the Constitution which holds it together, and that is a power which does not belong to any department of this Government, or to all of them united.

Treated as States

This is so plain that it has been acknowledged by all branches of the Federal Government. The Executive (my predecessor as well as myself) and the heads of all the Departments have uniformly acted upon the principle that the Union is not only undissolved, but indissoluble. Congress submitted an amendment of the Constitution to be ratified by the Southern States, and accepted their acts of ratification as a necessary and lawful exercise of their highest function. If they were not States, or were States out of the Union, their consent to a change in the fundamental law of the Union would have been nugatory, and Congress in asking it committed a political absurdity. The judiciary has also given the solemn sanction of its authority to the same view of the case. The judges of the Supreme Court have included the Southern States in their circuits, and they are constantly, *in banc* and elsewhere, exercising jurisdiction which does not belong to them unless those States are States of the Union.

If the Southern States are component parts of the Union, the Constitution is the supreme law for them, as it is for all the other States. They are bound to obey it, and so are we. The right of the Federal Government, which is clear and unquestionable, to enforce the Constitution upon them implies the correlative obligation on our part to observe its limitations and execute its guaranties. Without the Constitution we are nothing; by, through, and under the Constitution we are what it makes us. We may doubt the wisdom of the law, we may not approve of its provisions, but we can not violate it merely because it seems to confine our powers within limits narrower than we could wish. It is not a question of individual or class or sectional interest, much less of party predominance, but of duty—of high and sacred duty—which we are all sworn to perform. If we can not support the Constitution with the cheerful alacrity of those who love and believe in it, we must give to it as least the fidelity of public servants who act under solemn obligations and commands which they dare not disregard.

The constitutional duty is not the only one which requires the States to be restored. There is another consideration which, though of minor importance, is yet of great weight. On the 22d day of July, 1861, Congress declared by an almost unanimous vote of both Houses that the war should be condemned solely for the purpose of preserving the Union and maintaining the supremacy of the Federal Constitution and laws, without impairing the dignity, equality, and rights of the States or of individuals, and that when this was done the war should cease. I do not say that this declaration is personally binding on those who joined in making it, any more than individual members of Congress are personally bound to pay a public debt created under a law for which they voted. But it was a solemn, public, official pledge of the national honor, and I can not imagine upon what grounds the repudiation of it is to be justified. If it be said that we are not bound to keep faith with rebels, let it be remembered that this promise was not made to rebels only. Thousands of true men in the South were drawn to our standard by it, and hundreds of thousands in the North gave their lives in the belief that it would be carried out. It was made on the day after the first great battle of the war had been fought and lost. All patriotic and intelligent men then saw the necessity of giving such an assurance, and believed that without it the war would end in disaster to our cause. Having given that assurance in the extremity of our peril, the violation of it now, in the day of our power, would be a rude rending of that good faith which holds the moral world together; our country would cease to have any claim upon the confidence of men; it would make the war not only a failure, but a fraud. . . .

Unjust Punishment

I have no desire to save from the proper and just consequences of their great crime those who engaged in rebellion against the Government, but as a mode of punishment the measures under consideration are the most unreasonable that could be invented. Many of those people are perfectly innocent; many kept their fidelity to the Union untainted to the last; many were incapable of any legal offense; a large proportion even of the persons able to bear arms were forced into rebellion against their will, and of those who are guilty with their own consent the degrees of guilt are as various as the shades of their character and temper. But these acts of Congress confound them all together in one common doom. Indiscriminate vengeance upon classes, sects, and parties, or upon whole communities, for offenses committed by a portion of them against the governments to which they owed obedience was common in the barbarous ages of the world; but Christianity and civilization have made such progress that recourse to a punishment so cruel and unjust would meet with the condemnation of all unprejudiced and right-minded men. The punitive justice of this age, and especially of this country, does not consist in stripping whole States of their liberties and reducing all their people, without distinction, to the condition of slavery. It deals separately with each individual, confines itself to the forms of law, and vindicates its own purity by an impartial examination of every case before a competent judicial tribunal. If this does not satisfy all our desires with regard to Southern rebels, let us console ourselves by reflecting that a free Constitution, triumphant in war and unbroken in peace, is worth far more to us and our children than the gratification of any present feeling.

I am aware it is assumed that this system of government for the Southern States is not to be perpetual. It is true this military government is to be only provisional, but it is through this temporary evil that a greater evil is to be made perpetual. If the guaranties of the Constitution can be broken provisionally to serve a temporary purpose, and in a part only of the country, we can destroy them everywhere and for all time. Arbitrary measures often change, but they generally change for the worse. It is the curse of despotism that is has no halting place. The intermitted exercise of its power brings no sense of security to its subjects, for they can never know what more they will be called to endure when its red right hand is armed to plague them again. Nor is it possible to conjecture how or where power, unrestrained by law, may seek its next victims. The States that are still free may be enslaved at any moment; for if the Constitution does not protect all, it protects none.

48

VIEWPOINT 5

"I am satisfied that the mass of thinking men of the South accept the present situation of affairs in good faith."

The South Is Willing to Accept Reconstruction

Ulysses S. Grant (1822-1885)

Ulysses S. Grant was the commander of all U.S. armies during the Civil War and accepted the surrender of Robert E. Lee at Appomattox on April 9, 1865. One of the nation's most prominent men at the end of the war, Grant held few political convictions; those he did have corresponded with those of the Democrats.

In November 1865, President Andrew Johnson sent Grant to tour the South as an observer of the conditions in the former Confederacy. The attitude of the South toward reconstruction was an important factor in the planning of reconstruction policies. If the southern states were resistant to change—as the Radical Republicans claimed they were—the North would need to continue military rule and maintain federal agencies such as the Freedmen's Bureau, which was established to aid and protect the newly freed southern blacks. If, however, the southern states truly repented the rebellion and were willing to comply with the dictates of the North, they could be entrusted to carry out reconstruction with little federal intervention, a concept that appealed to the moderates.

On December 18, 1865, Grant sent the following report to Johnson, in which he stresses that the South was, indeed, ready to comply willingly with reconstruction. Grant also is critical of southern blacks and advocates a patronizing approach toward a people he suggests may be on the brink of extinction—a not uncommon opinion during a time when thousands of recently freed slaves roamed the South as landless and penniless refugees.

Ulysses S. Grant, *Report on Conditions in the South*, Washington, D.C., 1866.

$S_{ir:}$

In reply to your note of the 16th instant requesting a report from me giving such information as I may be possessed of coming within the scope of the inquiries made by the Senate of the United States in their resolution of the 12th instant, I have the honor to submit the following:

With your approval, and also that of the honorable secretary of war, I left Washington city on the 27th of last month for the purpose of making a tour of inspection through some of the Southern states, or states lately in rebellion, and to see what changes were necessary to be made in the disposition of the military forces of the country; how these forces could be reduced and expenses curtailed, etc.; and to learn, as far as possible, the feelings and intentions of the citizens of those states toward the general government.

The state of Virginia, being so accessible to Washington city, and information from this quarter, therefore, being readily obtained, I hastened through the state without conversing or meeting with any of its citizens. In Raleigh, North Carolina, I spent one day; in Charleston, South Carolina, two days; Savannah and Augusta, Georgia, each one day. Both in traveling and while stopping, I saw much and conversed freely with the citizens of those states, as well as with officers of the Army who have been stationed among them. The following are the conclusions come to by me.

A Fortunate Outcome

I am satisfied that the mass of thinking men of the South accept the present situation of affairs in good faith. The questions which have heretofore divided the sentiment of the people of the two sections—slavery and state's rights, or the right of a state to secede from the Union—they regard as having been settled forever by the highest tribunal—arms—that man can resort to. I was pleased to learn from the leading men whom I met that they not only accepted the decision arrived at as final but, now that the smoke of battle has cleared away and time has been given for reflection, that this decision has been a fortunate one for the whole country, they receiving like benefits from it with those who opposed them in the field and in council.

Four years of war, during which law was executed only at the point of the bayonet throughout the states in rebellion, have left the people possibly in a condition not to yield that ready obedience to civil authority the American people have generally been in the habit of yielding. This would render the presence of small garrisons throughout those states necessary until such time as labor returns to its proper channel and civil authority is fully established. I did not meet anyone, either those holding places under the government or citizens of the Southern states, who think it practicable to withdraw the military from the South at present. The white and the black mutually require the protection of the general government.

A Southerner's Opinion

Louisianian James D.B. De Bow was the editor of De Bow's Review, *the leading commercial newspaper in the South. On March 28, 1866, he testified before the Joint Committee on Reconstruction concerning the attitudes of the South toward blacks.*

I think if the whole regulation of the negroes, or freedmen, were left to the people of the communities in which they live, it will be administered for the best interest of the negroes as well as of the white men. I think there is a kindly feeling on the part of the planters towards the freedmen. They are not held at all responsible for anything that has happened. They are looked upon as the innocent cause. In talking with a number of planters, I remember some of them telling me they were succeeding very well with their freedmen, having got a preacher to preach to them and a teacher to teach them, believing it was for the interest of the planter to make the negro feel reconciled; for, to lose his services as a laborer for even a few months would be very disastrous. The sentiment prevailing is, that it is for the interest of the employer to teach the negro, to educate his children, to provide a preacher for him, and to attend to his physical wants. And I may say I have not seen any exception to that feeling in the south. Leave the people to themselves, and they will manage very well. The Freedmen's Bureau, or any agency to interfere between the freedman and his former master, is only productive of mischief.

There is such universal acquiescence in the authority of the general government throughout the portions of country visited by me that the mere presence of a military force, without regard to numbers, is sufficient to maintain order. The good of the country and economy require that the force kept in the interior, where there are many freedmen (elsewhere in the Southern states than at forts upon the seacoast no force is necessary), should all be white troops. The reasons for this are obvious without mentioning many of them. The presence of black troops, lately slaves, demoralizes labor, both by their advice and by furnishing in their camps a resort for the freedmen for long distances around. White troops generally excite no opposition, and therefore a small number of them can maintain order in a given district. Colored troops must be kept in bodies sufficient to defend themselves. It is not

51

the thinking men who would use violence toward any class of troops sent among them by the general government, but the ignorant in some places might; and the late slave seems to be imbued with the idea that the property of his late master should, by right, belong to him, or at least should have no protection from the colored soldier. There is danger of collisions being brought on by such causes.

My observations lead me to the conclusion that the citizens of the Southern states are anxious to return to self-government within the Union as soon as possible; that while reconstructing they want and require protection from the government; that they are in earnest in wishing to do what they think is required by the government, not humiliating to them as citizens, and that if such a course were pointed out they would pursue it in good faith. It is to be regretted that there cannot be a greater commingling, at this time, between the citizens of the two sections, and particularly of those entrusted with the lawmaking power.

The Freedmen's Bureau

I did not give the operations of the Freedmen's Bureau that attention I would have done if more time had been at my disposal. Conversations on the subject, however, with officers connected with the bureau lead me to think that in some of the states its affairs have not been conducted with good judgment or economy, and that the belief widely spread among the freedmen of the Southern states that the lands of their former owners will, at least in part, be divided among them has come from the agents of this bureau. This belief is seriously interfering with the willingness of the freedmen to make contracts for the coming year. In some form the Freedmen's Bureau is an absolute necessity until civil law is established and enforced, securing to the freedmen their rights and full protection. At present, however, it is independent of the military establishment of the country and seems to be operated by the different agents of the bureau according to their individual notions. Everywhere General [Oliver] Howard, the able head of the bureau, made friends by the just and fair instructions and advice he gave; but the complaint in South Carolina was that when he left, things went on as before.

Many, perhaps the majority, of the agents of the Freedmen's Bureau advise the freedmen that by their own industry they must expect to live. To this end they endeavor to secure employment for them and to see that both contracting parties comply with their engagements. In some instances, I am sorry to say, the freedman's mind does not seem to be disabused of the idea that a freedman has the right to live without care or provision for the future. The effect of the belief in division of lands is idleness and accumulation in camps, towns, and cities. In such cases I think it will be found that vice and disease will tend to the extermination or great reduction of the colored race. It cannot be expected that the opinions held by men at the South for years can be changed in a day, and therefore the freedmen require, for a few years, not only laws to protect them but the fostering care of those who will give them good counsel and on whom they rely.

The Freedmen's Bureau, being separated from the military establishment of the country requires all the expenses of a separate organization. One does not necessarily know what the other is doing or what orders they are acting under. It seems to me this could be corrected by regarding every officer on duty with troops in the Southern states as an agent of the Freedmen's Bureau, and then have all orders, from the head of the bureau sent through department commanders. This would create a responsibility that would secure uniformity of action throughout all the South; would insure the orders and instructions from the head of the bureau being carried out, and would relieve from duty and pay a large number of employees of the government.

VIEWPOINT 6

"There is . . . an entire absence of that national spirit which forms the basis of true loyalty and patriotism."

The South Is Unwilling to Accept Reconstruction

Carl Schurz (1829-1906)

A native of Germany, Carl Schurz was forced to flee his homeland because of his participation in the German revolutionary movement of 1848. After immigrating to the United States, he joined the anti-slavery movement and became involved in Republican politics. Schurz rose to the rank of major-general during the Civil War. In November 1865, he was sent by President Andrew Johnson as a special commissioner to report on the South. Unlike fellow commissioner Ulysses S. Grant, Schurz found that the attitude of the South was anything but conciliatory. In his 1865 report to the president, Schurz cautions that the southern states are reluctant to comply with reconstruction and are only submitting because of military intervention by the North. He argues that white Southerners continue to mistreat blacks and warns against "the establishment of a new form of servitude" closely resembling slavery. Schurz fell out of favor with Johnson due to this report, receiving a chilly reception at the White House. However, Schurz continued his successful political career, later serving as a U.S. senator and as secretary of the interior.

The continuance of the national control in the south, although it may be for a short period only, will cause some inconvenience and expense; but if thereby destructive collisions and anarchical

Excerpted from Carl Schurz, *Condition of the South*, Washington, D.C., 1866.

disorders can be prevented, justice secured to all men, and the return of peace and prosperity to all parts of this country hastened, it will be a paying investment. For the future of the republic, it is far less important that this business of reconstruction be done quickly than that it be well done. The matter well taken in hand, there is reason for hope that it will be well done, and quickly too. In days like these great changes are apt to operate themselves rapidly. At present the southern people assume that free negro labor will not work, and therefore they are not inclined to give it a fair trial. As soon as they find out that they must give it a fair trial, and that their whole future power and prosperity depend upon its success, they will also find out that it will work, at least far better than they have anticipated. Then their hostility to it will gradually disappear. This great result accomplished, posterity will not find fault with this administration for having delayed complete "reconstruction" one, two, or more years. . . .

In discussing the matter of negro suffrage I deemed it my duty to confine myself strictly to the practical aspects of the subject. I have, therefore, not touched its moral merits nor discussed the question whether the national government is competent to enlarge the elective franchise in the States lately in rebellion by its own act; I deem it proper, however, to offer a few remarks on the assertion frequently put forth, that the franchise is likely to be extended to the colored man by the voluntary action of the southern whites themselves. My observation leads me to a contrary opinion. Aside from a very few enlightened men, I found but one class of people in favor of the enfranchisement of the blacks: it was the class of Unionists who found themselves politically ostracised and looked upon the enfranchisement of the loyal negroes as the salvation of the whole loyal element. But their numbers and influence are sadly insufficient to secure such a result. The masses are strongly opposed to colored suffrage; anybody that dares to advocate it is stigmatized as a dangerous fanatic; nor do I deem it probable that in the ordinary course of things prejudices will wear off to such an extent as to make it a popular measure. Outside of Louisiana only one gentleman who occupied a prominent political position in the south expressed to me an opinion favorable to it. He declared himself ready to vote for an amendment to the constitution of his State bestowing the right of suffrage upon all male citizens without distinction of color who could furnish evidence of their ability to read and write, without, however, disfranchising those who are now voters and are not able to fulfill that condition. This gentleman is now a member of one of the State conventions, but I presume he will not risk his political standing in the south by moving such an amendment in that body.

The only manner in which, in my opinion, the southern people can be induced to grant to the freedman some measure of self-protecting power in the form of suffrage, is to make it a condition precedent to "readmission."

More Intolerable than Slavery

In the first years of Reconstruction, southern blacks held numerous meetings to discuss their situation and their future. The Convention of the Colored People of Virginia, held in August 1865, issued an "Address to the Loyal Citizens and Congress of the United States." The address includes the following assessment of southern white attitudes.

We, the undersigned members of a Convention of colored citizens of the State of Virginia, would respectfully represent that, although we have been held as slaves, and denied all recognition as a constituent of your nationality for almost the entire period of the duration of your Government, and that by *your permission* we have been denied either home or country, and deprived of the dearest rights of human nature: yet when you and our immediate oppressors met in deadly conflict upon the field of battle—the one to destroy and the other to save your Government and nationality, *we*, with scarce an exception, in our inmost souls espoused your cause, and watched, and prayed, and waited, and labored for your success. . . .

Well, the war is over, the rebellion is "put down," and we are *declared* free! Four fifths of our enemies are paroled or amnestied, and the other fifth are being pardoned, and the President [Andrew Johnson] has, in his efforts at the reconstruction of the civil government of the States, late in rebellion, left us entirely at the mercy of these subjugated but unconverted rebels, in *everything* save the privilege of bringing us, our wives and little ones, to the auction block. . . . We *know* these men—know them *well*—and we assure you that, with the majority of them, loyalty is only "lip deep," and that their professions of loyalty are used as a cover to the cherished design of getting restored to their former relations with the Federal Government, and then, by all sorts of "unfriendly legislation," to render the freedom you have given us more intolerable than the slavery they intended for us.

We warn you in time that our only safety is in keeping them under Governors of the *military persuasion* until you have so amended the Federal Constitution that it will prohibit the States from making any distinction between citizens on account of race or color.

I have to notice one pretended remedy for the disorders now agitating the south, which seems to have become the favorite plan of some prominent public men. It is that the whole colored population of the south should be transported to some place where they could live completely separated from the whites. It is hardly necessary to discuss, not only the question of right and justice, but the difficulties and expense necessarily attending the deportation of nearly four millions of people. But it may be asked, what would become of the industry of the south for many years, if the bulk of its laboring population were taken away? The south stands in need of an increase and not of a diminution of its laboring force to repair the losses and disasters of the last four years. Much is said of imported European laborers and northern men; this is the favorite idea of many planters who want such immigrants to work on their plantations. . . .

But whatever the efficiency of such expedients may be, the true problem remains, not how to remove the colored man from his present field of labor, but how to make him, where he is, a true freeman and an intelligent and useful citizen. The means are simple: protection by the government until his political and social status enables him to protect himself, offering to his legitimate ambition the stimulant of a perfectly fair chance in life, and granting to him the rights which in every just organization of society are coupled with corresponding duties.

The South Falls Short

I may sum up all I have said in a few words. If nothing were necessary but to restore the machinery of government in the States lately in rebellion in point of form, the movements made to that end by the people of the south might be considered satisfactory. But if it is required that the southern people should also accommodate themselves to the results of the war in point of spirit, those movements fall far short of what must be insisted upon.

The loyalty of the masses and most of the leaders of the southern people, consists in submission to necessity. There is, except in individual instances, an entire absence of that national spirit which forms the basis of true loyalty and patriotism.

The emancipation of the slaves is submitted to only in so far as chattel slavery in the old form could not be kept up. But although the freedman is no longer considered the property of the individual master, he is considered the slave of society, and all independent State legislation will share the tendency to make him such. The ordinances abolishing slavery passed by the conventions under the pressure of circumstances, will not be looked upon as barring the establishment of a new form of servitude.

Practical attempts on the part of the southern people to deprive the negro of his rights as a freeman may result in bloody collisions, and will certainly plunge southern society into restless fluctuations and anarchical confusion. Such evils can be prevented only by continuing the control of the national government in the States lately in rebellion until free labor is fully developed and firmly established, and the advantages and blessings of the new order of things have disclosed themselves. This desirable result will be hastened by a firm declaration on the part of the government, that national control in the south will not cease until such results are secured. Only in this way can that security be established in the south which will render numerous immigration possible, and such immigration would materially aid a favorable development of things.

The solution of the problem would be very much facilitated by enabling all the loyal and free-labor elements in the south to exercise a healthy influence upon legislation. It will hardly be possible to secure the freedman against oppressive class legislation and private persecution, unless he be endowed with a certain measure of political power.

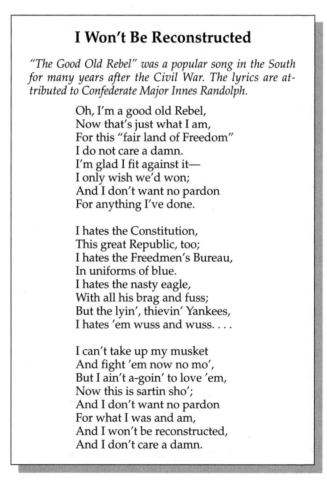

I Won't Be Reconstructed

"The Good Old Rebel" was a popular song in the South for many years after the Civil War. The lyrics are attributed to Confederate Major Innes Randolph.

Oh, I'm a good old Rebel,
Now that's just what I am,
For this "fair land of Freedom"
I do not care a damn.
I'm glad I fit against it—
I only wish we'd won;
And I don't want no pardon
For anything I've done.

I hates the Constitution,
This great Republic, too;
I hates the Freedmen's Bureau,
In uniforms of blue.
I hates the nasty eagle,
With all his brag and fuss;
But the lyin', thievin' Yankees,
I hates 'em wuss and wuss. . . .

I can't take up my musket
And fight 'em now no mo',
But I ain't a-goin' to love 'em,
Now this is sartin sho';
And I don't want no pardon
For what I was and am,
And I won't be reconstructed,
And I don't care a damn.

As to the future peace and harmony of the Union, it is of the highest importance that the people lately in rebellion be not permitted to build up another "peculiar institution" whose spirit is in conflict with the fundamental principles of our political system; for as long as they cherish interests peculiar to them in preference to those they have in common with the rest of the American people, their loyalty to the Union will always be uncertain.

I desire not to be understood as saying that there are no well-meaning men among those who were compromised in the rebellion. There are many, but neither their number nor their influence is strong enough to control the manifest tendency of the popular spirit. . . .

A Cautious Report

In submitting this report I desire to say that I have conscientiously endeavored to see things as they were, and to represent them as I saw them. I have been careful not to use stronger language than was warranted by the thoughts I intended to express. A comparison of the tenor of the annexed documents with that of my report, will convince you that I have studiously avoided overstatements. Certain legislative attempts at present made in the south, and especially in South Carolina, seem to be more than justifying the apprehensions I have expressed.

Conscious though I am of having used my best endeavors to draw, from what I saw and learned, correct general conclusions, yet I am far from placing too great a trust in my own judgment, when interests of such magnitude are at stake. I know that this report is incomplete, although as complete as an observation of a few months could enable me to make it. Additional facts might be elicited, calculated to throw new light upon the subject. Although I see no reason for believing that things have changed for the better since I left for the south, yet such may be the case. Admitting all these possibilities, I would entreat you to take no irretraceable step towards relieving the States lately in rebellion from all national control, until such favorable changes are clearly and unmistakably ascertained.

To that end, and by virtue of the permission you honored me with when sending me out to communicate to you freely and unreservedly my views as to measures of policy proper to be adopted, I would now respectfully suggest that you advise Congress to send one or more "investigating committees" into the southern States, to inquire for themselves into the actual condition of things, before final action is taken upon the readmission of such States to their representation in the legislative branch of the government, and the withdrawal of the national control from that section of the country.

CHAPTER 2

Moderate Reconstruction: The President Versus Congress

Chapter Preface

On March 13, 1868, for the first time in American history, a High Court of Impeachment convened to try a president of the United States for "high crimes and misdemeanors." The visitors' galleries of the Senate were jammed with spectators; demand for admittance to the galleries was so great that tickets had been issued and police had been summoned to disperse crowds of disappointed ticket seekers. Thaddeus Stevens, a leading Radical and one of the seven U.S. representatives chosen to prosecute the case, was in the throes of his final illness and had to be carried into the Senate. The acting president of the Senate, Radical Republican Benjamin Wade, was also the next in line to succeed President Andrew Johnson should he be removed from office; despite this conflict of interest, Wade had refused to abstain from taking part in the trial. President Johnson, the focus of all the commotion, wanted to appear before the court, but his lawyers feared Johnson's penchant for haranguing speeches would hurt his case and had persuaded him not to attend. Meanwhile, bookmakers' odds in Washington, D.C., were running heavily in favor of Johnson's conviction.

How had the government arrived at such a crisis? After all, many Radical Republicans had been so frustrated with President Abraham Lincoln's conciliatory attitude toward the South that they had barely managed to hide their jubilation when Lincoln was killed and Johnson—who advocated a harsh approach to reconstruction—took over the presidency in 1865. Representative George W. Julian wrote, "Hostility towards Lincoln's policy of conciliation and contempt for his weakness were undisguised. The universal feeling among radical men here is that his death is a god-send." Senator Wade, who three years later would be pressing for Johnson's impeachment, announced, "Johnson, we have faith in you. By the Gods, there will be no trouble now in running the government." The Radicals were overjoyed with Johnson's reply to Wade:

> I can only say you can judge my policy by the past. Everybody knows what that is. I hold this: . . . *treason* is a crime, and *crime* must be punished. The law provides for it and the courts are open. Treason must be made infamous and traitors impoverished.

However, it was not Johnson's past record but his future policy that would precipitate the crisis between the White House and

Congress. Lincoln had been assassinated while Congress was in adjournment, and although Johnson met with congressional members shortly after taking office, he chose not to call Congress into special session. On May 29, 1865, Johnson infuriated the Radical Republicans when he issued an amnesty proclamation that allowed most southern "traitors" to escape punishment by simply taking an oath of allegiance to the Union. The proclamation did specify fourteen classes of Southerners (primarily former Confederate officials and wealthy planters) who were required to apply directly to the president for pardons, but during the next few months Johnson would grant a steady stream of pardons to thousands of petitioners. Declaring reconstruction finished in Arkansas, Louisiana, Tennessee, and Virginia, Johnson provided the remaining seven southern states with provisional governments that were designed to complete reconstruction as quickly as possible. Congressional Radicals fumed while the new southern governments elected former Confederate leaders to the U.S. Senate.

When Congress finally assembled in December 1865, they refused to seat the new southern members and quickly formulated a response to Johnson's lenient reconstruction plans. The Freedmen's Bureau Bill, which would expand the powers of a federal agency designed to help the freed slaves, was overwhelmingly passed in Congress—and then vetoed by Johnson. In March 1866, Johnson also vetoed the Civil Rights Bill, which protected black rights and citizenship—but this time his veto was overridden by Congress. Congress sent the Fourteenth Amendment to the states for ratification in June; Johnson criticized the amendment and urged the states not to ratify it.

Two major race riots in Memphis and New Orleans during the spring and summer of 1866, in which policemen and whites indiscriminately murdered blacks, raised doubts over the effectiveness of Johnson's reconstruction plan. At the same time, campaigning began for the congressional elections in the fall. Johnson made a campaign trip to support candidates who agreed with his policies, but instead he damaged his own credibility by losing his temper during speeches, arguing with hecklers, and lambasting Radical Republican leaders. The elections resulted in a landslide victory for the Republicans, who gained a two-thirds majority in both the Senate and the House.

The Republicans used their majority to dismantle Johnson's reconstruction policy. Between March and July 1867, Congress passed three Reconstruction Acts, overriding a presidential veto each time. Under these acts, ten southern states (the eleventh, Tennessee, had been readmitted to the Union) were grouped into five military districts; black males in those states were given the vote; and whites who had taken part in the Confederacy were disfranchised. Congress and Johnson clashed further when John-son replaced some of the commanders of the military districts with politically conservative generals. In February 1868, when Johnson violated the Tenure of Office Act by removing Secretary of War Edwin Stanton without obtaining congressional consent, the Radicals seized their chance to impeach Johnson and replace him with one of their own.

"The distinction of race and color is, by the bill, made to operate in favor of the colored and against the white race."

The Civil Rights Bill of 1866 Should Not Be Enacted

Andrew Johnson (1808-1875)

After the assassination of Abraham Lincoln, many Radical Republicans initially believed that his successor, Andrew Johnson, would share their preference for a harsh and expansive reconstruction. Johnson, who grew up in extreme poverty in the South, was known for his intense hatred of the rich plantation owners and the southern aristocracy. He was a strong supporter of the Union and had fiercely denounced the secessionists as traitors. However, Johnson was also a Democrat with a deep commitment to states' rights and a former slaveowner who still held many racial prejudices. His presidency increasingly became a tug-of-war with Congress over policies of reconstruction.

In early 1866, Congress passed the Civil Rights Bill, which specified those civil rights of U.S. citizens that could not be obstructed due to race. The bill was designed in part to counteract the severe "Black Codes" that had been passed in several southern states after the end of the Civil War. These codes gave blacks stricter punishments than whites for the same criminal offenses, created a system of indentured apprenticeship that closely resembled slavery, and restricted the right of blacks to own firearms and to assemble freely. The Civil Rights Bill effectively nullified the Black Codes and established penalties of fines or imprisonment for any

Excerpted from Andrew Johnson's veto message to the U.S. Senate on March 27, 1866. Reprinted in *The Political History of the United States of America During the Period of Reconstruction*, Edward McPherson, ed., Solomons & Chapman, 1875.

person found guilty of depriving a citizen of civil rights because of race. Most importantly, the bill clearly stated that all blacks were now citizens.

On March 27, 1866, Johnson issued his veto of the Civil Rights Bill. In his explanation, Johnson argues that the former slaves should undergo the same process as foreigners of applying for citizenship and studying the principles of government. Citizenship, he further contends, is not necessary to ensure that the civil rights of blacks are protected. Additionally, Johnson objects to the amount of federal power implicit in the bill, claiming that it infringes on states' rights.

I regret that the bill which has passed both Houses of Congress, entitled "An act to protect all persons in the United States in their civil rights, and furnish the means of their vindication," contains provisions which I cannot approve, consistently with my sense of duty to the whole people, and my obligations to the Constitution of the United States. I am therefore constrained to return it to the Senate, the house in which it originated, with my objections to its becoming a law.

By the first section of the bill all persons born in the United States, and not subject to any foreign power, excluding Indians not taxed, are declared to be citizens of the United States. This provision comprehends the Chinese of the Pacific States, Indians subject to taxation, the people called Gipsies, as well as the entire race designated as blacks, people of color, negroes, mulattoes, and persons of African blood. Every individual of these races, born in the United States, is by the bill made a citizen of the United States. It does not purport to declare or confer any other right of citizenship than federal citizenship. It does not purport to give these classes of persons any *status* as citizens of States, except that which may result from their *status* as citizens of the United States. The power to confer the right of State citizenship is just as exclusively with the several States as the power to confer the right of federal citizenship is with Congress.

Acquiring Citizenship

The right of federal citizenship thus to be conferred on the several excepted races before mentioned, is now, for the first time, proposed to be given by law. If, as is claimed by many, all persons who are native-born already are, by virtue of the Constitution, citizens of the United States, the passage of the pending bill cannot be necessary to make them such. If, on the other hand, such persons are not citizens, as may be assumed from the proposed legislation to make them such, the grave question presents itself, whether, when eleven of the thirty-six States are unrepresented in Congress at the present time, it is sound policy to make our entire colored population and all other excepted classes citizens of the United States? Four millions of them have just emerged from slavery into freedom. Can it be reasonably supposed that they possess the requisite qualifications to entitle them to all the privileges and immunities of citizens of the United States? Have the people of the several States expressed such a conviction? It may also be asked whether it is necessary that they should be declared citizens, in order that they may be secured in the enjoyment of the civil rights proposed to be conferred by the bill? Those rights are, by federal as well as State laws, secured to all domiciled aliens and foreigners, even before the completion of the process of naturalization; and it may safely be assumed that the same enactments are sufficient to give like protection and benefits to those for whom this bill provides special legislation. Besides, the policy of the Government, from its origin to the present time, seems to have been that persons who are strangers to and unfamiliar with our institutions and our laws should pass through a certain probation, at the end of which, before attaining the cov-

The Civil Rights Bill of 1866

The Civil Rights Bill of 1866 gave the first statutory definition of the rights of U.S. citizens. The first article of the bill, excerpted below, extended citizenship to all native-born blacks, regardless of whether they had been born free or slave.

Be it enacted by the Senate and House of Representatives of the United States of America in Congress assembled, That all persons born in the United States and not subject to any foreign power, excluding Indians not taxed, are hereby declared to be citizens of the United States; and such citizens, of every race and color, without regard to any previous condition of slavery or involuntary servitude, except as a punishment for crime whereof the party shall have been duly convicted, shall have the same right, in every State and Territory in the United States, to make and enforce contracts, to sue, be parties, and give evidence, to inherit, purchase, lease, sell, hold, and convey real and personal property, and to full and equal benefit of all laws and proceedings for the security of person and property, as is enjoyed by white citizens, and shall be subject to like punishment, pains, and penalties, and to none other, any law, statute, ordinance, regulation, or custom, to the contrary notwithstanding.

eted prize, they must give evidence of their fitness to receive and to exercise the rights of citizens, as contemplated by the Constitution of the United States. The bill, in effect, proposes a discrimination against large numbers of intelligent, worthy, and patriotic foreigners, and in favor of the negro, to whom, after long years of bondage, the avenues to freedom and intelligence have just now been suddenly opened. He must, of necessity, from his previous unfortunate condition of servitude, be less informed as to the nature and character of our institutions than he who, coming from abroad, has to some extent, at least, familiarized himself with the principles of a government to which he voluntarily intrusts "life, liberty, and the pursuit of happiness." Yet it is now proposed, by a single legislative enactment, to confer the rights of citizens upon all persons of African descent born within the extended limits of the United States, while persons of foreign birth, who make our land their home, must undergo a probation of five years, and can only then become citizens upon proof that they are "of good moral character, attached to the principles of the Constitution of the United States, and well disposed to the good order and happiness of the same."

States' Rights

The first section of the bill also contains an enumeration of the rights to be enjoyed by these classes, so made citizens, "in every State and Territory in the United States." These rights are, "to make and enforce contracts, to sue, be parties, and give evidence; to inherit, purchase, lease, sell, hold, and convey real and personal property;" and to have "full and equal benefit of all laws and proceedings for the security of person and property as is enjoyed by white citizens." So, too, they are made subject to the same punishments, pains, and penalties in common with white citizens, and to none other. Thus a perfect equality of the white and colored races is attempted to be fixed by federal law in every State of the Union, over the vast field of State jurisdiction covered by these enumerated rights. In no one of these can any State ever exercise any power of discrimination between the different races. In the exercise of State policy over matters exclusively affecting the people of each State, it has frequently been thought expedient to discriminate between the two races. By the statutes of some of the States, northern as well as southern, it is enacted, for instance, that no white person shall intermarry with a negro or mulatto. Chancellor [James] Kent [of the New York State Court of Chancery] says, speaking of the blacks, that "marriages between them and the whites are forbidden in some of the States where slavery does not exist, and they are prohibited in all the slave-holding States; and when not absolutely contrary to law, they are revolting, and regarded as an offence against public decorum."

I do not say that this bill repeals State laws on the subject of marriage between the two races; for, as the whites are forbidden to intermarry with the blacks, the blacks can only make such contracts as the whites themselves are allowed to make, and therefore cannot, under this bill, enter into the marriage contract with the whites. I cite this discrimination, however, as an instance of the State policy as to discrimination, and to inquire whether, if Congress can abrogate all State laws of discrimination between the two races in the matter of real estate, of suits, and of contracts generally, Congress may not also repeal the State laws as to the contract of marriage between the two races? Hitherto every subject embraced in the enumeration of rights contained in this bill has been considered as exclusively belonging to the States. They all relate to the internal police and economy of the respective States. They are matters which in each State concern the domestic condition of its people, varying in each according to its own peculiar circumstances and the safety and well-being of its own citizens. I do not mean to say that upon all these subjects there are not federal restraints—as, for instance, in the State power of legislation over contracts, there is a federal limitation that no State shall pass a law impairing the obligations of contracts; and, as to crimes, that no State shall pass an *ex post facto* law; and, as to money, that no State shall make anything but gold and silver a legal tender. But where can we find a federal prohibition against the power of any State to discriminate, as do most of them, between aliens and citizens, between artificial persons called corporations and natural persons, in the right to hold real estate? If it be granted that Congress can repeal all State laws discriminating between whites and blacks in the subjects covered by this bill, why, it may be asked, may not Congress repeal, in the same way, all State laws discriminating between the two races on the subjects of suffrage and office? If Congress can declare by law who shall hold lands, who shall testify, who shall have capacity to make a contract in a State, then Congress can by law also declare who, without regard to color or race, shall have the right to sit as a juror or as a judge, to hold any office, and, finally, to vote, "in every State and Territory of the United States." As respects the Territories, they come within the power of Congress, for as to them the law-making power is the federal power; but as to the States no similar provision exists vesting in Congress the power "to make rules and regulations" for them. . . .

Fraught with Evil

I do not propose to consider the policy of this bill. To me the details of the bill seem fraught with evil. The white race and the black race of the South have hitherto lived together under the relation of master and slave—capital owning labor. Now, suddenly, that relation is changed, and, as to ownership, capital and labor are divorced. They stand now each master of itself. In this new relation, one being necessary to the other, there will be a new adjustment, which both are deeply interested in making harmonious. Each has equal power in settling the terms, and, if left to the laws that regulate capital and labor, it is confidently believed that they will satisfactorily work out the problem. Capital, it is true, has more intelligence, but labor is never so ignorant as not to understand its own interests, not to know its own value, and not to see that capital must pay that value.

Southern Protest

Many Southerners were opposed to the passage of the Civil Rights Act of 1866. In an article from the Charleston (S.C.) Courier, *published six days after the bill was passed into law over the president's veto, Julius J. Fleming expresses the South's dissatisfaction with the fact that the states of the former Confederacy were barred from representation in Congress and therefore had no say over the passage of this legislation.*

The [Civil Rights] Bill has passed. In vain the president's veto. In vain the voice of reason and the protest of patriotism. It has become a law—a law specially obnoxious and known to be so to the very states excluded from representation and allowed no voice in its passage. A measure pronounced by prominent statesmen to be most fatal to liberty and certainly most damaging to our great unrepresented southern domain. Its leading provisions regarded by learned jurists as directly at war with the first principles of this government. . . .

This will necessitate additional state legislation. Our own legislature must undo much of its last winter's work. The freedmen's code and its adjunct machinery, considered by some at the time an abortion, must be decently buried. Under the high pressure now brought to bear, we have no option. No state law must be left on the statute which does not accord with the express will and decree of Congress. There must be no more class legislation, no discrimination in codes or courts on account of color, but equality before the law must be everywhere recognized. . . . It devolves upon us to fall in promptly at the word of congressional command.

This bill frustrates this adjustment. It intervenes between capital and labor, and attempts to settle questions of political economy through the agency of numerous officials, whose interest it will be to foment discord between the two races; for as the breach widens their employment will continue, and when it is closed their occupation will terminate.

In all our history, in all our experience as a people, living under federal and State law, no such system as that contemplated by the details of this bill has ever before been proposed or adopted. They establish for the security of the colored race safeguards which go infinitely beyond any that the General Government has ever provided for the white race. In fact, the distinction of race and color is, by the bill, made to operate in favor of the colored and against the white race. They interfere with the municipal legislation of the States, with the relations existing exclusively between a State and its citizens, or between inhabitants of the same State—an absorption and assumption of power by the General Government which, if acquiesced in, must sap and destroy our federative system of limited powers, and break down the barriers which preserve the rights of the States. It is another step, or rather stride, towards centralization, and the concentration of all legislative powers in the national Government. The tendency of the bill must be to resuscitate the spirit of rebellion, and to arrest the progress of those influences which are more closely drawing around the States the bonds of union and peace.

To Protect and Defend

My lamented predecessor, in his proclamation of the 1st of January, 1863, ordered and declared that all persons held as slaves within certain States and parts of States therein designated were, and thenceforward should be free, and, further, that the executive government of the United States, including the military and naval authorities thereof, would recognize and maintain the freedom of such persons. This guarantee has been rendered especially obligatory and sacred by the amendment of the Constitution abolishing slavery throughout the United States. I, therefore, fully recognize the obligation to protect and defend that class of our people, whenever and wherever it shall become necessary, and to the full extent compatible with the Constitution of the United States.

Entertaining these sentiments, it only remains for me to say, that I will cheerfully co-operate with Congress in any measure that may be necessary for the protection of the civil rights of the freedmen, as well as those of all other classes of persons throughout the United States, by judicial process, under equal and impartial laws, in conformity with the provisions of the Federal Constitution.

VIEWPOINT 2

"It is manifest that, unless this bill can be passed, nothing can be done to protect the freedmen in their liberty and their rights."

The Civil Rights Bill of 1866 Should Be Enacted

Lyman Trumbull (1813-1896)

Senator Lyman Trumbull of Illinois began his political career as a Democrat, but his antislavery views led him to join the Republicans in the 1850s. Originally a lawyer, Trumbull became a justice of the Illinois Supreme Court and in 1855 was elected to the U.S. Senate. A prominent politician, Trumbull was the head of the Senate Judiciary Committee during the Civil War and submitted the resolution from which the Thirteenth Amendment (abolishing slavery in the United States) was drafted. Trumbull also sponsored the Civil Rights Bill that President Andrew Johnson vetoed in March 1866.

In his April 4, 1866, speech to the Senate, Trumbull objects to Johnson's veto, supporting his reasoning by quoting Johnson's earlier argument against a veto by President James Buchanan. In defense of the bill, Trumbull asserts that a national law must be established to protect the civil rights of blacks. He insists that states have no right to deny an individual's constitutional rights because of race; therefore, the bill does not violate states' rights. Although Trumbull stops short of advocating black suffrage, he emphasizes that the citizenship of the former slaves must be established by law in order to protect their civil rights.

On April 8, 1866, Congress overrode Johnson's veto and passed the Civil Rights Act.

Lyman Trumbull, *Congressional Globe*, 39th Cong., 1st sess., 1866, pp. 1755-61.

Mr. President, I fully share with the President of the United States the regret expressed that he was unable to sign the bill "to protect all persons in the United States in their civil rights and secure the means of their vindication." I regret it on my own account because the just expectations raised when this bill was presented to the President before its introduction into the Senate have been disappointed. I regret it on the President's account because it is calculated to alienate him from those who elevated him to power and would gladly have rallied around his administration to sustain him in the principles upon which he was elected. But above all, sir, I regret it for liberty's sake, to secure which to ourselves and our posterity this government was founded. Yet, if the bill is unconstitutional or unjust to the whole people, I would not have had the President approve it. . . .

Gladly would I refrain from speaking of the spirit of [President Andrew Johnson's veto] message, of the dangerous doctrines it promulgates, of the inconsistencies and contradictions of its author, of his encroachments upon the constitutional rights of Congress, of his assumption of unwarranted powers, which, if persevered in and not checked by the people, must eventually lead to a subversion of the government and the destruction of liberty.

A Difference of Opinion

Congress, in the passage of the bill under consideration, sought no controversy with the President. So far from it, the bill was proposed with a view to carry out what were supposed to be the views of the President and was submitted to him before its introduction into the Senate. I am not about to relate private declarations of the President, but it is right that the American people should know that the controversy which exists between him and Congress in reference to this measure is of his own seeking. Soon after Congress met it became apparent that there was a difference of opinion between the President and some members of Congress in regard to the condition of the rebellious states and the rights to be secured to freedmen.

The President in his annual message had denied the constitutional power of the general government to extend the elective franchise to Negroes, but he was equally decided in the assertion of the right of every man to life, liberty, and the pursuit of happiness. This was his language:

> But while I have no doubt that now, after the close of the war, it is not competent for the general government to extend the elective franchise in the several states, it is equally clear that good faith requires the security of the freedmen in their liberty and their property.

There were some members of Congress who expressed the opinion that in the reorganization of the rebellious states the right of suffrage should be extended to the colored man, though this was not the prevailing sentiment of Congress. All were anxious for reorganization of the rebellious states and their admission to full participation in the federal government as soon as these relations could be restored with safety to all concerned. Feeling the importance of harmonious action between the different departments of the government and an anxious desire to sustain the President, for whom I had always entertained the highest respect, I had frequent interviews with him during the early part of the session.

Senator Lyman Trumbull disagreed with President Andrew Johnson on many political issues, but in 1868 he opposed Johnson's impeachment.

Without mentioning anything said by him, I may with propriety state that, acting from the considerations I have stated and believing that the passage of a law by Congress, securing equality in civil rights when denied by state authorities to freedmen and all other inhabitants of the United States, would do much to relieve anxiety in the North, to induce the Southern states to secure these rights by their own action, and thereby remove many of the obstacles to an early reconstruction, I prepared the bill substantially as it is now returned with the President's objections. After the bill was introduced and printed, a copy was furnished him; and, at a subsequent period, when it was reported that he was hesitating about signing the Freedmen's Bureau Bill, he was informed of the condition of the Civil Rights Bill then pending in the House, and a hope expressed that if he had objections to any of its provisions he would make them known to its friends that they might be remedied, if not destructive of the measure; that there was believed to be no disposition on the part of Congress, and certainly none on my part, to have bills presented to him which he could not approve.

Civil Rights

He never indicated to me, nor, so far as I know, to any of its friends, the least objection to any of the provisions of the bill till after its passage. And how could he, consistently with himself? The bill was framed, as was supposed, in entire harmony with his views, and certainly in harmony with what he was then and has since been doing in protecting freedmen in their civil rights all through the rebellious states. It was strictly limited to the protection of the civil rights belonging to every freeman, the birthright of every American citizen, and carefully avoided conferring or interfering with political rights or privileges of any kind.

The bill neither confers nor abridges the rights of anyone but simply declares that in civil rights there shall be an equality among all classes of citizens and that all alike shall be subject to the same punishment. Each state, so that it does not abridge the great fundamental rights belonging, under the Constitution, to all citizens, may grant or withhold such civil rights as it pleases; all that is required is that, in this respect, its laws shall be impartial.

And yet this is the bill now returned with the President's objections; and such objections! What are they? That:

> In all our history, in all our experience as a people, living under federal and state laws, no such system as that contemplated by the details of this bill has ever before been proposed or adopted. . . .

He says "the tendency of this bill must be to resuscitate the spirit of the rebellion." What assumption in one who denies the authority to punish those who violate United States laws under color of state authority—a doctrine from which the rebellion sprung and in entire harmony with the declaration of Mr. [James] Buchanan, that there was no power to coerce a state.

Johnson's Own Words

But, sir, out of the mouth of Senator Andrew Johnson I will prove that President Andrew Johnson has violated the spirit of the Constitution, if not its letter, in vetoing this bill. It will be remembered that the bill passed both houses of Congress by more than a two-thirds majority—the vote in the Senate being, yeas 33

74

As Free As White Men

Blacks began to call for their full civil rights even before the end of the Civil War. On March 5, 1865, the New Orleans Tribune, the first black-owned newspaper in the South, published an editorial demanding equal treatment and the right to vote.

We ask justice—full justice—for all.

For colored soldiers, who partake of the perils of our armies on the battlefield, we want equal treatment with the white soldiers. We claim for them fair chance for promotion, fair board of examination, and admission of colored officers to all positions and ranks according to their merit and valor.

For colored laborers we want entire freedom and self-disposal of themselves. We want that they be as free as white men in contracting for their labor, going from place to place, and enjoying the earnings of their toils. . . .

For colored men in general, we claim the right of suffrage, and thereby the right of self-taxation and self-government, which is conferred upon the whites. We claim that privilege on the broad ground that they are men and they are American citizens.

These are the principles we have at any time advocated and defended. We do not care for the obstacles we may find in our way, or the enemies we may arraign against us. The men who oppose such a platform can only be the enemies of our race. Do not say that we are going too fast or going too far. We ask any candid man: is freedom complete? Is the black in the full enjoyment of all he has a right to obtain? If not, why should we stop in our efforts to have justice done to our race?

to nays 12, and, in the House, yeas 111, nays 38. I will read from the remarks of Senator Andrew Johnson on the veto of the Homestead Bill by Mr. Buchanan:

The President of the United States *presumes*—yes, sir, I say *presumes*—to dictate to the American people and to the two houses of Congress, in violation of the spirit, if not the letter, of the Constitution, that this measure shall not become a law. Why do I say this? I ask, is there any difference in the spirit of the Constitution whether a measure is sanctioned by a two-thirds vote before its passage or afterward? When a measure has been vetoed by the President, the Constitution requires that it shall be reconsidered and passed by a two-thirds vote in order to become a law. But here, in the teeth of the Executive, there was a two-thirds vote in favor of this bill. The vote was 36 to 2 in this body. The two houses have said that this bill is constitutional and right. In the other house, reflecting the popular sentiment of the nation, the vote was 112 to 51—ten more than the two-thirds majority which the Constitution requires; and when there is a two-thirds vote for a measure, I say it is against the spirit of the Constitution for the Executive to say, "No, you shall not have this measure; I will take all the chances of vetoing it."

Apply this language to the facts connected with this bill and then say who has violated the spirit of the Constitution.

This bill in no manner interferes with the municipal regulations of any state which protects all alike in their rights of person and property. It could have no operation in Massachusetts, New York, Illinois, or most of the states of the Union. How preposterous, then, to charge that unless some state can have and exercise the right to punish somebody or to deny somebody a civil right on account of his color, its rights as a state will be destroyed. It is manifest that, unless this bill can be passed, nothing can be done to protect the freedmen in their liberty and their rights.

Whatever may have been the opinion of the President at one time as to "good faith requiring the security of the freedmen in their liberty and their property," it is now manifest from the character of his objections to this bill that he will approve no measure that will accomplish the object. That the second clause of the [Thirteenth] constitutional amendment gives this power, there can be no question. Some have contended that it gives the power even to confer the right of suffrage. I have not thought so, because I have never thought suffrage any more necessary to the liberty of a freedman than of a nonvoting white, whether child or female. But his liberty under the Constitution he is entitled to, and whatever is necessary to secure it to him he is entitled to have, be it the ballot or the bayonet. If the bill now before us, and which goes no further than to secure civil rights to the freedman, cannot be passed, then the constitutional amendment proclaiming freedom to all the inhabitants of the land is a cheat and a delusion.

I cannot better conclude what I have to say than in the language of Mr. Johnson on the occasion of the veto of the Homestead Bill, when, after stating that the fact that the President was inconsistent and changed his opinion with reference to a great measure and a great principle is no reason why a senator or representative who had acted understandingly should change his opinion, he said:

> I hope the Senate and House of Representatives, who have sanctioned this bill by more than a two-thirds majority, will, according to the Constitution, exercise their privilege and power and let the bill become a law of the land, according to the high behest of the American people.

VIEWPOINT 3

"This [proposed amendment] is but another attempt to consolidate the power of the States in the Federal Government. It is another step to an imperial despotism."

The Fourteenth Amendment Violates States' Rights

Andrew J. Rogers (1828-1900)

Even before the Civil Rights Bill was passed by Congress in April 1866, many Radical Republicans worried that the bill did not go far enough. Although the bill firmly established black citizenship and equal rights, it contained no provision to ensure its enforcement. An amendment to the Constitution, many felt, was necessary to secure citizenship and equality for the former slaves. Because the president has no authority over the passing of an amendment, some also saw this approach as a way to circumvent President Andrew Johnson's opposition to civil rights. Accordingly, members of the Joint Committee on Reconstruction began work on a proposed Fourteenth Amendment to the Constitution.

On February 26, 1866, Representative John A. Bingham of Ohio submitted his draft of the proposed amendment, which authorized Congress to protect the civil rights of all U.S. citizens, to the House of Representatives. After Bingham finished speaking, Andrew J. Rogers, a Democratic representative from New Jersey and a minority member of the Republican-controlled Joint Committee, took the floor in opposition to the amendment. In his speech to the House, Rogers insists that the organic federal law (the U.S. Constitution) does not allow the federal government to determine

Andrew J. Rogers, *Congressional Globe*, 39th Cong., 1st sess., February 26, 1866, pp. 150-51.

which state laws are permissible. If the Civil Rights Bill is constitutional, Rogers contends, there should be no need for a constitutional amendment to enforce it. Rogers also advocates restricting the rights of blacks, particularly the right to vote and to hold political office. According to Rogers, individual state governments have the right to segregate schools, ban interracial marriage, prohibit blacks from owning property, and pass other discriminatory laws without interference from the federal government.

No resolution proposing an amendment to the Constitution of the United States had been offered to this Congress more dangerous to the liberties of the people and the foundations of this Government than the pending resolution [Fourteenth Amendment]. When sifted from top to bottom it will be found to be the embodiment of centralization and the disfranchisement of the States of those sacred and immutable State rights which were reserved to them by the consent of our fathers in our organic law.

The Organic Law

When the gentleman [Ohio representative John A. Bingham] says the proposed amendment is intended to authorize no rights except those already embodied in the Constitution, I give him the plain and emphatic answer—if the Constitution provides the requirements contained in this amendment, why, in this time of excitement and public clamor, should we attempt to again ingraft upon it what is already in it? . . .

The gentleman takes the position that there is nothing in this proposed amendment with regard to privileges and immunities of citizens of the several States attempted to be ingrafted in the instrument, except those which already exist in it. If those rights already exist in the organic law of the land, I ask him, what is the necessity of so amending the Constitution as to authorize Congress to carry into effect a plain provision which now, according to his views, inheres in the very organic law itself?

I know what the gentleman will attempt to say in answer to that position: that because the Constitution authorizes Congress to carry the powers conferred by it into effect, privileges and immunities are not considered within the meaning of powers, and therefore Congress has no right to carry into effect what the Constitution itself intended when it provided that citizens of each State should have all privileges and immunities of citizens in the several States.

Now, sir, the answer to that argument is simply this: that when the Constitution was framed and ratified, its makers did not intend to lodge in the Congress of the United States any power to override a State and settle by congressional legislation the rights, privileges, and immunities of citizens in the several States. That matter was left entirely for the courts, to enforce the privileges and immunities of the citizens under that clause of the organic law. Although our forefathers, in their wisdom, after having exacted and wrested from Great Britain State rights, saw fit to incorporate in the Constitution such a principle in regard to citizens of the several States, yet they never intended to give to Congress the power, by virtue of that clause, to control the local domain of a State or the privileges and immunities of citizens in the State, even though they had come from another State. . . .

But this proposed amendment goes much further than the Constitution goes in the language which it uses with regard to the privileges and immunities of citizens in the several States. It proposes so to amend it that all persons in the several States shall by act of Congress have equal protection in regard to life, liberty, and property. If the bill to protect all persons in the United States in their civil rights and furnish the means of their vindication, which has just passed the Senate by almost the entire vote of the Republican party be constitutional, what, I ask, is the use of this proposed amendment? What is the use of authorizing Congress to do more than Congress has already done, so far as one branch is concerned, in passing a bill to guaranty civil rights and immunities to the people of the United States without distinction of race or color? If it is necessary now to amend the Constitution of the United States in the manner in which the learned gentleman [Bingham] who reported this amendment proclaims, then the vote of the Senate of the United States in passing that bill guarantying civil rights to all without regard to race or color was an attempt to project legislation that was manifestly unconstitutional, and which this proposed amendment is to make legal. . . .

Are Blacks Citizens?

My only hope for liberty is in the full restoration of all the States, with the rights of representation in the Congress of the United States upon no condition but to take the oath laid down in the Constitution. In the legislation by the States they should look to the protection, security, advancement, and improvement, physically and intellectually, of all classes, as well the blacks as the whites. Negroes should have the channels of education opened to them by the States, and by the States they should be protected in life, liberty, and property, and by the States should be allowed all the rights of being witnesses, of suing and being sued, of contracting, and doing every act or thing that a white man is authorized by law to do. But to give to them the right of suffrage, and hold office, and marry whites, in my judgment is dangerous and never ought to be extended to them by any State. However, that is a matter belonging solely to the sovereign will of the States. I have faith in the people, and dark and gloomy as the hour is, I do not despair of free government. I plant myself upon the will of God to work out a bright destiny for the American people. . . .

The Proposed Amendment

John A. Bingham, a member of the Joint Committee on Reconstruction, authored the following proposal for the Fourteenth Amendment and reported it to Congress on February 26, 1866. Although this initial draft was not accepted by Congress, it became the foundation for the civil rights portions of the Fourteenth Amendment adopted by Congress in 1866 and ratified in 1868.

Resolved by the Senate and House of Representatives of the United States of America in Congress assembled, (two thirds of both Houses concurring,) That the following article be proposed to the Legislatures of the several States as an amendment to the Constitution of the United States, which, when ratified by three fourths of the said Legislatures, shall be valid as part of said constitution, namely:
ARTICLE—. The Congress shall have power to make all laws which shall be necessary and proper to secure to the citizens of each State all privileges and immunities of citizens in the several States, and to all persons in the several States equal protection in the rights of life, liberty, and property.

Who gave the Senate the constitutional power to pass that bill guarantying equal rights to all, if it is necessary to amend the organic law in the manner proposed by this joint resolution? This is but another attempt to consolidate the power of the States in the Federal Government. It is another step to an imperial despotism. It is but another attempt to blot out from that flag the eleven stars that represent the States of the South and to consolidate in the Federal Government, by the action of Congress, all the powers claimed by the Czar of Russia or the Emperor of the French. It provides that all persons in the several States shall have equal protection in the right of life, liberty, and property. Now, it is claimed by gentlemen upon the other side of the House [Republicans] that negroes are citizens of the United States. Suppose that in the State of New Jersey negroes are citizens, as they are claimed to be by the other side of the House, and they change their residence to the State of South Carolina, if this amendment be passed Congress can pass under it a law compelling South Carolina to grant to negroes every right accorded to white people there; and as white men there have the right to marry white women, negroes, under this amendment, would be entitled to the same right; and thus miscegenation and mixture of the races could be authorized in any State, as all citizens under this amendment are entitled to the same privileges and immunities, and the same protection in life, liberty, and property. . . .

The organic law says that no person but a natural-born citizen, or a citizen when it was made, shall be eligible to the office of President. This amendment would make all citizens eligible, negroes as well as whites. For if negroes are citizens, they are natural born, because they are the descendants of ancestors for several generations back, who were born here as well as themselves. The negroes cannot be citizens in a new State in which they may take up their residence unless they are entitled to the privileges and immunities of the citizens resident in that State. Most of the States make a distinction in the rights of married women. This would authorize Congress to repeal all such distinctions.

Marriage is a contract as set down in all the books from the Year-books down to the present time. A white citizen of any State may marry a white woman; but if a black citizen goes into the same State he is entitled to the same privileges and immunities that white citizens have, and therefore under this amendment a negro might be allowed to marry a white woman. I will not go for an amendment of the Constitution to give a power so dangerous, so likely to degrade the white men and women of this country, which would put it in the power of fanaticism in times of excitement and civil war to allow the people of any State to mingle and mix themselves by marriage with negroes so as to run the pure white blood of the Anglo-Saxon people of the country into the black blood of the negro or the copper blood of the Indian.

Sovereignty of the States

Now, sir, the words "privileges and immunities" in the Constitution of the United States have been construed by the courts of the several States to mean privileges and immunities in a limited extent. . . . Those words, as now contained in the Constitution of the United States, were used in a qualified sense, and subject to the local control, dominion, and the sovereignty of the States. But this act of Congress proposes to amend the Constitution so as to take away the rights of the States with regard to the life, liberty, and property of the people, so as to enable and empower Congress to pass laws compelling the abrogation of all the statutes of the States which make a distinction, for instance, between a crime committed by a white man and a crime committed by a black man, or allow white people privileges, immunities, or property not allowed to a black man.

Take the State of Kentucky, for instance. According to her laws, if a negro commits a rape upon a white woman he is punished by death. If a white man commits that offense, the punishment is imprisonment. Now, according to this proposed amendment, the Congress of the United States is to have the right to repeal the law of Kentucky and compel that State to inflict the same punishment upon a white man for rape as upon a black man.

According to the organic law of Indiana a negro is forbidden to come there and hold property. This amendment would abrogate and blot out forever that law, which is valuable in the estimation of the sovereign people of Indiana.

In the State of Pennsylvania there are laws which make a distinction with regard to the schooling of white children and the schooling of black children. It is provided that certain schools shall be designated and set apart for white children, and certain other schools designated and set apart for black children. Under this amendment, Congress would have power to compel the State to provide for white children and black children to attend the same school, upon the principle that all the people in the several States shall have equal protection in all the rights of life, liberty, and property, and all the privileges and immunities of citizens in the several States.

The effect of this proposed amendment is to take away the power of the States; to interfere with the internal police and regulations of the States; to centralize a consolidated power in this Federal Government which our fathers never intended should be exercised by it.

VIEWPOINT 4

"The adoption of the proposed amendment will take from the States no rights that belong to the States."

The Fourteenth Amendment Does Not Violate States' Rights

John A. Bingham (1815-1900)

John A. Bingham was a Republican representative from Ohio and had served as special judge advocate in the trial of the conspirators in the assassination of Abraham Lincoln. A member of the Joint Committee on Reconstruction, Bingham was involved in the preparation of the proposed Fourteenth Amendment to the Constitution. The amendment went through many rewritings between January 1866, when a first draft was submitted to Congress, and June 1866.

On February 26, 1866, Bingham submitted his revision of the first draft to the House of Representatives. Bingham's proposed amendment assigned to Congress the power to make laws ensuring the civil rights of all citizens and to provide equal protection of life, liberty, and prosperity, regardless of race. Two days later, Bingham defended the proposed amendment against the attacks of Democrats who, like Andrew J. Rogers, believed the amendment would infringe on states' rights. Bingham castigates the "gentlemen" of Congress who declare their approval of equal rights while simultaneously refusing to give the federal government the power to enforce civil rights legislation. Without the amendment, he insists, the southern states will be free to violate the constitutional rights of blacks without fear of federal intervention.

John A. Bingham, *Congressional Globe*, 39th Cong., 1st sess., February 28, 1866, pp. 157-60.

Although Bingham's draft was also sent back for revisions, the Fourteenth Amendment was eventually accepted by both houses of Congress on June 13, 1866; it was ratified in July 1868.

The people of the United States have intrusted to the present Congress in some sense the care of the Republic, not only for the present, but for all the hereafter. [The Joint Committee on Reconstruction] would not have sent to this House for its consideration this proposition [Fourteenth Amendment] but for the conviction that its adoption by Congress and its ratification by the people of the United States is essential to the safety of all the people of every State. I repel the suggestion made here in the heat of debate, that the committee or any of its members who favor this proposition seek in any form to mar the Constitution of the country, or take away from any state any right that belongs to it, or from any citizen of any State any right that belongs to him under that Constitution. The proposition pending before the House is simply a proposition to arm the Congress of the United States, by the consent of the people of the United States, with the power to enforce the bill of rights as it stands in the Constitution today. . . .

Gentlemen admit the force of the provisions in the bill of rights, that the citizens of the United States shall be entitled to all the privileges and immunities of citizens of the United States in the several States, and that no person shall be deprived of life, liberty, or property without due process of law; but they say, "We are opposed to its enforcement by act of Congress under an amended Constitution, as proposed." That is the sum and substance of all the argument that we have heard on this subject. Why are gentlemen opposed to the enforcement of the bill of rights, as proposed? Because they aver it would interfere with the reserved rights of the States! Who ever before heard that any State had reserved to itself the right, under the Constitution of the United States, to withhold from any citizen of the United States within its limits, under any pretext whatever, any of the privileges of a citizen of the United States, or to impose upon him, no matter from what State he may have come, any burden contrary to that provision of the Constitution which declares that the citizen shall be entitled in the several States to all the immunities of a citizen of the United States?

Enforcing the Constitution

What does the word immunity in your Constitution mean? Exemption from unequal burdens. Ah! say gentlemen who oppose this amendment, we are not opposed to equal rights; we are not opposed to the bill of rights that all shall be protected alike in life, liberty, and property; we are only opposed to enforcing it by national authority, even by the consent of the loyal people of all the States. . . .

Why, I ask, should not the "injunctions and prohibitions," addressed by the people in the Constitution to the States and the Legislatures of States, be enforced by the people through the proposed amendment? By the decisions read the people are without remedy. It is admitted . . . that the State Legislatures may by direct violations of their duty and oaths avoid the requirements of the Constitution, and thereby do an act which would break up any government.

Those oaths have been disregarded; those requirements of our Constitution have been broken; they are disregarded to-day in Oregon; they are disregarded to-day, and have been disregarded for the last five, ten, or twenty years in every one of the eleven States recently in insurrection.

The question is, simply, whether you will give by this amendment to the people of the United States the power, by legislative enactment, to punish officials of States for violation of the oaths enjoined upon them by their Constitution? That is the question, and the whole question. The adoption of the proposed amendment will take from the States no rights that belong to the States. They elect their Legislatures; they enact their laws for the punishment of crimes against life, liberty, or property; but in the event of the adoption of this amendment, if they conspire together to enact laws refusing equal protection to life, liberty, or property, the Congress is thereby vested with power to hold them to answer before the bar of the national courts for the violation of their oaths and of the rights of their fellow-men. Why should it not be so? That is the question. Why should it not be so? Is the bill of rights to stand in our Constitution hereafter, as in the past five years within eleven States, a mere dead letter? It is absolutely essential to the safety of the people that it should be enforced.

Unity of the People

Mr. Speaker, it appears to me that this very provision of the bill of rights brought in question this day, upon this trial before the House, more than any other provision of the Constitution, makes that unity of government which constitutes us one people, by which and through which American nationality came to be, and only by the enforcement of which can American nationality continue to be.

The imperishable words of [George] Washington ought to be in the minds of all of us touching this great question whether the unity of the Government shall be enforced hereafter by just penal enactments when the Legislatures of States refuse to do their duty or keep inviolate their oath. Washington, speaking to you and to me and to the millions who are to come after us, says:

> The unity of the Government which constitutes you one people is a main pillar in the edifice of your real independence, the support of your tranquillity at home, your peace abroad, of your safety, or your prosperity, of that very liberty which you so highly prize.

Is it not essential to the unity of the people that the citizens of each State shall be entitled to all the privileges and immunities of citizens in the several States? Is it not essential to the unity of the Government and the unity of the people that all persons, whether citizens or strangers, within this land, shall have equal protection in every State in this Union in the rights of life and liberty and property?

Why, sir, what an anomaly is presented today to the world! We have the power to vindicate the personal liberty and all the personal rights of the citizen on the remotest sea, under the frowning batteries of the remotest tyranny on this earth, while we have not the power in time of peace to enforce the citizens' rights to life, liberty, and property within the limits of South Carolina after her State government shall be recognized and her constitutional relations restored. . . .

As the whole Constitution was to be the supreme law in every State, it therefore results that the citizens of each State, being citizens of the United States, should be entitled to all the privileges and immunities of citizens of the United States in every State, and all persons, now that slavery has forever perished, should be entitled to equal protection in the rights of life, liberty, and property.

As a further security for the enforcement of the Constitution, and especially of this sacred bill of rights, to all the citizens and all the people of the United States, it is further provided that the members of the several State Legislatures and all executive and judicial officers, both of the United States and of the several States, shall be bound by oath or affirmation to support this Constitution. The oath, the most solemn compact which man can make with his Maker, was to bind the State Legislatures, executive officers, and judges to sacredly respect the Constitution and all the rights secured by it. And yet there is still another provision lest a State Legislature, with the approval of a State Executive, should, in disregard of their oath, invade the rights of any citizen or person by unjust legislation, violative alike of the Constitution and the rights secured by it, which is very significant and not to be overlooked, which is,

> And the judges of every State shall be bound by the Constitu-

Mending the Constitution

By May of 1866, Congress was considering the final version of the proposed Fourteenth Amendment. In a speech delivered on May 8, 1866, Representative Thaddeus Stevens warns his colleagues that a future majority of Democrats in Congress could easily overturn the Civil Rights Act of 1866. Stevens advocates adopting the Fourteenth Amendment as a much surer safeguard of civil rights.

I can hardly believe that any person can be found who will not admit that every one of these provisions [of the Fourteenth Amendment] is just. They are all asserted, in some form or other, in our DECLARATION or organic law. But the Constitution limits only the action of Congress, and is not a limitation on the States. This amendment supplies that defect, and allows Congress to correct the unjust legislation of the States, so far that the law which operates upon one man shall operate *equally* upon all. Whatever law punishes a white man for a crime shall punish the black man precisely in the same way and to the same degree. Whatever law protects the white man shall afford "equal" protection to the black man. . . . These are great advantages over their present [black] codes. Now different degrees of punishment are inflicted, not on account of the magnitude of the crime, but according to the color of the skin. Now color disqualifies a man from testifying in courts, or being tried in the same way as white men. I need not enumerate these partial and oppressive laws. Unless the Constitution should restrain them those States will all, I fear, keep up this discrimination, and crush to death the hated freedmen. Some answer, "Your civil rights bill secures the same things." That is partly true, but a law is repealable by a majority. And I need hardly say that the first time that the South with their copperhead allies obtain the command of Congress it will be repealed. The veto of the President and their votes on the bill are conclusive evidence of that. . . . This amendment once adopted cannot be annulled without two thirds of Congress.

tion of the United States, anything in the constitution and laws of any State to the contrary notwithstanding.

With these provisions in the Constitution for the enforcement in every State of its requirements, is it surprising that the framers of the Constitution omitted to insert an express grant of power in Congress to enforce by penal enactment these great canons of the supreme law, securing to all the citizens in every State all the privileges and immunities of citizens, and to all the people all the sacred rights of person—those rights dear to freemen and formidable only to tyrants—and of which the fathers of the Republic spoke, after God had given them the victory, in that memorable address in which they declared, "Let it be remembered that the rights for which America has contended were the rights of human nature"? Is it surprising that essential as they held the full security to all citizens of all the privileges and immunities of citizens, and to all the people the sacred rights of person, that having proclaimed them they left their lawful enforcement to each of the States, under the solemn obligation resting upon every State officer to regard, respect, and obey the constitutional injunction?

Protection of Rights

What more could have been added to that instrument to secure the enforcement of these provisions of the bill of rights in every State, other than the additional grant of power which we ask this day? Nothing at all. And I am perfectly confident that that grant of power would have been there but for the fact that its insertion in the Constitution would have been utterly incompatible with the existence of slavery in any State; for although slaves might not have been admitted to be citizens they must have been admitted to be persons. That is the only reason why it was not there. There was a fetter upon the conscience of the nation; the people could not put it there and permit slavery in any State thereafter. Thank God, that fetter has been broken; it has turned to dust before the breath of the people, speaking as the voice of God and solemnly ordaining that slavery is forever prohibited everywhere within the Republic except as punishment for crime on due conviction. Even now for crimes men may be enslaved in States, notwithstanding the new amendment.

As slaves were not protected by the Constitution, there might be some color of excuse for the slave States in their disregard for the requirement of the bill of rights as to slaves and refusing them protection in life or property; though, in my judgment, there could be no possible apology for reducing men made like themselves, in the image of God, to a level with the brutes of the field, and condemning them to toil without reward, to live without knowledge, and die without hope.

But, sir, there never was even colorable excuse, much less apology, for any man North or South claiming that any State Legislature or State court, or State Executive, has any right to deny protection to any free citizen of the United States within their limits in the rights of life, liberty, and property. Gentlemen who oppose this amendment oppose the grant of power to enforce the bill of rights. Gentlemen who oppose this amendment simply declare to these rebel States, go on with your confiscation statutes, your statutes of banishment, your statues of unjust imprisonment, your statutes of murder and death against men because of their loyalty to the Constitution and Government of the United States. . . .

I speak in behalf of this amendment in no party spirit, in no spirit of resentment toward any State or the people of any State, in no spirit of innovation, but for the sake of a violated Constitution and a wronged and wounded country whose heart is now smitten with a strange, great sorrow. I urge the amendment for the enforcement of these essential provisions of your Constitution, divine in their justice, sublime in their humanity, which declare that all men are equal in the rights of life and liberty before the majesty of American law.

Representatives, to you I appeal, that hereafter, by your act and the approval of the loyal people of this country, every man in every State of the Union, in accordance with the written words of your Constitution, may, by the national law, be secured in the equal protection of his personal rights. Your Constitution provides that no man, no matter what his color, no matter beneath what sky he may have been born, no matter in what disastrous conflict or by what tyrannical hand his liberty may have been cloven down, no matter how poor, no matter how friendless, no matter how ignorant, shall be deprived of life or liberty or property without due process of law—law in its highest sense, that law which is the perfection of human reason, and which is impartial, equal, exact justice; that justice which requires that every man shall have his right; that justice which is the highest duty of nations as it is the imperishable attribute of the God of nations.

VIEWPOINT 5

"With such treachery in such a cause there can be no parley."

President Johnson Should Be Impeached

Charles Sumner (1811-1874)

By 1868, President Andrew Johnson and the Republican-held Congress had spent three years battling over reconstruction legislation. The Freedmen's Bureau Act, the Civil Rights Act, the Reconstruction Acts: All had been vetoed by Johnson, and every veto had been overridden by Congress. The Tenure of Office Act, also passed over a presidential veto, prohibited the president from removing federal officials without the Senate's approval. Johnson tested this new act by dismissing Secretary of War Edwin Stanton. Four days later, the House of Representatives responded by voting to impeach Johnson.

The trial of Andrew Johnson was held in the Senate in March 1868, and Senator Charles Sumner of Massachusetts was among those arguing for conviction. Sumner, a powerful Radical, was the leader of the antislavery contingent in Congress and the first prominent official to support emancipation. In 1856, Sumner was beaten with a cane by an outraged southern congressman; his injuries were so severe that he left public life for three years to recuperate. Yet when he returned to the Senate floor, Sumner remained as outspoken as ever, combating Johnson's reconstruction program. In the speech that follows, Sumner compares Johnson to Confederate Rebels and slaveholders, insisting that the Union is in jeopardy every day that Johnson remains president. He accuses Johnson of usurping the powers belonging to Congress. Johnson has become a dictator, Sumner declares, who must be removed from office for the country's good.

Excerpted from *Trial of Andrew Johnson*, vol. 3, Benjamin P. Poore, ed., Washington, D.C., 1868.

This is one of the last great battles with slavery. Driven from these legislative chambers, driven from the field of war, this monstrous power has found a refuge in the executive mansion, where, in utter disregard of the Constitution and laws, it seeks to exercise its ancient, far-reaching sway. All this is very plain. Nobody can question it. Andrew Johnson is the impersonation of the tyrannical slave power. In him it lives again. He is the lineal successor of John C. Calhoun and Jefferson Davis; and he gathers about him the same supporters.

Original partisans of slavery, North and South; habitual compromisers of great principles; maligners of the Declaration of Independence; politicians without heart; lawyers for whom a technicality is everything, and a promiscuous company who at every stage of the battle have set their faces against equal rights; these are his allies. It is the old troop of slavery, with a few recruits, ready as of old for violence—cunning in device and heartless in quibble. With the President at their head, they are now entrenched in the executive mansion.

Not to dislodge them is to leave the country a prey to one of the most hateful tyrannies of history. Especially is it to surrender the Unionists of the Rebel states to violence and bloodshed. Not a month, not a week, not a day should be lost. *The safety of the republic requires action at once.* The lives of innocent men must be rescued from sacrifice.

Barefaced Treachery

I would not in this judgment depart from that moderation which belongs to the occasion; but God forbid that, when called to deal with so great an offender, I should affect a coldness which I cannot feel. Slavery has been our worst enemy, assailing all, murdering our children, filling our homes with mourning, and darkening the land with tragedy; and now it rears its crest anew, with Andrew Johnson as its representative. Through him it assumes once more to rule the republic and to impose its cruel law.

The enormity of his conduct is aggravated by his barefaced treachery. He once declared himself the Moses of the colored race. Behold him now the Pharaoh. With such treachery in such a cause there can be no parley. Every sentiment, every conviction, every vow against slavery must now be directed against him. Pharaoh is at the bar of the Senate for judgment.

The formal accusation is founded on certain recent transgressions, enumerated in articles of impeachment, but it is wrong to suppose that this is the whole case. It is very wrong to try this impeachment merely on these articles. It is unpardonable to higgle over words and phrases when, for more than two years, the tyrannical pretensions of this offender, now in evidence before the Senate . . . have been manifest in their terrible, heartrending consequences. . . .

THIS LITTLE BOY WOULD PERSIST IN HANDLING BOOKS ABOVE HIS CAPACITY.

AND THIS WAS THE DISASTROUS RESULT.

Stock Montage, Inc.

In this cartoon from 1868, President Andrew Johnson is depicted as a child whose attempts to handle the Constitution result in his own downfall.

This usurpation, with its brutalities and indecencies, became manifest as long ago as the winter of 1866, when, being President, and bound by his oath of office to preserve, protect, and defend the Constitution, and to take care that the laws are faithfully executed, he took to himself legislative powers in the reconstruction of the Rebel states; and, in carrying forward this usurpation, nullified an act of Congress, intended as the cornerstone of Reconstruction, by virtue of which Rebels are excluded from office under the government of the United States; and, thereafter, in vindication of this misconduct, uttered a scandalous speech in which he openly charged members of Congress with being assassins, and mentioned some by name. Plainly he should have been impeached and expelled at that early day. The case against him was complete. . . .

Meanwhile, the President proceeded in his transgressions. There is nothing of usurpation which he has not attempted. Beginning with an assumption of all power in the Rebel states, he has shrunk from nothing in the maintenance of this unparalleled assumption. This is a plain statement of fact. Timid at first, he grew bolder and bolder. He saw too well that his attempt to substitute himself for

Congress in the work of reconstruction was sheer usurpation, and, therefore, by his secretary of state, did not hesitate to announce that "it must be distinctly understood that the restoration will be *subject to the decision of Congress."* On two separate occasions, in July and September 1865, he confessed the power of Congress over the subject; but when Congress came together in December, this confessor of congressional power found that he alone had this great prerogative. According to his newfangled theory, Congress had nothing to do but admit the states with the governments which had been instituted through his will alone. . . .

Had this assumption of power been incidental, for the exigency of the moment, as under the pressure of war, and especially to serve the cause of human rights, to which before his elevation the President had professed such vociferous devotion, it might have been pardoned. It would have passed into the chapter of unauthorized acts which a patriot people had condoned. But it was the opposite in every particular. Beginning and continuing in usurpation, it was hateful beyond pardon because it sacrificed the rights of Unionists, white and black, and was in the interest of the rebellion and of those very Rebels who had been in arms against their country.

Rebels in Power

More than one person was appointed provisional governor who could not take the oath of office required by act of Congress. Other persons in the same predicament were appointed in the revenue service. The effect of these appointments was disastrous. They were in the nature of notice to Rebels everywhere, that participation in the rebellion was no bar to office. If one of their number could be appointed governor, if another could be appointed to a confidential position in the Treasury Department, then there was nobody on the long list of blood who might not look for preferment. And thus all offices from governor to constable were handed over to a disloyal scramble.

Rebels crawled forth from their retreats. Men who had hardly ventured to expect their lives were now candidates for office, and the rebellion became strong again. The change was felt in all the gradations of government, whether in states, counties, towns, or villages. Rebels found themselves in places of trust, while the truehearted Unionists, who had watched for the coming of our flag and ought to have enjoyed its protecting power, were driven into hiding places. All this was under the auspices of Andrew Johnson. It was he who animated the wicked crew. He was at the head of the work. Loyalty everywhere was persecuted. White and black, whose only offense was that they had been true to their country, were insulted, abused, murdered. There was no safety for the loyal man except within the flash of our bayonets. The story is as authentic as hideous. . . .

The officers he had appointed in defiance of law were paid also in the same defiance. Millions of property were turned over without consideration to railroad companies whose special recommendation was their participation in the rebellion. The Freedman's Bureau, that sacred charity of the republic, was despoiled of its possessions for the sake of Rebels, to whom their forfeited estates were given back after they had been vested by law in the United States. The proceeds of captured and abandoned property, lodged under the law in the national Treasury, were ravished from their place of deposit and sacrificed. Rebels were allowed to fill the antechambers of the executive mansion and to enter into his counsels. The pardoning power was prostituted, and pardons were issued in lots to suit Rebels, thus grossly abusing that trust whose

Articles of Impeachment

President Andrew Johnson was tried on eleven articles of impeachment. Adopted on March 2, 1868, the first nine articles dealt with various aspects of Johnson's violation of the 1867 Tenure of Office Act. The last two articles, added the next day, accused Johnson of maligning Congress in his public speeches.

ARTICLE I

That said Andrew Johnson, President of the United States, on [February 21, 1868], at Washington, in the District of Columbia, unmindful of the high duties of his office, of his oath of office, and of the requirement of the Constitution that he should take care that the laws be faithfully executed, did unlawfully, and in violation of the Constitution and laws of the United States issue an order in writing for the removal of Edwin M. Stanton from the office of Secretary for the Department of War, said Edwin M. Stanton having been theretofore duly appointed and commissioned by and with the advice and consent of the Senate of the United States, as such Secretary. . . .

ARTICLE X

That said Andrew Johnson, President of the United States, unmindful of the high duties of his office, and the dignity and proprieties thereof, and of the harmony and courtesies which ought to exist and be maintained between the executive and legislative branches of the government of the United States, designing and intending to set aside the rightful authority and powers of Congress . . . [did] make and deliver, with a loud voice, certain intemperate, inflammatory, and scandalous harangues, and did therein utter loud threats and bitter menaces, as well against Congress as the laws of the United States duly enacted thereby, amid the cries, jeers, and laughter of the multitudes then assembled.

discreet exercise is so essential to the administration of justice. The powers of the Senate over appointments were trifled with and disregarded by reappointing persons who had been already rejected, and by refusing to communicate the names of others appointed by him during the recess. The veto power conferred by the Constitution as a remedy for ill-considered legislation was turned by him into a weapon of offense against Congress and into an instrument to beat down the just opposition which his usurpation had aroused. The power of removal, which patriot Presidents had exercised so sparingly, was seized as an engine of tyranny and openly employed to maintain his wicked purposes by the sacrifice of good citizens who would not consent to be his tools. . . .

Laws enacted by Congress for the benefit of the colored race, including that great statute for the establishment of the Freedman's Bureau, and that other great statute for the establishment of civil rights, were first attacked by his veto; and, when finally passed by the requisite majority over his veto, were treated by him as little better than dead letters, while he boldly attempted to prevent the adoption of a constitutional amendment by which the right of citizens and the national debt were placed under the guarantee of irrepealable law.

During these successive assumptions, usurpations, and tyrannies, utterly without precedent in our history, this deeply guilty man ventured upon public speeches, each an offense to good morals, where, lost to all shame, he appealed in coarse words to the coarse passions of the coarsest people, scattering firebrands of sedition, inflaming anew the rebel spirit, insulting good citizens, and, with regard to officeholders, announcing in his own characteristic phrase that he would "kick them out"—the whole succession of speeches being from their brutalities and indecencies in the nature of a "criminal exposure of his person," indictable at common law, for which no judgment can be too severe. But even this revolting transgression is aggravated when it is considered that through these utterances the cause of justice was imperiled and the accursed demon of civil feud was lashed again into vengeful fury.

All these things from beginning to end are plain facts, already recorded in history and known to all. And it is further recorded in history and known to all, that, through these enormities, any one of which is enough for condemnation, while all together present an aggregation of crime, untold calamities have been brought upon our country; disturbing business and finance; diminishing the national revenues; postponing specie payments; dishonoring the Declaration of Independence in its grandest truths; arresting the restoration of the Rebel states; reviving the dying rebellion, and instead of that peace and reconciliation so much longed for, sowing strife and wrong, whose natural fruit is violence and blood.

The Tenure of Office Act

For all these, or any one of them, Andrew Johnson should have been impeached and expelled from office. The case required a statement only, not an argument. Unhappily this was not done. As a petty substitute for the judgment which should have been pronounced, and as a bridle on presidential tyranny in "kicking out of office," Congress enacted a law known as the Tenure of Office Act, passed March 2, 1867, over his veto by the vote of two-thirds of both houses. And in order to prepare the way for impeachment, by removing certain scruples of technicality, its violation was expressly declared to be a high misdemeanor.

The President began at once to chafe under its restraint. Recognizing the act and following its terms, he first suspended Mr. [Edwin] Stanton from office, and then, on his restoration by the Senate, made an attempt to win General [Ulysses S.] Grant into a surrender of the department so as to oust Mr. Stanton and to render the restoration by the Senate ineffectual. Meanwhile, [General Philip] Sheridan in Louisiana, [General John] Pope in Alabama, and [General Daniel] Sickles in South Carolina, who, as military commanders, were carrying into the pacification of these states all the energies which had been so brilliantly displayed in the war, were pursued by the same vindictive spirit.

They were removed by the President, and rebellion throughout that whole region clapped its hands. This was done in the exercise of his power as commander in chief. At last, in his unappeased rage, he openly violated the Tenure of Office Act so as to bring himself under its judgment by the defiant attempt to remove Mr. Stanton from the War Department, without the consent of the Senate, and the appointment of Lorenzo Thomas, adjutant general of the United States, as secretary of war *ad interim*.

The Grand Inquest of the nation, which had slept on so many enormities, was awakened by this open defiance. The gauntlet was flung into its very chamber, and there it lay on the floor. The President, who had already claimed everything for the executive with impunity, now rushed into conflict with Congress on the very ground selected in advance by the latter. The field was narrow, but sufficient. There was but one thing for the House of Representatives to do. Andrew Johnson must be impeached, or the Tenure of Office Act would become a dead letter, while his tyranny would receive a letter of license, and impeachment as a remedy for wrongdoing would be blotted from the Constitution.

"I cannot agree to destroy the harmonious working of the Constitution for the sake of getting rid of an unacceptable President."

Johnson Should Not Be Impeached

James Grimes (1816-1872)

President Andrew Johnson's struggles with Congress over reconstruction policies culminated in his trial on eleven articles of impeachment, held by the Senate in March 1868. The strongest charge against Johnson was his violation of the Tenure of Office Act, which prohibited the president from dismissing federal officers without obtaining the consent of Congress. However, Johnson's refusal to cooperate with Congress in the matter of reconstruction was the primary reason that the Radical Republicans pushed for his impeachment. In many respects, the Tenure of Office Act had been devised as a trap for Johnson; the members of Congress had known that Johnson would defy the act, giving them grounds for impeachment.

During the trial, a crucial question was whether Johnson's violation of the Tenure of Office Act amounted to the "high crimes and misdemeanors" necessary for a conviction and removal from the presidency. Senator James Grimes of Iowa, a moderate Republican, was among those who debated that Johnson had committed no such crimes. In his address to the Senate, Grimes argues that the Tenure of Office Act is unconstitutional. Furthermore, he insists, it is the president's duty to challenge any unconstitutional act. Grimes also maintains that elections, not impeachment trials, are the proper method for removing unpopular presidents from office. In May 1868, Grimes cast the deciding vote for the acquittal of President Johnson.

Excerpted from *Trial of Andrew Johnson*, vol. 3, Benjamin P. Poore, ed., Washington, D.C., 1868.

The President of the United States stands at the bar of the Senate charged with the commission of high crimes and misdemeanors. The principal offense charged against him is embodied in various forms in the first eight articles of impeachment. This offense is alleged to consist in a violation of the provisions of the 1st Section of an act of Congress entitled "An act regulating the tenure of certain civil offices," approved March 2, 1867, in this, that on the 21st day of February, 1868, the President removed, or attempted to remove, Edwin M. Stanton from the office of secretary for the Department of War, and issued a letter of authority to General Lorenzo Thomas as secretary for the Department of War *ad interim*.

The House of Representatives charge in their three first articles that the President attempted to remove Mr. Stanton, and that he issued his letter of authority to General Thomas with an intent to violate the law of Congress, and with the further "intent to violate the Constitution of the United States." The President, by his answer, admits that he sought to substitute General Thomas for Mr. Stanton at the head of the Department of War; but insists that he had the right to make such substitution under the laws then and now in force, and denies that in anything that he has done or attempted to do he intended to violate the laws or the Constitution of the United States. . . .

The first section of this act reads as follows:

> That every person holding any civil office to which he has been appointed by and with the advice and consent of the Senate, and every person who shall hereafter be appointed to any such office and shall become duly qualified to act therein, is and shall be entitled to hold such office until a successor shall have been in a like manner appointed and duly qualified, except as herein otherwise provided.

Then comes what is "otherwise provided":

> *Provided*, that the secretaries of state, of the treasury, of war, of the Navy, and of the interior, the postmaster general, and the attorney general shall hold their offices respectively for and during the term of the President by whom they may have been appointed, and for one month thereafter, subject to removal by and with the advice and consent of the Senate. . . .

It is clear to my mind that the proviso does not include, and was not intended to include, Mr. Stanton's case. It is not possible to apply to his case the language of the proviso unless we suppose it to have been intended to legislate him out of office; a conclusion, I consider, wholly inadmissible. He was appointed by President Lincoln during his first term of office. He cannot hereafter go out of office at the end of the term of the President by whom he was appointed. That term was ended before the law was passed. The proviso, therefore, cannot have been intended to make a rule for his case; and it is shown that it was not intended.

Congressional Usurpation

The steadily increasing power of Congress during Reconstruction alarmed many political leaders. In a speech delivered on March 11, 1868, Samuel J. Tilden, the head of the New York State Democratic Party, accuses Congress not only of unfounded impeachment proceedings against President Johnson but also of attempting to obstruct the separation of powers among the three branches of federal government.

Congress is systematically breaking down all the divisions of power between the co-ordinate departments of the Federal Government which the Constitution established, and which have always been considered as essential to the very existence of constitutional representative government. . . .

Congress has stripped the President of his constitutional powers over his subordinates in the executive function, and even over his own confidential advisers, and vested these powers in the Senate. It is now exercising the power of removing from office the President elected by the people and appointing another in his place, under the form of a trial, but without the pretence of actual crime, or anything more than a mere difference of opinion.

It has menaced the Judiciary: at one time proposing to create by law an incapacity in the Supreme Court to act by a majority in any case where it should disagree with Congress; at another time proposing to divest that tribunal of jurisdiction, exercised by it from the foundation of the government, to decide between an ordinary law and the Constitution, which is the fundamental and supreme law. . . .

These changes are organic. They would revolutionize the very nature of the government. They would alter every important part of its structure on which its authors relied to secure good laws and good administration, and to preserve civil liberty. They would convert it into an elective despotism.

This was plainly declared in debate by the conference committee, both in the Senate and in the House of Representatives, when the proviso was introduced and its effect explained. The meaning and effect of the proviso were then explained and understood to be that the only tenure of the secretaries provided for by this law was a tenure to end with the term of service of the President by whom they were appointed; and, as this new tenure could not include Mr. Stanton's case, it was here explicitly declared that it did not include it.

Believing, as I do, that the orders of the President for the removal of Mr. Stanton and the designation of General Thomas to act *ad interim* were legal orders, it is manifestly impossible for me to attach to them any idea of criminal conspiracy. If those orders had not been, in my judgment, lawful, I should not have come to the conclusion, upon the evidence, that any actual intent to do an unlawful act was proved. . . .

I come now to the question of intent. Admitting that the President had no power under the law to issue the order to remove Mr. Stanton and appoint General Thomas secretary for the Department of War *ad interim*, did he issue those orders with a manifest *intent* to violate the laws and "the Constitution of the United States" as charged in the articles, or did he issue them, as he says he did, with a view to have the constitutionality of the Tenure of Office Act judicially decided? It is apparent to my mind that the President thoroughly believed the Tenure of Office Act to be unconstitutional and void. He was so advised by every member of his Cabinet when the bill was presented to him for his approval in February 1867. . . .

I cannot believe it to be our duty to convict the President of an infraction of a law when, in our consciences, we believe the law itself to be invalid, and therefore having no binding effect. If the law is unconstitutional, it is null and void, and the President has committed no offense and done no act deserving of impeachment. . . .

It is not denied, I think, that the constitutional validity of this law could not be tested before the courts unless a case was made and presented to them. No such case could be made unless the President made a removal. That act of his would necessarily be the basis on which the case would rest. He is sworn to "preserve, protect, and defend the Constitution of the United States." He must *defend* it against all encroachments from whatever quarter.

A question arose between the Legislative and Executive departments as to their relative powers in the matter of removals and appointments to office. That question was—Does the Constitution confer on the President the power which the Tenure of Office Act seeks to take away? It was a question manifestly of construction and interpretation. The Constitution has provided a common arbiter in such cases of controversy—the Supreme Court of the United States. Before that tribunal can take jurisdiction a removal must be made. The President attempted to give the court jurisdiction in that way. For doing so he is impeached. . . .

The President's Duty

This was a *punitive* statute. It was directed against the President alone. It interfered with the prerogatives of his department as recognized from the foundation of the government. It wrested from him powers which, according to the legislative and judicial construction of eighty years, had been bestowed upon him by the Constitution itself. In my opinion, it was not only proper but it was his duty to cause the disputed question to be determined in the manner and by the tribunal established for such purposes. This government can only be preserved and the liberty of the people maintained by preserving intact the coordinate branches of it—legislative, executive, judicial—alike. I am no convert to any doctrine of the omnipotence of Congress. . . .

Mr. Johnson's character as a statesman, his relations to political parties, his conduct as a citizen, his efforts at reconstruction, the exercise of his pardoning power, the character of his appointments, and the influences under which they were made are not before us on any charges and are not impugned by any testimony.

Nor can I suffer my judgment of the law governing this case to be influenced by political considerations. I cannot agree to destroy the harmonious working of the Constitution for the sake of getting rid of an unacceptable President. Whatever may be my opinion of the incumbent, I cannot consent to trifle with the high office he holds. I can do nothing which, by implication, may be construed into an approval of impeachments as a part of future political machinery.

However widely, therefore, I may and do differ with the President respecting his political views and measures, and however deeply I have regretted, and do regret, the differences between himself and the Congress of the United States, I am not able to record my vote that he is guilty of high crimes and misdemeanors by reason of those differences. I am acting in a judicial capacity, under conditions whose binding obligation can hardly be exceeded, and I must act according to the best of my ability and judgment, and as they require. If, according to their dictates, the President is guilty, I *must* say so; if, according to their dictates, the President is not guilty, I *must* say so.

In my opinion, the President has not been guilty of an impeachable offense by reason of anything alleged in either of the articles preferred against him at the bar of the Senate by the House of Representatives.

CHAPTER 3

Radical Reconstruction

Chapter Preface

Much to the disappointment of the Radical Republicans, the impeachment trial of President Andrew Johnson for high crimes and misdemeanors ended with Johnson's acquittal on May 28, 1868. However, although the Radical Republicans failed in their attempt to remove Johnson from office, they did succeed in wresting away Johnson's control over reconstruction. During the remaining ten months of his term, Johnson had little influence over reconstruction and no chance of being nominated for the 1868 presidential election. General Ulysses S. Grant, the Republican candidate who would become the next president, was a popular wartime hero but had no political experience and no solid political allegiance to either party. More moderate than the Radical Republicans, Grant would nevertheless give the congressional Radicals primary control over reconstruction during his two presidential terms. Due to these developments, the Radical Republicans in Congress were the primary architects of reconstruction policy from 1868 to 1874.

Of the ten southern states affected by the Reconstruction Acts, all save Texas held state constitutional conventions during the winter of 1867–1868. Because the Reconstruction Acts temporarily disfranchised most of the white population, there were black electoral majorities or strong minorities in the southern states, and black delegates made up a significant proportion of the constitutional conventions. Among other innovations, the new constitutions created state public school systems (which had been virtually nonexistent in the prewar South), abolished imprisonment for debt, guaranteed equal protection under the law regardless of race, and reduced the number of crimes punishable by death. Once a new constitution had been ratified by the state's electorate and the state had fulfilled all the requirements of the Reconstruction Acts, Congress readmitted the state to the Union. Arkansas, Louisiana, Alabama, Georgia, Florida, North Carolina, and South Carolina were readmitted by the summer of 1868, in time to take part in the presidential elections. However, the political disabilities that restricted former Confederates (most of whom were Democrat) from voting and holding political office were not automatically lifted when the states were readmitted, which resulted in new "reconstruction" state governments that consisted primarily of Republican politicians.

Since its founding in 1854, when it had risen from the ashes of the defunct Whig Party, the Republican Party had generally been a northern party. In fact, during the Civil War the Confederate government had considered the Republican Party a subversive and treasonous organization, and throughout Reconstruction, most Southerners would regard the Republicans unwanted Yankee intruders. During Reconstruction, the Republican Party of the South consisted of three elements: northern immigrants, known as carpetbaggers; southern anti-secessionists, often former Whigs, who were called scalawags; and blacks, who were dedicated in their support of the party that had brought them emancipation, suffrage, and civil rights. Many Southerners detested being ruled by carpetbagger, scalawag, and black politicians and accused them of plundering the South through widespread graft and fraud.

Southerners became increasingly resentful of what they saw as crooked and unwanted Republican rule forced upon them and took a number of steps to combat it. Largely disqualified from voting themselves, some Democrats courted black voters while others resorted to rigging elections. White supremacist organizations, including the Ku Klux Klan, grew in popularity. Political dissension between Democrats and Republicans was often a factor in race riots, such as the 1870 election campaign riot in Eutaw, Alabama, and the 1871 riot in Meridian, Mississippi. The Democrats saw themselves as "the white man's party" and urged their constituents "to rally on the color line"—that is, to maintain the separation between the "black Republicans" and the white Democrats.

Southern resistance hampered the progress of Radical Reconstruction. The spread of violence led to the passage of three Enforcement Acts, which authorized the use of federal forces to keep the peace. When Georgia's state legislature expelled its black members in 1868, the state was placed back under military rule until 1870, when it was once again declared "reconstructed." However, despite the remaining problems, by 1870 all eleven states of the former Confederacy had been readmitted to the Union, and by 1872 voting and office-holding privileges had been restored to the previously disfranchised white Southerners.

VIEWPOINT 1

"The carpet-bag element . . . [has been] the prolific source of a great deal of trouble and prejudice and bitterness."

Carpetbaggers Have Harmed the South

William Manning Lowe (1842-1881)

"Carpetbagger," a derogatory term used to describe Northerners who relocated to the South after the Civil War, implied that these Northerners only owned enough possessions to carry in a carpetbag and had moved to the South for personal gain and enrichment. Largely despised in the South, carpetbaggers were accused of ransacking the state treasuries and blamed for the widespread corruption that followed the war.

The Fourteenth Amendment and the Reconstruction Acts of 1867 restricted ex-Confederates (the majority of white Southerners) from holding political office and even voting. Carpetbaggers often filled this political vacuum, but many Southerners chafed under northern rule. Other carpetbaggers were teachers or clergy who had come South to educate and aid the ex-slaves, an objective that was resented and feared by much of the white South. Those native Southerners who supported Radical Reconstruction measures were often referred to as scalawags (good-for-nothing rascals).

On October 13, 1871, former Confederate colonel and Alabama lawyer William Manning Lowe was questioned about southern opinions of carpetbaggers by members of the Joint Select Committee to Inquire into the Condition of Affairs in the Late Insurrectionary States. In the following viewpoint, which contains excerpts from his testimony, Lowe is critical of Alabama's U.S. sena-

William Manning Lowe, from *Testimony Taken by the Joint Select Committee to Inquire into the Condition of Affairs in the Late Insurrectionary States: Alabama*, vol. 2, Washington, DC: GPO, 1872.

tors Willard Warner and George Spencer, who were originally from Ohio and New York, respectively. However, Lowe specifies that he does not consider another Northerner, Captain Lionel W. Day, a carpetbagger because Day supports the Democratic Party.

I regard the most aggravating and disagreeable fact in the whole business of reconstruction to have been the intrusion of what is known in the South as the carpet-bag element. General [George] Spencer and General [Willard] Warner were elected to the Senate of the United States, . . . both of them men recently coming into the State, and men whom we supposed and whom we considered as the representatives of the negro race, in combined hostility to the white race. . . .

Question. Were the county officers of the same stripe?

Answer. I believe so, sir; they were in a great degree of the same character. . . . The carpet-bag element took the lead in the formation of the [new state] constitution, and in holding all the offices, and in carrying the State back in the reconstruction policy, and I regard that as the prolific source of a great deal of trouble and prejudice and bitterness. . . .

Question. Is there any prejudice at all in this State against northern men who came here for the purpose of carrying on business, and following any avocation, and to mingle their fortunes with those of the people of this State as citizens?

Answer. No, sir; on the contrary, there is a very earnest desire that they shall come. . . .

Question. You have used the epithets "carpet-baggers," and "scalawags," repeatedly, during the course of your testimony. I wish you would give us an accurate definition of what a carpet-bagger is and what a scalawag is.

Answer. Well, sir, the term carpet-bagger is not applied to northern men who come here to settle in the South, but a carpet-bagger is generally understood to be a man who comes here for office sake, of an ignorant or bad character, and who seeks to array the negroes against the whites; who is a kind of political dry-nurse for the negro population, in order to get office through them.

Question. Then it does not necessarily suppose that he should be a northern man?

Answer. Yes, sir; it does suppose that he is to be a northern man, but it does not apply to all northern men that come here.

Question. If he is an intelligent, educated man, and comes here for office, then he is not a carpet-bagger, I understand?

Answer. No, sir; we do not generally call them carpet-baggers.

Question. If he is a northern man possessed of good character and seeks office he is not a carpet-bagger?

Answer. Mr. Chairman, there are so few northern men who come here of intelligence and character, that join the republican party and look for office alone to the negroes, that we have never made a class for them. I have never heard them classified. . . . But the term "carpet-bagger" was applied to the office-seeker from the North who comes here seeking office by the negroes, by arraying their political passions and prejudices against the white people of the community.

Cartoonist Thomas Nast satirized Carl Schurz, a former Union general who had moved to the South, in this 1872 caricature depicting Schurz as a carpetbagger. Nast commented, "The bag in front of him, filled with others' faults, he always sees. The one behind him, filled with his own faults, he never sees."

Question. The man in addition to that, under your definition, must be an ignorant man and of bad character?

Answer. Yes, sir; he is generally of that description. We regard any man as a man of bad character who seeks to create hostility between the races.

Question. Do you regard any republican as a bad character who seeks to obtain the suffrages of the negro population?

Answer. We regard any republican or any man as a man of bad character, whether he is native or foreign born, who seeks to obtain office from the negroes by exciting their passions and prejudices against the whites. We think that a very great evil—very great. We are very intimately associated with the negro race; we have a large number in the country, and we think it essential that we shall live in peace together.

Question. Do you regard Senators Warner and Spencer as in the category of carpet-baggers?

Answer. Yes, sir. . . .

Question. Do you regard Senator Spencer as an ignorant man and of bad character?

Answer. I have a very slight acquaintance with General Spencer; I know him; I do not think him an ignorant man; I think him, with the authority of those who know him intimately and well, to be an unprincipled man. Ex-Governor William H. Smith, of this State, in the last campaign, published a letter . . . containing a statement to the effect that Senator Spencer lived upon the passions and prejudices of the races; that the breath of peace would leave him on the surface, neglected and despised.

Question. I am not asking for Governor Smith's opinion, but your own?

Answer. Well, sir, I believe Governor Smith.

Question. Did Senator Spencer seek to array the negroes against the whites?

Answer. Yes, sir. One of his shysters and agents here, in the last election when I was a candidate, circulated the most infamous lies about me all over the county, to the effect that I would deprive the colored people of the substance of personal freedom if I got into office, although I told them the contrary; that I would deprive them of suffrage if I got into office; that I would do everything to injure them in person and property. His agents who were in his confidence did this. They told me they were in his confidence, and I have no doubt they did it to subserve his political interests. . . .

Scalawags

Question. Having given a definition of the carpet-bagger, you may now define scalawag.

Answer. A scalawag is his subservient tool and accomplice, who is a native of the country.

Question. How many of the white race in the county of Madison vote the republican ticket?

Answer. I do not think, and I have very accurate means of judging, that a hundred ever voted it.

Question. You class them all as carpet-baggers and scalawags?

Answer. Yes, sir.

Question. Are all of them seeking office?

Answer. No, sir.

Question. Are all of them ignorant men and of bad character?

Answer. No, sir.

Question. Are all of them natives of the Northern States?

Answer. No, sir.

Question. Why do you classify them as carpet-baggers and

scalawags?

Answer. I have told you that I classified as carpet-baggers those who came down here, who come within that definition, coming down here and seeking office from the negroes by arraying their passions and prejudices against the white people. I classed the others as scalawags. They are more or less scalawaggers, according to the part they play in this political programme.

Rapacious Adventurers

The Mississippi elections of 1875 were marked by fraud and violence on the part of white Democrats. In response, the U.S. Congress established a committee to inquire into the elections. The following excerpt from the committee's minority report places the blame for the unrest on unscrupulous carpetbag politicians.

Unfortunately the new and arbitrary political conditions imposed upon both races by the will of Congress were disturbed by the presence of a class of unscrupulous, needy, and rapacious adventurers who came down [to Mississippi] to fill the political offices. . . . The result was, as the testimony everywhere discloses, that the State and Federal offices to which any considerable emolument was attached fell into the hands of white men newly arrived within the borders of the State, ignorant and unsympathetic of the wishes and feelings of the white population, and bent wholly upon using the political material which they found ready at their hands in the shape of masses of ignorant, superstitious, and suspicious negroes to sustain themselves in office and power. Instead of encouraging the colored population to relations of amity and confidence with the whites who gave them employment and furnished them with the means of subsistence, it has been plainly the object and intent of these political adventurers to increase the distrust between the races, and to encourage on the part of the blacks and intensify the instinct and feeling of race opposition. In this, by means of low arts, they have been, unhappily, too successful, and the negroes of the State of Mississippi have been banded together in an unthinking mass, under the lead and blind control of a handful of northern strangers, with here and there a native white man.

Question. What proportion of this one hundred white men who vote the republican ticket are seeking office?

Answer. It would be impossible for me to say. I believe that there are very few of them that would decline to serve their country in a lucrative office if they could get it. . . .

Question. How do you classify Captain [Lionel W.] Day, who is clerk, I believe, of the district court of the United States, and *ex officio* commissioner?

Answer. He has never been politically classed. He never took any part in politics at all.

Question. Does he hold office under the Federal Government?

Answer. Yes, sir.

Question. Do you regard him as a carpet-bagger?

Answer. No, sir.

Question. A northern man?

Answer. Yes, sir.

Question. Did he come here seeking office?

Answer. No, sir.

Question. Did he come into the State seeking an office?

Answer. No, sir; I do not think he did. I do not know that he did.

Question. Has he not held office in some capacity all through since he came?

Answer. I do not know. I never knew him until he came here.

Question. What distinguishes him from the genuine carpet-bagger?

Answer. Because he does not associate with the negroes; he does not seek their society, politically or socially; he has nothing to do with them any more than any other white gentleman in the community.

Question. He votes with the democratic party? . . .

Answer. I think he did.

Question. Was he not a democratic delegate to [the state constitutional] convention?

Answer. Yes, sir; he was spoken of as a candidate himself, but he did not desire the nomination. He told me he did not want it. He said he did not think it was reputable for a northern man to come down here and be seeking offices that southern men could hold, and he preferred his name should not be mentioned.

Question. As I want to get at the true definition of these terms, I will inquire of you if a northern man comes into Alabama intent upon obtaining office, and seeks to obtain an office through the instrumentality of the democratic organization, is he a carpet-bagger?

Answer. No, sir; the term is never applied to a democrat under any circumstances. . . . No democrat who seeks office through the virtue, intelligence, and property of the country, who says, "Gentleman, your best men are disfranchised by the act of Congress; I do not care particularly about office, but as you cannot hold it I will go there, knock your chains off, and get you a chance."

VIEWPOINT 2

"What the South needs is emigrants with carpet bags well filled with capital to revive industry, organize labor, and develop her resources."

Carpetbaggers Have Helped the South

Oliver Morton (1823-1877)

Southerners had their reasons for despising carpetbaggers—the northern men who moved to the South after the war, became involved in southern politics, and often promoted Radical Republican ideals. To Southerners, carpetbaggers were an unwelcome reminder of their recent defeat by the North. They resented Northerners' controlling their public offices, especially at a time when the majority of white southern men were disenfranchised according to the disabilities placed on former Confederates in the Fourteenth Amendment. Carpetbag politicians could not possibly represent the feelings and beliefs of their southern constituencies, Southerners felt, especially when most carpetbaggers were Radical Republicans in a region that was largely Southern Democrat. Furthermore, carpetbaggers were suspected of everything from fraud and corruption to instigating race wars between blacks and whites.

Most northern Republicans, however, did not view the matter in this way. They saw a defeated and ravaged South, full of untrustworthy former Rebels, that desperately needed an infusion of northern enterprise and Republican sentiments. They believed that Southerners' complaints about carpetbaggers had their roots in southern prejudice against the North and were not due to any actual wrongdoing on the part of the carpetbagger governments.

The viewpoint that follows contains excerpts from an 1871 speech given by Senator Oliver Morton of Indiana, a leading Radical Republican who was prominent in the impeachment trial of

Oliver Morton, from *Great Debates in American History*, vol. 8, Marion Mills Miller, ed., Current Literature Co., 1913.

President Andrew Johnson and who later served on the electoral commission in the disputed presidential contest of 1876. In his address, Morton argues that the war-torn South needs the influx of northern newcomers—with their large capital and boundless energy—to aid in rebuilding its economy and political structure. Criticizing those who claim Northerners have no right to move South or take part in southern government, Morton reminds his listeners that the Constitution guarantees the right to emigrate from state to state.

When the war ended many men who had been in the Union army remained in the South, intending to make it their home and identify themselves with its fortunes. Others emigrated from the North, taking with them large capital, believing that the South presented fine prospects for business, individual success, and general prosperity. In the reconstruction of the Southern States it so happened, and was, in fact, necessary, that many of these men should be elected to office and take a leading part in the government of the States in which they settled. This was their right and the natural result of the circumstances by which they were surrounded; but they were denounced as adventurers and intruders, and the odious slang of "carpetbaggers" was reechoed by the Democracy of the North, who sent word to the South that these men had no rights they were bound to respect.

Free to Emigrate

Emigration is a part of the genius of the American people. They are composed of those who came from abroad or their descendants. To emigrate from State to State, and there to enjoy all the privileges and immunities of citizens of the United States, is guaranteed by the Constitution, and it is an odious and anti-American doctrine that a man has no right to be elected to an office in a State because he was not born in it or has not lived in it many years. When we consider the circumstances under which the Territories were settled and new States formed, the rapid transition of our population from one part of the country to another, we shall comprehend the infamy and villainy of this slang against "carpet-baggers."

Why, sir, it is the same spirit in another form which a few years ago attempted to deny equal political rights to men of foreign birth and insisted that the offices should be held only by those who were born upon the soil; and it is humiliating that any portion of the people of the North should endeavor to excite the people of the South against their own citizens who have gone there to find homes. What the South needs is emigrants with carpet bags well filled with capital to revive industry, organize labor, and develop her resources; and the howl against this class of citizens is insane and suicidal.

"This society was purely a police organization to keep the peace, to prevent disturbances in our State."

The Ku Klux Klan Is a Peacekeeping Organization

John Brown Gordon (1823-1904)

Founded as a social fraternity in Tennessee in 1866, the Ku Klux Klan—a secret group based on the concept of white supremacy—spread rapidly throughout the South. Thousands of southern whites, including many respectable and influential citizens, joined the Klan and similar secret organizations, such as the White League and the Knights of the White Camelia. During the late 1860s and early 1870s, reports began to filter out of the South about whippings and lynchings administered to blacks, carpetbaggers, and scalawags by mysterious night-riding groups of disguised men. In 1871 the U.S. Congress established the Joint Select Committee to Inquire into the Condition of Affairs in the Late Insurrectionary States, the primary purpose of which was to investigate the secret organizations. For several months, the committee held hearings throughout the southern states, interviewing witnesses and compiling information on the activities of the Klan and similar groups.

The following viewpoint contains excerpts from the committee's questioning of John Brown Gordon, a former lieutenant general in the Confederate Army and a wealthy Atlanta lawyer who belonged to the Georgia Klan. (Although Gordon declined to name his organization to the Joint Select Committee, his biographer, Ralph Lowell Eckert, has verified that Gordon was a prominent member of the Klan.) In his testimony, Gordon contends that

John Brown Gordon, from *Testimony Taken by the Joint Select Committee to Inquire into the Condition of Affairs in the Late Insurrectionary States: Alabama*, vol. 1, Washington, DC: GPO, 1872.

the secret orders arose in response to the growing membership of blacks in the Union League, a political group organized by northern Republicans during a time in which most white Southerners were disenfranchised and prohibited from holding political office. Gordon asserts that the secret orders were formed because southern whites feared they would be attacked by recently freed slaves and were merely intended to keep the peace. Any violence against blacks or Northerners, he avers, was committed not by the secret societies but by individuals acting alone.

After the end of Reconstruction in 1877, Gordon entered politics, eventually serving as governor of Georgia and in the U.S. Senate.

Question. What do you know of any combinations in Georgia, known as Ku-Klux, or by any other name, who have been violating the law?

Answer. I do not know anything about any Ku Klux organization, as the papers talk about it. I have never heard of anything of that sort except in the papers and by general report; but I do know that an organization did exist in Georgia at one time. I know that in 1868—I think that was the time—I was approached and asked to attach myself to a secret organization in Georgia. I was approached by some of the very best citizens of the State—some of the most peaceable, law-abiding men, men of large property, who had large interests in the State. The object of this organization was explained to me at the time by these parties; and I want to say that I approved of it most heartily. I would approve again of a similar organization, under the same state of circumstances.

Question. Tell us about what that organization was.

Answer. The organization was simply this—nothing more and nothing less: it was an organization, a brotherhood of the property-holders, the peaceable, law-abiding citizens of the State, for self-protection. The instinct of self-protection prompted that organization; the sense of insecurity and danger, particularly in those neighborhoods where the negro population largely predominated. The reasons which led to this organization were three or four. The first and main reason was the organization of the Union League, as they called it, about which we knew nothing more than this: that the negroes would desert the plantations, and go off at night in large numbers; and on being asked where they had been, would reply, sometimes, "We have been to the muster;" sometimes, "We have been to the lodge;" sometimes, "We have been to the meet-

115

ing." Those things were observed for a great length of time. We knew that the "carpet-baggers," as the people of Georgia called these men who came from a distance and had no interest at all with us; who were unknown to us entirely; who from all we could learn about them did not have any very exalted position at their homes—these men were organizing the colored people. We knew that beyond all question. We knew of certain instances where great crimes had been committed; where overseers had been driven from plantations, and the negroes had asserted their right to hold the property for their own benefit. Apprehension took possession of the entire public mind of the State. Men were in many instances afraid to go away from their homes and leave their wives and children, for fear of outrage. Rapes were already being committed in the country. There was this general organization of the black race on the one hand, and an entire disorganization of the white race on the other hand. We were afraid to have a public organization; because we supposed it would be construed at once, by the authorities at Washington, as an organization antagonistic to the Government of the United States. It was therefore necessary, in order to protect our families from outrage and preserve our own lives, to have something that we could regard as a brotherhood—a combination of the best men of the country, to act purely in self-defense, to repel the attack in case we should be attacked by these people. That was the whole object of this organization. I never heard of any disguises connected with it; we had none, very certainly. This organization, I think, extended nearly all over the State. It was, as I say, an organization purely for self-defense. It had no more politics in it than the organization of the Masons. I never heard the idea of politics suggested in connection with it.

A Peace Police Organization

Question. Did it have any antagonism toward either the State or the Federal Government?

Answer. None on earth—not a particle. On the contrary, it was purely a peace police organization, and I do know of some instances where it did prevent bloodshed on a large scale. I know of one case in Albany, Georgia, where, but for the instrumentality of this organization, there would have been, beyond all doubt, a conflict, growing out of a personal difficulty between a black man and a white man. The two races gathered on each side, but this organization quelled the trouble easily and restored peace, without any violence to anybody, and without a particle of difficulty with either the black race or the white. They stopped one just as much as they did the other. This society was purely a police organization to keep the peace, to prevent disturbances in our State. That was the motive that actuated me in going into it, and that was the whole object of the organization, as explained to me by these persons who approached me. I approved of the object.

Question. You had no riding about at nights?

Answer. None on earth. I have no doubt that such things have occurred in Georgia. It is notoriously stated—I have no personal knowledge of anything of the kind, but I have reason to believe it—that disguised parties have committed outrages in Georgia; but we have discovered in some cases that these disguised parties did not belong to any particular party. We have demonstrated that beyond all question in some cases, by bringing to trial and conviction parties who belonged, for instance, to the radical [Republican] party, who had in disguise committed outrages in the State. There is not a good man in Georgia who does not deplore that thing just as much as any radical deplores it. When I use the

At the Mercy of Ignorance

U.S. senator James Chesnut of South Carolina resigned his seat in 1860 in order to help organize the Confederacy. Eleven years later, Chesnut was interviewed by the Joint Select Committee to Inquire into the Condition of Affairs in the Late Insurrectionary States about the formation of the secret organizations in South Carolina.

There is a deep dissatisfaction . . . in the hearts of the people of this State. . . . The government of this State, has been very bad. . . . The people having been accustomed heretofore to a well-ordered civil government, and . . . to self-government, suddenly found themselves in a condition where their whole system, social and political, was subverted, and this government put over them and exercised without intelligence and without integrity. . . . That is the main cause which has produced that discontent in the State. . . . My attention was first attracted to that shortly after the arming of the militia of this State, and a large number of instances of the burning of barns and dwellings, gin-houses and stables, etc., in the country. Then followed the arming of the . . . colored militia . . . the white people were not armed, and in the main were excluded from organization. . . .

Three hundred thousand white people here around us, who had been accustomed to self-government, who had had an orderly government and had participated in that government, whose property had been taxed only by those who paid the taxes, beheld the whole thing suddenly subverted and themselves placed at the mercy of ignorance and of corruption, foreign, and domestic. These people are under an absolute despotism, and you will find that the countries where governments are most despotic are precisely those in which secret associations appear; associations of parties . . . seeking redress for real or fancied wrongs which they think cannot be avenged through the government. That is the true secret of all this thing.

term "radical," I do not mean to reflect upon the republican party generally; but in our State a republican is a very different sort of a man from a republican generally in the Northern States. In our State republicanism means nothing in the world but creating disturbance, riot, and animosity, and filching and plundering. That is what it means in our State—nothing else; there is no politics in it. In the North the thing is very different. There men can differ in politics, and yet have the kindliest relations; in Georgia we cannot do it unless we are willing to countenance all sorts of outrages upon our people. There are genteel republicans in Georgia, who are just as safe as any one else; who travel all over the State; who occupy high positions, and are never insulted in the street, the cars, or anywhere else. If there is any organization in Georgia for the purpose of putting down republicanism there, why does it not attack the leaders of that party? It strikes me as the very highest commentary upon the law-abiding spirit of the people of Georgia that such men as I could name—men in high position who have plundered our people by the million—still live and are countenanced on the streets, have no insults offered to them. The truth is simply this: that individuals in Georgia of all parties and all colors have, I suppose, committed outrage; but such affairs have been purely personal, just as they are when they occur anywhere else in the United States. I do not believe any more crimes have been committed in Georgia than in any other community of the same number anywhere else in the country. That is my honest conviction. I do not believe that any crime has ever been committed by this organization of which I have spoken, and of which I was a member. I believe it was purely a peace police—a law-abiding concern. That was its whole object, and it never would have existed but for the apprehension in the minds of our people of a conflict in which we would have had no sympathy and no protection. We apprehended that the sympathy of the entire Government would be against us; and nothing in the world but the instinct of self-protection prompted that organization. We felt that we must at any cost protect ourselves, our homes, our wives and children from outrage. We would have preferred death rather than to have submitted to what we supposed was coming upon us. At this time I do not believe any such organization exists, or has existed for a long time. I have not heard of it for two years, I am certain.

Self-Protection Is No Longer Needed

Question. Why did it cease to exist; why did it pass away?

Answer. Well, sir, it just dissolved because the courts became generally established; and though the courts were in the hands of the opposite party, our people believed they were trying to do

118

justice; that a general protection was extended over us. Our people thought we could get justice at the hands of these judges; though they were of the opposite party, and though negroes were on the juries, we were satisfied that in the existing condition of things we were safe. Since Governor [Rufus] Bullock's election [in 1868] I have not heard anything of that organization. I am not sure that it did not pass away with his election. It certainly has not existed since within my knowledge; and I think I would have known it if it had. I think that my position would have brought it to my knowledge if any such organization had existed for several years past. As I have stated, the only reason it has passed away is, I think, because the people felt safe. Courts were established and police regulations were generally instituted.

You must remember that we were in a state of anarchy there for a long time. We had no law but drum-head courts-martial. Our people were entirely powerless to do anything. We always felt that if the Federal troops were kept in our midst we would be protected. I want to state that with great emphasis. Our people have always felt that if the white troops of the Federal Army could have been stationed in our midst in those negro belts we would have been safe. But the troops were perhaps two hundred miles away; and before they could have been brought to our relief the whole neighborhood might have been slaughtered. We then believed that such a thing might occur on almost any night. Such was the condition of things in Georgia at that time. I do not believe that it exists now, or has existed for two years. To my certain knowledge this organization never did exist as a political organization. I do not know what may have been the case elsewhere; but very certainly there was no politics in this thing in Georgia, so far as I had anything to do with it; and I think that the organization was of the same character all over the State—probably over the South wherever it existed. We never called it Ku-Klux, and therefore I do not know anything about Ku-Klux.

VIEWPOINT 4

"The Klan, in carrying out the purposes for which it was organized and armed, inflicted summary vengeance on the colored citizens."

The Ku Klux Klan Is a Terrorist Organization

The Federal Grand Jury

Ulysses S. Grant, elected U.S. president in 1868, had campaigned on the slogan "Let Us Have Peace." However, extensive reports of violent vigilante groups in the South led Congress to pass the Third Enforcement Act (also known as the Ku Klux Act) in April 1871. This law empowered the president to employ federal forces to protect terrorized communities and to suspend the writ of habeas corpus, allowing for imprisonment without charges. In October 1871, violence in South Carolina—the state where the Ku Klux Klan was most active—became so rampant that Grant invoked the powers of the Third Enforcement Act, sent federal troops to occupy nine counties, and suspended the writ of habeas corpus in these counties. Shortly thereafter, a federal grand jury was convened in Columbia, South Carolina, to conduct investigations into offenses committed by the state's Klan.

The following viewpoint is excerpted from the grand jury's report to the judges of the U.S. Circuit Court in Columbia. In this report, the members of the jury maintain that the Klan has been responsible for numerous murders and hundreds of whippings, both of blacks and white Radical Republicans. The jury contends that, far from being a peacekeeping organization during a time of lawlessness, the Klan actually has disrupted civil law and left the state's citizens without protection. The federal government should punish those guilty of atrocities against blacks, the jury recommends, in part to avoid retaliation by blacks against their

House of Representatives, *Report of the Federal Grand Jury to the Judges of the U.S. Circuit Court, Columbia, S.C.*, 42nd Cong., 2nd sess., 1872, H. Rept. 22, pt. 1, 48-49.

white persecutors.

According to historian Eric Foner, a few dozen of the worst offenders in the South Carolina Klan were eventually brought to trial and sentenced to prison; however, as many as 2,000 Klansmen fled the state and escaped punishment.

In closing the labors of the present term, the grand jury beg leave to submit the following presentment.

During the whole session we have been engaged in investigations of the most grave and extraordinary character—investigations of the crimes committed by the organization known as the Ku Klux Klan. The evidence elicited has been voluminous, gathered from the victims themselves and their families, as well as those who belong to the Klan and participated in its crimes. The jury has been shocked beyond measure at the developments which have been made in their presence of the number and character of the atrocities committed, producing a state of terror and a sense of utter insecurity among a large portion of the people, especially the colored population. The evidence produced before us has established the following facts:

1. That there has existed since 1868, in many counties of the state [South Carolina], an organization known as the "Ku Klux Klan," or "Invisible Empire of the South," which embraces in its membership a large proportion of the white population of every profession and class.

2. That this Klan [is] bound together by an oath, administered to its members at the time of their initiation into the order, of which the following is a copy:

OBLIGATION

I [name], before the immaculate Judge of Heaven and earth, and upon the Holy Evangelists of Almighty God, do, of my own free will and accord, subscribe to the following sacredly binding obligation:

1. We are on the side of justice, humanity, and constitutional liberty, as bequeathed to us in its purity by our forefathers.

2. We oppose and reject the principles of the Radical Party.

3. We pledge mutual aid to each other in sickness, distress, and pecuniary embarrassment.

4. Female friends, widows, and their households shall ever be special objects of our regard and protection.

Any member divulging, or causing to be divulged, any of the foregoing obligations, shall meet the fearful penalty and traitor's doom, which is Death! Death! Death!

That, in addition to this oath, the Klan has a constitution and bylaws, which provides, among other things, that each member shall furnish himself with a pistol, a Ku Klux gown, and a signal instrument. That the operations of the Klan were executed in the night, and were invariably directed against members of the Republican Party by warnings to leave the country, by whippings, and by murder.

Culver Pictures, Inc.

North Carolina Klansmen prepare to lynch John Campbell for being a Republican. Campbell was rescued by federal agents, one of whom took the photograph on which this 1871 engraving is based.

3. That in large portions of the counties of York, Union, and Spartanburgh, to which our attention has been more particularly called in our investigations during part of the time for the last eighteen months, the civil law has been set at defiance and ceased to afford any protection to the citizens.

4. That the Klan, in carrying out the purposes for which it was organized and armed, inflicted summary vengeance on the colored citizens of these counties by breaking into their houses at the

dead of night, dragging them from their beds, torturing them in the most inhuman manner, and in many instances murdering them; and this, mainly, on account of their political affiliations. Occasionally, additional reasons operated, but in no instance was the political feature wanting.

5. That for this condition of things, for all these violations of law and order and the sacred rights of citizens, many of the leading men of those counties were responsible. It was proven that large numbers of the most prominent citizens were members of the order. Many of this class attended meetings of the Grand Klan. At a meeting of the Grand Klan held in Spartanburgh County, at which there were representatives from the various dens of Spartanburgh, York, Union, and Chester counties, in this state, besides a number from North Carolina, a resolution was adopted that no raids should be undertaken or anyone whipped or injured by members of the Klan without orders from the Grand Klan. The penalty for violating this resolution was 100 lashes on the bare back for the first offense; and for the second, death.

This testimony establishes the nature of the discipline enforced in the order, and also the fact that many of the men who were openly and publicly speaking against the Klan, and pretending to deplore the work of this murderous conspiracy, were influential members of the order and directing its operations, even in detail.

Whippings and Murders

The jury has been appalled as much at the number of outrages as at their character, it appearing that 11 murders and over 600 whippings have been committed in York County alone. Our investigation in regard to the other counties named has been less full; but it is believed, from the testimony, that an equal or greater number has been committed in Union, and that the number is not greatly less in Spartanburgh and Laurens.

We are of the opinion that the most vigorous prosecution of the parties implicated in these crimes is imperatively demanded; that without this there is great danger that these outrages will be continued, and that there will be no security to our fellow citizens of African descent.

We would say further that unless the strong arm of the government is interposed to punish these crimes committed upon this class of citizens, there is every reason to believe that an organized and determined attempt at retaliation will be made, which can only result in a state of anarchy and bloodshed too horrible to contemplate.

VIEWPOINT 5

"What is needed is a thorough enforcement of the law, protection to all citizens; especially in their rights of personal security."

More Federal Intervention Is Needed in the South

Joseph Gurney Cannon (1836-1926)

Throughout Reconstruction, recalcitrant white Southerners used a variety of means to circumvent Radical Reconstruction measures and to deny blacks their newly legislated civil rights. Faced with southern resistance to the new Fourteenth and Fifteenth Amendments, which made blacks citizens and gave black men the right to vote, Congress passed a series of acts that provided for the enforcement of the amendments. The First Enforcement Act, passed on May 30, 1870, authorized the federal government to prosecute state officials who prohibited blacks from voting or from holding political office. Passed on February 28, 1871, the Second Enforcement Act allowed for federal supervision of elections and returns in areas where election fraud was prevalent. On April 20, 1871, the Third Enforcement Act—commonly called the Ku Klux Act—was passed. This act prohibited the secret organizations of the South and gave the president the authority to use federal troops to quell these groups and to keep the peace.

In 1875, the U.S. House of Representatives debated a new Enforcement Bill, which if enacted would extend provisions of the previous Enforcement Acts to cover more jurisdictions in the South and would authorize the president to suspend the writ of habeas corpus, the power to do so under the Third Enforcement

Joseph Gurney Cannon, *Congressional Record*, 43rd Cong., 2nd sess., February 27, 1875, pp. 1885-1911.

Act having expired in 1872. Joseph Gurney Cannon, Republican representative from Illinois, spoke on the House floor supporting the bill on February 27, 1875. Cannon cites his recent experiences as a member of a congressional committee investigating violence in the South to support his belief that it is necessary to pass the Fourth Enforcement Bill. Blacks receive no justice in the southern courts, Cannon insists, and therefore need the protection of the federal government. Cannon also points out that the recent congressional elections resulted in a Democratic landslide, and the new majority party is not likely to pass measures protecting southern blacks. Therefore, if the Republicans want to pass this legislation, Cannon urges, they must do so immediately, before the new Congress convenes.

Trained as a lawyer, Cannon served in the House of Representatives for most of his career and held the powerful position of Speaker of the House from 1903 to 1911.

I had the honor to be designated by the House as one of a special committee during the present session to proceed to the State of Alabama for the purpose of taking testimony concerning the condition of alleged outrages in the State and make report in the premises to the House. Prior to that committees had been appointed to make similar inquiries in the States of Mississippi, Louisiana, and Arkansas, all of these committees have performed the duties with which they were charged, and have made reports to the House. . . .

Defiance in the South

I can only pause long enough to refer to the fact that bad men, organized and armed, stand ready, in defiance of all law, to go from Texas to Mississippi, from Mississippi to Alabama, and from all of these States to Louisiana, to subvert all law, both State and Federal, and with a strong hand hunt down republicans, kill negroes, burn churches and school-houses, depose officers of a State or county, or subvert and revolutionize a State government. The testimony of the different investigating committees shows all this and much more. I do not mean to say that all democrats in Alabama and elsewhere South commit these outrages or approve them. On the contrary, there are many good men South, democrats, who deplore this condition of society. But it is also true that these bad men are sufficient in numbers to boldly and defiantly commit all these acts and so control public opinion that

125

"OF COURSE HE WANTS TO VOTE THE DEMOCRATIC TICKET"

DEMOCRAT "REFORMER:" "You're as free as air, ain't you? Say you are, or I'll blow yer black head off."

This cartoon by Arthur Burdett Frost portrays one type of intimidation used by southern whites against blacks. The caption reads, "Of course he wants to vote the Democratic ticket! You're free as air, ain't you? Say you are, or I'll blow yer black head off!"

no redress whatever for outrages of this kind can be had in the courts. And while I have no doubt, so far as judges of courts are concerned, in most instances, that they declare the law correctly when called upon to make rulings, yet cases ordinarily can only be disposed of with the aid of juries and healthy public opinion. With the foregoing state of society as a rule, the juries will not or do not help administer the law so as to protect republican citizens, especially negroes, in their rights, so far as personal security is concerned, and punish men who commit political crimes heretofore spoken of; and while Justice may perhaps be still, so far as the judges are concerned, represented with her eyes bandaged, holding the balances, yet she should also be represented as bound both hand and foot by public opinion, and powerless to make and enforce her decrees; and, strange as it may appear, the testimony shows since the war but one white man has been convicted for homicide of a negro in the whole State of Alabama, yet when our democratic friends are called upon to explain, justify, or condemn this state of affairs, they generally deny, or if they admit in part seek to palliate or justify, by saying that the people of Alabama have been under the rule of the republican carpet-baggers, who are fattening upon the misfortunes of the people, and that those manifestations are only the violent protests of a generous people against such a state of things. . . .

Grave responsibilities are resting upon the people of Alabama and other Southern States. Many of the whites are ignorant and lawless, and most of the negroes are ignorant, ordinarily well disposed, but owing to their poverty and former condition many of them incline to commit petit larcenies and smaller grades of offenses. What is needed is a thorough enforcement of the law, protection to all citizens; especially in their rights of personal security, and general education, and until all these are given I do not see much chance for prosperity in the South. But our democratic friends tell us that the difficulty is that the negroes are ignorant and will not divide their votes between the parties, but insist on voting the republican ticket. I have no doubt it would be better if all parties would acknowledge the equality of all men before the law in practice as well as theory; and until this is done by democrats South, instead of resorting to force and intimidation, how can they expect the negroes will vote with them, and how can they criticise with justice the negroes for not dividing their votes between the two parties when the more intelligent whites are seeking to divide on the color line, and resort to ostracism, proscription, and some of them to murder and assassination to accomplish their purpose? . . .

I have no patience with some gentlemen who admit the necessity for action, but quietly fold their arms, while the blood of the slain cries from the ground and the moan of the widow and orphan are heard as protests against the most foul taking-off of the husband and father, and search with a microscope for a fancied want of power to legislate, or cry conciliation and peace, peace, when there is no peace for these citizens of the United States, if they persist in exercising their rights in voting as they see proper, but the peace of the grave. . . .

The Majority Are Against Reconstruction

Gentlemen on the other side say, however, why not leave this legislation to the next Congress? I will tell them, among others, for the reason that the House of Representatives in the next Congress is composed of many men, enough to make a majority, who the history of the last fourteen years shows will not favor legislation to secure the equality of all before the law, many of whom from the North the records of this House show to have done all they dared do to embarrass the United States in putting down the rebellion, and many of whom from the South sought the life of the nation by war, and nearly all of whom, both from the North and South, have made war on reconstruction, upon the adoption of the [Fourteenth and Fifteenth] constitutional amendments, and from time to time have opposed all legislation to insure a free ballot; who in 1871 first denied the existence of the Ku-Klux and their outrages, and if possible more bitterly denounced the Ku-Klux act than they do this proposed legislation; who have for ten years from time to time ignored, apologized for, or defended ostracism, proscription, riot, murder, and assassination; and who can only hope to get into power and control the United States by a united South, which is only possible by a reign of terror in many parts of the South, under which a free ballot cannot be had. . . .

In conclusion, I want to say in all kindness to gentlemen, North and South, that in my opinion there neither can nor ought to be peace and prosperity until all citizens, as a rule, wherever they may be throughout the Union, are equal before the law in fact as well as in theory.

"In the midst of peace we propose to enact a new force bill, with cruel and unusual penalties, and to suspend the writ of habeas corpus, . . . *that sole and simple barrier between liberty and despotism."*

Additional Federal Intervention in the South Is Unnecessary

Henry Lillie Pierce (1825-1896)

The Enforcement Acts, which were passed in 1870 and 1871 to counteract violent white supremacists in the South, enabled the federal government to intervene in state affairs in order to protect the legal rights and the physical safety of white Republicans and blacks. However, despite the obvious unrest occurring in various sections of the South, many people believed that the Enforcement Acts were too severe—more appropriate for times of war than during peace—and constituted too large an infringement of states' rights.

For example, the Enforcement Acts inflicted heavy fines and imprisonment for violations of the Fourteenth and Fifteenth Amendments; they also took jurisdiction in these cases away from the southern state courts and gave it to Republican-controlled federal courts. Under the acts, the president had the power to suspend the writ of habeas corpus, which meant southern citizens could be arrested without any charges' being brought against them. The president was also empowered to declare martial law and to send federal troops to maintain order. President Ulysses S. Grant used

Henry Lillie Pierce, *Congressional Record*, 43rd Cong., 2nd sess., February 27, 1875, pp. 1885-1911.

this authority in 1871 when he sent troops to dispel the Klan in South Carolina and again in 1874 to settle disputed elections and ensuing violence in Arkansas and Louisiana.

Most southern whites chafed under the restrictions of the Enforcement Acts, which they perceived as yet another case of post-war northern vindictiveness. By 1875, even many Republicans were concerned over the extent of federal intervention in southern affairs and began to defect from the party line. Henry Lillie Pierce, a Republican representative from Boston, Massachusetts, was among those who argued that the time had come to decrease federal intrusion in the South. In his speech of February 27, 1875, Pierce accuses his fellow Republicans of attempting to use the Enforcement Bill to retain Republican electoral majorities in the South. He insists that the Radical Republicans are endeavoring to push the bill through in the last days of the congressional session only because Democrats have won a majority in recent elections and will control the next House. However, Pierce maintains, the first three Enforcement Acts provide the president with enough power to maintain order in the South; no further measures are needed.

Although the Enforcement Bill did pass in the House, it reached the Senate too late for a vote and was never enacted.

Mr. Speaker, I deplore the introduction of this measure into this House in the last hours of an expiring Congress; for in my judgment it is ill-timed, unnecessary, and worse than useless. Impressed with its injustice and impolicy, I should fall short of my duty did I content myself with giving a silent vote against it. It is a political measure, intended, as its advocates aver, to secure in the country the ascendency of the political party to which they belong. To this end it provides for the increase of the power of the President, and clothes him with additional authority to interfere in the internal affairs of the several States. For one I am opposed to this increase and to this interference. Nothing but an exigency of the gravest character would justify special legislation of this kind at the very close of the session of a House of Representatives that is to be succeeded by one of adverse political opinion.

Are we not at the bottom working simply and solely for the continuance of political party supremacy? Are we not aiming, or do not those who advocate this bill aim, if not exclusively, mainly at party success by this instrumentality? Is not that in fact the motive to the introduction of the bill? Sir, gentlemen know it is. We are told, by high authority, that one hundred and thirty-eight electoral votes of the reconstructed States rightfully belong to the republican party; and that if the bill now pending in the House becomes a law it will secure these votes to that party, and otherwise they will be lost.

Extreme Penalties

The pretense of redressing personal grievances and protecting individual liberty by this bill is not sufficiently plausible to free the action of its supporters from this criticism. I assert, Mr. Speaker, that we have ample legislation already; sufficiently rigorous and effective laws to accomplish all that is necessary in the Southern States. The Revised Statutes [Enforcement Acts] not only permit, but by implication enjoin upon the President and subordinate authorities the suppression of insurrectionary manifestations; the protection of the States against domestic violence and the rights of citizens in the exercise of suffrage. Why, then, add to the laws this extreme power, these extreme penalties? Are we mindful that constitutional liberty has meaning or force? Do we consider the States as provinces of the General Government that we may obtrude upon them at our pleasure our officers, civil and military, sending them all through the country with utter disregard for their authorities?

If domestic violence exists in the Southern States, the President is empowered to crush it. He has exercised his powers in Louisiana, Arkansas, and other States; and certainly order and tranquillity reign in Arkansas and in Louisiana. We hear of none but political troubles to-day. And yet in the midst of peace we propose to enact a new force bill, with cruel and unusual penalties, and to suspend the writ of *habeas corpus*, that great writ of personal privilege and personal protection, that sole and simple barrier between liberty and despotism that distinguishes this nation and Great Britain from all other nations of the world.

Sir, it is not in the interest of the republican party that this should be done. The people I more immediately represent and the people of Massachusetts as well ask for no such violent remedy. They do not believe the occasion for it exists; and with all kindness toward those who are managing and urging this measure, I say that I doubt if in their heart of hearts these gentlemen believe that any such occasion exists now or is likely to arise in the future.

CHAPTER 4

The New Social Order

Chapter Preface

On March 29, 1865, only a month after Charleston, South Carolina, was captured by Union forces, an exuberant parade of four thousand blacks wound through the streets of the city. Among the groups marching in this "jubilee of freedom" were the Twenty-first United States Colored Troops, ten companies of firemen, members of various other trades carrying their tools, a musical band, and eighteen hundred singing schoolchildren whose banner read, "We Know No Master but Ourselves." As the *New York Daily Tribune* reported, the parade also included a large cart drawn by horses:

> On this cart was an auctioneer's block and a black man with a bell represent[ing] a Negro trader. This man had himself been sold several times and two women and a child who sat on the block had also been knocked down at auction in Charleston. As the cart moved along, the mock-auctioneer rang his bell and cried out: "How much am I offered for this good cook? She is an excellent cook, gentlemen." . . . Women burst into tears as they saw this tableau and forgetting that it was a mimic scene, shouted wildly: *"Give me back my children! Give me back my children!"*

Closely following the auctioneer's block was a procession of mourners dressed in black and a coffin labeled with the sign "Slavery is dead."

By the time the Thirteenth Amendment was ratified on December 18, 1865, slavery was indeed dead. The process of legally abolishing slavery had begun with Abraham Lincoln's Emancipation Proclamation of January 1, 1863, which was a wartime measure that only freed slaves living in Confederate territory. However, when it became apparent that the loyal border states would not end slavery of their own accord, Congress drafted the Thirteenth Amendment, which permanently abolished slavery throughout the United States. Black reaction to emancipation was swift: Thousands took to the road, testing the boundaries of their freedom and searching for lost family members who had been sold away. Couples legalized their marriages, and former slaves chose their own surnames. Black children came to school in droves, and often their parents and grandparents attended as well. Some freed slaves agreed to work—for wages—for their former owners, while others found new employers. Many women, eager to set up their own households and care for their own children, refused to continue working outside the home at all. The 250,000 free blacks in the North were also jubilant over slavery's demise. They no longer needed to fear the white slavecatchers who kidnapped northern blacks, and they hoped that nationwide emancipation would be the first step toward granting blacks citizenship, equality, and civil rights.

For though slavery was dead, racial prejudice was very much alive, in both the North and the South. Prior to the Civil War, free blacks in most northern states had not been allowed to vote, to serve on a jury, or to attend public schools. Many white Americans assumed that changes in black status would stop with emancipation and that racial discrimination would continue in the South as it had in the North. In fact, most white Southerners had a difficult time accepting that their black employees could not be treated as slaves; the Freedmen's Bureau received numerous complaints from blacks who were whipped for "sassing" their employers or for taking time off work to care for their sick children. During 1865 and 1866, several southern states passed laws called Black Codes, which, as historian Kenneth M. Stampp notes,

> were not designed to help the Negro through the admittedly difficult transition from the status of slave to that of a responsible freeman. They were not intended to prepare him for a constructive role in the social, political, and economic life of the South. Few believed that such a role was possible. Rather, the purpose of the Black Codes was to keep the Negro, as long as possible, exactly what he was: a propertyless rural laborer under strict controls, without political rights, and with inferior legal rights.

The harshness of the Black Codes shocked the North. Clearly, the Thirteenth Amendment had not been enough to protect the liberty of the freed slaves. As Congress moved to pass legislation that would safeguard the rights of blacks, it became increasingly obvious that the end of slavery had not ended the debate over "the black question" after all. Instead, emancipation raised new questions about the role of blacks in American society, the proper interaction between whites and blacks, and the exact boundaries of equality. In many respects, this debate would be a defining moment in American history, a time when Americans would be required to decide whether the ideals of justice and equality that the nation was founded on would be extended to all people, regardless of race.

VIEWPOINT 1

"Where universal suffrage is the rule, where that is the fundamental idea of the government, to rule us out is to make us an exception, to brand us with the stigma of inferiority."

Blacks Should Have the Right to Vote

Frederick Douglass (1817-1895)

Born in Maryland to a white father and a slave mother, Frederick Douglass escaped from slavery in 1838 and soon became a prominent abolitionist, lecturing throughout the North and in England. Douglass also published his autobiography, *The Narrative of the Life of Frederick Douglass*, in 1845 and *The North Star*, an abolitionist newspaper, from 1847 to 1863. Unlike some abolitionists, Douglass was not content with mere emancipation; he insisted that their work would not be done until the right of blacks to all civil liberties, including the vote, was firmly secured.

On January 26, 1865, Douglass delivered a speech entitled "What the Black Man Wants" to the members of the Massachusetts Anti-Slavery Society. Taking issue with those abolitionists who felt black enfranchisement should be gradual, Douglass calls for immediate suffrage for black men. Not only are blacks prepared for the responsibility of suffrage, Douglass insists, but once armed with the vote, they will be able to stand on their own, without any differential treatment. Especially in the South, Douglass maintains, blacks must be invested with the vote in order to protect themselves from vindictive whites.

From 1870 to 1874, Douglass published the *New National Era*, a weekly newspaper in which he continued to advocate the rights of blacks. He later served as the marshal of the District of Columbia and as the first U.S. minister to Haiti.

Abridged from Frederick Douglass, "What the Black Man Wants," *The Liberator*, February 1865. Reprinted in *The Frederick Douglass Papers*, series 1, vol. 4, *Speeches, Debates, and Interviews*, John W. Blassingame and John R. McKivigan, eds., Yale University Press, 1991.

I have had but one idea for the last three years to present to the American people, and the phraseology in which I clothe it is the old abolition phraseology. I am for the "immediate, unconditional and universal" enfranchisement of the black man, in every State of the Union. (Loud applause.) Without this, his liberty is a mockery; without this, you might as well almost retain the old name of slavery for his condition; for, in fact, if he is not the slave of the individual master, he is the slave of society, and holds his liberty as a privilege, not as a right. He is at the mercy of the mob, and has no means of protecting himself.

The Time Is Ripe

It may be objected, however, that this pressing of the negroes' right to suffrage is premature. Let us have slavery abolished, it may be said, let us have labor organized, and then, in the natural course of events, the right of suffrage will be extended to the negro. I do not agree with this. The constitution of the human mind is such, that if it once disregards the conviction forced upon it by a revelation of truth, it requires the exercise of a higher power to produce the same conviction afterwards. The American people are now in tears. The Shenandoah has run blood—the best blood of the North. All around Richmond the blood of New England and of the North has been shed—of your sons, your brothers, and your fathers. We all feel, in the existence of this rebellion, that judgments terrible, widespread, far-reaching, overwhelming, are abroad in the land; and we feel, in view of these judgments, just now, a disposition to learn righteousness. This is the hour. Our streets are in mourning, tears are falling at every fireside, and under the chastisement of this rebellion, we have almost come up to the point of conceding this great, this all-important right of suffrage. I fear that if we fail to do it now, if Abolitionists fail to press it now, we may not see, for centuries to come, the same disposition that exists at this moment. (Applause.) Hence, I say, now is the time to press this right.

It may be asked, "Why do you want it? Some men have got along very well without it. Women have not this right." Shall we justify one wrong by another? That is a sufficient answer. Shall we at this moment justify the deprivation of the negro of the right to vote because some one else is deprived of that privilege? I hold that women as well as men have the right to vote (applause), and my heart and my voice go with the movement to extend suffrage to woman. But that question rests upon another basis than that on which our right rests. We may be asked, I say, why we want it. I will tell you why we want it. We want it because it is our *right*, first of all. (Applause.) No class of men can, without insulting their own nature, be content with any deprivation of their rights. We want it, again, as a means for educating our race. Men are so constituted that they derive their conviction of their own possibilities largely from the estimate formed of them by others. If nothing is expected of a people, that people will find it difficult to contradict that expectation. By depriving us of suffrage, you affirm our incapacity to form an intelligent judgment respecting public men and public measures; you declare before the world that we are unfit to exercise the elective franchise, and by this means lead us to undervalue ourselves, to put a low estimate upon ourselves, and to feel that we have no possibilities like other men. Again, I want the elective franchise, for one, as a colored man, because ours is a peculiar government, based upon a peculiar idea, and that idea is universal suffrage. If I were in a monarchical government, or an autocratic or aristocratic Government, where the few bore rule and the many were subject, there would be no special stigma resting upon me because I did not exercise the elective franchise. It would do me no great violence. Mingling with the mass, I should partake of the strength of the mass; I should be supported by the mass, and I should have the same incentives to endeavor with the mass of my fellow-men; it would be no particular burden, no particular deprivation. But here, where universal suffrage is the rule, where that is the fundamental idea of the government, to rule us out is to make us an exception, to brand us with the stigma of inferiority, and to invite to our heads the missiles of those about us. Therefore I want the franchise for the black man.

There are, however, other reasons, not derived from any consideration merely of our rights, but arising out of the condition of the South and of the country . . . considerations which must arrest the attention of statesmen. I believe that when the tall heads of this rebellion shall have been swept down, as they will be swept down, when the [Jefferson] Davises and [Robert A.] Toombses and [Alexander H.] Stephenses and others who are leading in this rebellion shall have been blotted out, there will be this rank undergrowth of treason, to which reference has been made, growing up there, and interfering with and thwarting the quiet operation of the Federal Government in those States. You will see those traitors handing down from sire to son the same malignant spirit which they have manifested and which they are now exhibiting, with malicious hearts, broad blades and bloody hands in the field, against our sons and brothers. That spirit will still remain; and whoever sees the Federal Government extended over those Southern States will see that government in a strange land and not only in a strange land but in an enemy's land. A postmaster of the United States in the South will find himself surrounded by

National Black Suffrage

Black enfranchisement was a gradual process: Only a few northern states allowed blacks to vote at the beginning of Reconstruction, and the Reconstruction Acts of 1867 provided for black suffrage in the South alone. Although many politicians felt that the Fourteenth Amendment implicitly gave blacks the vote, eventually it became clear that a specific amendment was necessary to secure black suffrage throughout the nation. On January 29, 1869, Republican Samuel Shellabarger addressed the U.S. House of Representatives in favor of the Fifteenth Amendment and national black suffrage.

By our reconstruction laws—now accepted by the country as permanent—we have required the reconstructed States to submit to equal suffrage. We have done this mainly, I admit, because it was absolutely impossible to organize or guarantee republican governments down there at all unless we enabled the only loyal race there was there to vote. This fact, distinguishing the Northern from the Southern States, might, perhaps, justify us in requiring temporarily of them what we did not accept for ourselves. But, if this be so, it can only be temporarily so; if, indeed, as we all devoutly hope, general loyalty is ultimately to come back to the South. We must, therefore, speedily either let the South disfranchise its colored races if they will, or else enfranchise our own, or else compel a submission by sister States to a rule of elective franchise pronounced by ourselves dangerous and ruinous to us. To so compel them permanently to submit to what we refuse ourselves to accept is dishonor—a dishonor which will soon become revolting to the sense of fair play for which the American people are not undistinguished, and will shock the moral sense of mankind. This consideration has exceeding force in impelling us to at once make the law of enfranchisement national, universal.

a hostile spirit; a collector in a Southern port will find himself surrounded by a hostile spirit; a United States marshal or United States judge will be surrounded there by a hostile element. That enmity will not die out in a year, will not die out in an age. . . . They will endeavor to circumvent, they will endeavor to destroy the peaceful operation of this government. Now, where will you find the strength to counterbalance this spirit, if you do not find it in the negroes of the South! They are your friends, and have always been your friends. They were your friends even when the Government did not regard them as such. They comprehended the genius of this war before you did. It is a significant fact, it is a marvellous fact, it seems almost to imply a direct interposition of Providence, that this war, which began in the interest of slavery on both sides, bids fair to end in the interests of liberty on both sides. (Applause.) It was begun, I say, in the interest of slavery, on both sides. The South was fighting to take slavery out of the Union and the North fighting to keep it in the Union; the South fighting to get it beyond the limits of the United States Constitution, and the North fighting to retain it within those limits, the South fighting for new guarantees and the North fighting for the old guarantees;—both despising the negro, both insulting the negro. Yet the negro, apparently endowed with wisdom from on high, saw more clearly the end from the beginning than we did. When [William H.] Seward said the status of no man in the country would be changed by the war, the negro did not believe him. (Applause.) When our generals sent their underlings in shoulder straps to hunt the flying negro back from our lines into the jaws of slavery from which he had escaped, the negroes thought that a mistake had been made, and that the intentions of the Government had not been rightly understood by our officers in shoulder straps, and they continued to come into our lines, threading their way through bogs and fens, over briars and thorns, fording streams, swimming rivers, bringing us tidings as to the safe path to march, and pointing out the dangers that threatened us. They are our only friends in the South, and we should be true to them in this their trial hour, and see to it that they have the elective franchise.

The Fallacy of Inferiority

I know that we are inferior to you in some things—virtually inferior. We walk about among you like dwarfs among giants. Our heads are scarcely seen above the great sea of humanity. The Germans are superior to us; the Irish are superior to us; the Yankees are superior to us (laughter); they can do what we cannot, that is, what we have not hitherto been allowed to do. But, while I make this admission, I utterly deny that we are originally, or naturally, or practically, or in any way, or in any important sense, inferior to anybody on this globe. . . .

It is said that we are ignorant; I admit it. But if we know enough to be hung, we know enough to vote. If the negro knows enough to pay taxes to support the Government, he knows enough to vote—taxation and representation should go together. If he knows enough to shoulder a musket and fight for the flag, fight for the Government, he knows enough to vote. If he knows as much when he is sober as an Irishman knows when drunk, he knows enough to vote, on good American principles. (Laughter and applause.)

But I was saying that you needed a counterpoise in the persons of the slaves to the enmity that would exist at the South after the rebellion is put down. I hold that the American people are bound, not only in self-defence, to extend this right to the freedmen of the South, but they are bound by their love of country and by all their regard for the future safety of those Southern States to do this—to do it as a measure essential to the preservation of peace there. But I will not dwell upon this. I put it to the American sense of honor. The honor of a nation is an important thing. It is said in the Scriptures, "What doth it profit a man if he gain the whole world, and lose his own soul!" It may be said also, what doth it profit a nation if it gain the whole world, but lose its honor? I hold that the American Government has taken upon itself a solemn obligation of honor to see that this war, let it be long or let it be short, let it cost much, or let it cost little,—that this war shall not cease until every freedman at the South has the right to vote. (Applause.) It has bound itself to do it. What have you asked the black men of the South, the black men of the whole country to do? Why, you have asked them to incur the deadly enmity of their masters, in order to befriend you and to befriend this government. You have asked us to call down, not only upon ourselves, but upon our children's children, the deadly hate of the entire Southern people. You have called upon us to turn our backs upon our masters, to abandon their cause and espouse yours; to turn against the South and in favor of the North; to shoot down the Confederacy and uphold the flag—the American flag. You have called upon us to expose ourselves to all the subtle machinations of their malignity for all time. And now, what do you propose to do when you come to make peace? To reward your enemies, and trample in the dust your friends? Do you intend to sacrifice the very men who have come to the rescue of your banner in the South and incurred the lasting displeasure of their masters thereby? Do you intend to sacrifice them, and reward your enemies? Do you mean to give your enemies the right to vote, and take it away from your friends? Is that wise policy? Is that honorable? Could American honor withstand such a blow? I do not believe you will do it. I think you will see to it that we have the right to vote. There is something too mean in looking upon the negro when you are in trouble as a citizen, and when you are free from trouble as an alien. When this nation was in trouble, in its early struggles, it looked upon the negro as a citizen. In 1776, he was a citizen. At the time of the formation of the Constitution, the negro had the right to vote in eleven States out of the old thirteen. In your trouble you have made us citizens. In 1812, Gen. [Andrew] Jackson addressed us as citizens, "fellow citizens." He wanted us to fight. We were citizens then! And now, when you come to frame a conscription bill, the negro is a citizen again. He has been a citizen just three times in the history of this government, and it has always been in time of trouble. In time of trouble we are citizens. Shall we be citizens in war, and aliens in peace? Would that be just?

Less Sympathy, More Rights

I ask my friends who are apologizing for not insisting upon this right, where can the black man look in this country for the assertion of this right if he may not look to the Massachusetts Anti-Slavery Society? Where under the whole heavens can he look for sympathy in asserting this right if he may not look to this platform? Have you lifted us up to a certain height to see that we are men, and then are any disposed to leave us there, without seeing that we are put in possession of all our rights? We look naturally to this platform for the assertion of all our rights, and for this one especially. I understand the anti-slavery societies of this country to be based on two principles—first, the freedom of the blacks of this country; and, second, the elevation of them. Let me not be misunderstood here. I am not asking for sympathy at the hands of Abolitionists, sympathy at the hands of any. I think the American people are disposed often to be generous rather than just. . . . What I ask for the negro is not benevolence, not pity, not sympathy, but simply *justice*. (Applause.) The American people have always been anxious to know what they shall do with us. . . . Everybody has asked the question, and they learned to ask it early of the abolitionists: "What shall we do with the negro?" I have had but one answer from the beginning. Do nothing with us! Your doing with us has already played the mischief with us. Do nothing with us! If the apples will not remain on the tree of their own strength, if they are worm-eaten at the core, if they are early ripe and disposed to fall, let them fall! I am not for tying or fastening them on the tree in any way, except by nature's plan, and if they will not stay there let them fall. And if the negro cannot stand on his own legs, let him fall also. All I ask is, give him a chance to stand on his own legs! Let him alone! If you see him on his way to school, let him alone,—don't disturb him! If you see him going to the dinner table at a hotel, let him go! If you see him going to the ballot box, let him alone!—don't disturb him! (Applause.) If you see him going into a workshop, just let him alone,—your interference is doing him positive injury. . . . Let him live or die by that. If you will only untie his hands, and give him a chance, I think he will live.

VIEWPOINT 2

*"The negroes are not the equals of white Americans,
and are not entitled by any right, natural or acquired,
to participate in the Government of this country."*

Blacks Should Not
Have the Right to Vote

Benjamin M. Boyer (1823-1887)

Although northern states had abolished slavery long before the
Civil War, in 1866 only five allowed blacks to vote on equal terms
with whites. Hoping to set an example, Radical Republicans proposed a bill to enfranchise blacks in the District of Columbia.

On January 10, 1866, Pennsylvania Democrat Benjamin M.
Boyer spoke on the House floor, explaining his opposition to the
measure. Boyer attacks the Radical Republican interpretation of
the axiom "all men are created equal," arguing that the Founding
Fathers never intended for suffrage to be extended to blacks.
While Boyer concedes that all races share some basic rights, he argues that biological and cultural differences create inequalities
that cannot be ignored. Moreover, he suggests that enforcing
black enfranchisement in regions where white public opinion is
strongly against it would endanger, not protect, blacks. Boyer
concludes that black suffrage should be granted gradually—if at
all—as blacks proved themselves capable of the "intellectual and
moral capacity" to participate in the democratic process.

The District of Columbia suffrage bill passed the House of Representatives, but it met with disapproval from moderate Republicans and was allowed to die in a Senate committee without coming to a vote.

Benjamin M. Boyer, *Congressional Globe*, 39th Cong., 1st sess., January 10, 1866, pp. 100-101.

Mr. Speaker, however atrocious some gentlemen in this House may pronounce the sentiment that this is a white man's Government, and although I have lately heard in this Hall even the spirit of the illustrious dead condemned to everlasting fire for denying while upon earth the equality of the races, I am constrained notwithstanding to assume the responsibility of a respectful but firm and earnest opposition to this bill. I am opposed to it, sir, not only upon special and local grounds, but also upon the broad general principle that this is, and of right ought to be, a white man's Government.

Public Opinion

Sir, it is proposed by this bill to confer the elective franchise upon the colored population of the District of Columbia, and to elevate at once, without any qualification or preparation, a heterogeneous mass of about thirty thousand negroes and mulattoes to a complete political equality with the white inhabitants. It is proposed to do this, too, in opposition to the known wishes of a large majority of the citizens of the District, and in the face of an election held here only a few days ago in which the vote against negro suffrage was nearly unanimous. . . .

It would ill become us to fasten, by our votes, upon the people of this District, against their consent, a measure which the people of our own States have already pronounced a political degradation, and have provided against its infliction upon *them* by constitutional enactments. In eighteen out of twenty-five States now represented in this Congress negroes and mulattoes are not allowed to vote. In some of the others there are special restrictions imposed. In three of the States—Connecticut, Wisconsin, and Minnesota—elections were recently held, in which the people by heavy majorities decided against negro suffrage. Yet in each of the States the number of colored persons is comparatively small, while here it probably equals one third of the entire population.

In all the States the people have settled this question for themselves, and I claim the same privilege for the people of the District of Columbia. . . .

But we were told the other day by my distinguished colleague, the chairman of the committee on reconstruction, [Mr. Thaddeus Stevens,] that "to say so is political blasphemy." And in support of his position he said further that "our fathers repudiated the whole doctrine of the legal superiority of races." But the truth is too plain for discussion, that our fathers recognized and practiced directly the opposite doctrine, and even fortified by the bulwarks of the Constitution itself the subjection of the inferior race. No

143

man can read with open eyes and candid mind the Constitution of the United States, as made by our fathers, and fail to see that this Government was intended by its founders to be a white man's Government. It was on this very account that the early abolitionists denounced it as a covenant with hell, and the advocates of the higher law proposed to trample it under foot.

We Will Not Submit Quietly

Southern opposition to black suffrage was intensified because of the disfranchisement of white Southerners who had taken part in the Confederacy, which encompassed the majority of the white population. In 1868, the Democratic Party of South Carolina submitted an appeal to the U.S. Congress concerning the new state constitution, which provided unqualified suffrage for black men but enforced the federal restrictions on former Rebels.

[The South Carolina State] Constitution enfranchises every male negro over the age of twenty-one, and disfranchises many of the purest and best white men of the State. The negro being in a large numerical majority, as compared with the whites, the effect is that the new Constitution establishes in this State negro supremacy, with all its train of countless evils. A superior race—a portion, Senators and Representatives, of the same proud race to which it is your pride to belong—is put under the rule of an inferior race—the abject slaves of yesterday, the flushed freedmen of to-day. And think you that there can be any just, lasting reconstruction on this basis? The Committee respectfully reply, in behalf of their white fellow-citizens, that this cannot be. We do not mean to threaten resistance by arms. But the white people of our State will never quietly submit to negro rule. We may have to pass under the yoke you have authorized, but by moral agencies, by political organization, by every peaceful means left us, we will keep up this contest until we have regained the heritage of political control handed down to us by an honored ancestry. This is a duty we owe to the land that is ours, to the graves that it contains, and to the race of which you and we are alike members—the proud Caucasian race, whose sovereignty on earth God has ordained, and they themselves have illustrated on the most brilliant pages of the world's history.

Arguments derived from the phraseology of the Declaration of American Independence would scarcely need a refutation, were it not for the pertinacity with which they are thrust upon us. If, however, by the expression therein contained, that "all men are created free and equal," we are to infer that the illustrious slaveholders who helped to frame that instrument intended to assert the political equality of the races, we must believe also the monstrous anomaly that they intended to proclaim their daily life a continuous lie and their supremacy over the negro a most atrocious and wicked usurpation. If so, what blasphemy would have been their appeal to the Supreme Judge of the world for the rectitude of their intentions, and what mockery to profess as they did a decent respect for the opinions of mankind. . . .

We find in the constitutions of many of the States the same words so much dwelt upon by the advocates of negro equality; and further on in the same constitutions we find words expressly excluding the negro from all participation in the government.

The constitution of Connecticut, adopted in 1818, says, "that all men, when they form a social compact, are equal in rights; and that no men or set of men are entitled to exclusive public emoluments or privileges in the community." But this declaration did not prevent the insertion of a clause in the same instrument confining the elective franchise to the *white* male citizens of the State.

Mr. Speaker [Schuyler Colfax], in the constitution of your own State of Indiana, adopted as late as 1851, I find these same talismanic words, "All men are created equal." But further on in the same constitution I find these other words, "No negro or mulatto shall have the right of suffrage." And in another place these additional words, "No negro or mulatto shall come into or settle in the State after the adoption of this constitution." And this last prohibition is enforced by heavy pains and penalties. Surely it will not be pretended that the intelligent people of Indiana intended to make a public proclamation of their injustice by asserting the equality of the negro, while by their organic law they denied to him all the rights of an equal, and even a home within the limits of their community.

In the constitution of the State of Oregon, adopted in 1857, there are these words: "We declare all men, when they form a social compact, are equal in rights." But in the same instrument we find also these other words, "No negro, Chinaman, or mulatto shall have the right of suffrage."

And Kansas, too, in her constitution, adopted in 1859, declares that "all men are possessed of equal and inalienable rights." But by the constitution of Kansas white male persons alone can vote.

In the constitution of the State of Iowa, adopted in 1857, are contained these words: "All men are by nature free and equal." But whether the right of suffrage should be confined to whites was submitted to a vote of the people of the State, and they decided that in that State white persons alone should vote. Yet the whole colored population of Iowa at that time did not exceed a thousand. . . .

All men have indeed in some sense been created equal; but to apply this in its broadest signification, so as to ignore all national and ethnological inequalities among men, would involve the grossest absurdity. All men were endowed by their Creator with the equal right to receive, to do, and to enjoy according to their several capacities and in subservience to the common good. All men are equally entitled by nature to the enjoyment of "life, liberty, and the pursuit of happiness," but it does not follow from this that different races of men can all enjoy these blessings together in the same community and in the same form of government upon terms of complete equality. If it be true, as is affirmed by the greatest of the Apostles, that "God hath made of one blood all the nations of men," the same high authority informs us also that "he hath determined the bounds of their habitation." There is one extensive region of the earth where, all things considered, the negro is the superior of the white man, and where his race, defended by natural laws, has successfully defied the invading legions of conquering Rome and all the efforts of European enterprise. In Ethiopia the negro is and must ever continue to be the ruling race. But laws of Providence as imperative as those which have set apart Ethiopia for *him* will in the end preserve this Government for white men and their posterity, notwithstanding all the morbid excitements of this hour and all the temporary evils to which they are likely to lead. The ordinances of nature are not to be repealed by acts of Congress.

A War of Races

On October 3, 1865, President Andrew Johnson held an interview with Massachusetts abolitionist George L. Stearns, in which Johnson voiced his opposition to the enfranchisement of blacks. Johnson believed that the freed slaves would vote as their former masters dictated, which he feared would cause conflict between blacks and poor southern whites.

It would not do to let the negro have universal suffrage now; it would breed a war of races. There was a time in the Southern States when the slaves of large owners looked down upon non-slave owners because they did not own slaves; . . . this has produced hostility between the mass of the whites and the negroes. The outrages are mostly from non-slave holding whites against the negro, and from the negro upon the non-slaveholding whites. The negro will vote with the late master, whom he does not hate, rather than with the non-slaveholding white, whom he does hate. Universal suffrage will create another war, not against us, but a war of races.

Of the same nature as the argument just answered is the one derived from that clause in the Constitution of the United States which guarantees to all the States a republican form of government. Strangely enough, it is insisted that to make a State republican in form its negro population must vote. But of this principle the founders of our Republic must surely have lived and died in blissful ignorance, for they certainly acted and talked as if they imagined they were living in republican communities, even when surrounded by negro slaves. If the negro has a natural right to vote because he is a human inhabitant of a community professing to be republican, then women should vote, for the same reason; and the New England States themselves are only *pretended* republics, because their women, who are in a considerable majority, are denied the right of suffrage.

Some of the reformers do say that after the negro will come the women. But I protest against this inverse order of merit; and if both are to vote I claim precedence for the ladies. There is one sense in which I will admit that negro votes will be needed at the South to make *Republican* States. And that is the sense in which the term "Republican" was used by my colleague [Mr. Thaddeus STEVENS] in his speech already referred to, when, with even more than his characteristic candor, he assigned a reason for the coercion of southern communities into the adoption of negro suffrage. Said he:

> If they should grant the right of suffrage to persons of color, I think there would always be Union white men enough in the South aided by the blacks to divide the representation, and thus continue the Republican ascendency.

But I deny that to be the precise form of republican government guarantied by the Constitution.

An Inferior Race

It is common for the advocates of negro suffrage to assume that the *color* of the negro is the main obstacle to his admission to political equality; and the gentleman from Iowa [Mr. James F. WILSON] dwelt long upon that argument. But it is not the complexion of the negro that degrades him, and I grant that it is but a shallow argument that goes no deeper than his skin. If he is to be excluded from equality in the Government it is not because he is black, nor because he has long heels and woolly hair, nor because the bones of his cranium are thick and inclose a brain averaging by measurement fewer cubic inches in volume than the skulls of white Americans, (although that fact is significant,) nor because of his odor, (although that is not always agreeable,) nor because his facial outline does not conform to our ideas of beautiful humanity. All these considerations I am willing to discard from the argument. But if the peculiarities I have mentioned are the outward badges of a race by nature inferior in mental caliber, and lacking that vim, pluck, and pose of character which give force

147

and direction to human enterprise, and which are essential to the safety and progress of popular institutions, then the negroes are not the equals of white Americans, and are not entitled by any right, natural or acquired, to participate in the Government of this country. . . .

They are but superficial thinkers who imagine that the organic differences of races can be obliterated by the education of the schools. The qualities of races are perpetuated by descent, and are the result of historical influences reaching far back into the generations of the past. An educated negro is a negro still. The cunning chisel of a [Antonio] Canova could not make an enduring Corinthian column out of a block of anthracite; not because of its color, but on account of the structure of its substance. He might indeed with infinite pains give it the form, but he could not impart to it the strength and adhesion of particles required to enable it to brave the elements, and the temple it was made to support would soon crumble into ruin. . . .

It is argued that suffrage is necessary to the black man to enable him to protect himself against the oppression of the whites. But I do not think that this has been the experience of the country. In Pennsylvania we had, at the date of the last census, a colored population of 56,949, which since then has largely increased. They are there excluded from the polls; but in all my experience in the courts of my State, which has not been inconsiderable, I cannot recall to mind a single instance where justice was denied to a negro because of his complexion. I am satisfied that in those localities where such prejudice is allowed to corrupt the streams of justice you would only add force and acrimony to its operation by establishing a political rivalship between the races. The true friends of the negro race should save them from the fate which would be sure to follow. There is much to be done for the negro in which all parties can unite. In his emancipation the whole country has acquiesced, and a constitutional amendment enables Congress to secure to him the full measure of his liberty in all the States. It is our duty now to provide for his education, and to encourage and aid him in his efforts at improvement. Let the courts be opened to him; let his contracts be enforced, his labor protected, and his rights of property respected. Let public schools be provided for him; and after he shall have been first developed to the full measure of his intellectual and moral capacity there will be still time enough to decide the question whether he shall be a ruler in the land.

VIEWPOINT 3

"Nothing will make men so industrious and moral as to let them feel that they are above want and are the owners of the soil which they till."

Southern Land Should Be Given to the Freed Slaves

Thaddeus Stevens (1792-1868)

Thaddeus Stevens began life as a sickly, lame child in a fatherless and poverty-ridden home. His upbringing instilled in him an intense dislike of aristocracy; he was also an early and passionate opponent of slavery. A lawyer and a steel magnate, Stevens was first elected to the U.S. House of Representatives in 1849 and held his seat almost continuously until his death in 1868.

During the Reconstruction era, Stevens was the leader of the Radical Republicans in the U.S. House of Representatives. As the chairman of the Joint Committee on Reconstruction, Stevens advocated a harsh reconstruction policy for the Confederate states and favored extensive changes in the South. Among the measures that Stevens supported was the confiscation of the plantations belonging to the wealthiest Southerners and the division of these lands among the freed slaves in lots of 40 acres. The remaining land would then be sold—in plots no larger than 500 acres—to the highest bidders. The proceeds of the sale would be used to pay the war debt and to support Union veterans and their families.

In his speech to the House on March 19, 1867, Stevens proposed a land reform bill that would provide land for the freed slaves and destroy the plantation-based aristocracy of the South. It is unjust and cruel, Stevens argues, to emancipate a people without

Thaddeus Stevens, *Congressional Globe*, 40th Cong., 1st sess., March 19, 1867, pp. 204-207.

giving them the land necessary for them to become self-sufficient. Blacks have earned the land through generations of unpaid toil, he asserts. Furthermore, Stevens suggests, the poor southern whites—whose land will not be confiscated—will only benefit from the restructuring of the South's agricultural system. Steven's vision of a new South did not come about; his land reform bill was defeated in Congress.

This bill is important to several classes of people.

It is important to our wounded and maimed soldiers, who are unable to work for their living, and whose present pensions are wholly inadequate to their support. It is important to those bereaved wives and parents whose habiliments of woe are to be seen in every house, and proclaim the cruel losses which have been inflicted on them by the murderous hands of traitors.

It is important to the loyal men, North and South, who have been plundered and impoverished by rebel raiders and rebel Legislatures.

It is important to four millions of injured, oppressed, and helpless men, whose ancestors for two centuries have been held in bondage and compelled to earn the very property a small portion of which we propose to restore to them, and who are now destitute, helpless, and exposed to want and starvation under the deliberate cruelty of their former masters.

It is also important to the delinquents whose property it takes as a fine—a punishment for the great crime of making war to destroy the Republic, and for prosecuting the war in violation of all the rules of civilized warfare. It is certainly too small a punishment for so deep a crime, and too slight a warning to future ages. . . .

The cause of the war was slavery. We have liberated the slaves. It is our duty to protect them, and provide for them while they are unable to provide for themselves. Have we not a right, in the language of [Emerich de] Vattel, "to do ourselves justice respecting the object which has caused the war," by taking lands for homesteads for these "objects" of the war?

Have we not a right, if we chose to go to that extent, to indemnify ourselves for the expenses and damages caused by the war? We might make the property of the enemy pay the $4,000,000,000 which we have expended, as well as the damages inflicted on loyal men by confiscation and invasion, which might reach $1,000,000,000 more. This bill is merciful, asking less than one tenth of our just claims.

We could be further justified in inflicting severe penalties upon this whole hostile people as "a fierce and savage people," as an "obstinate enemy," whom it is a duty to tame and punish. Our future safety requires stern justice. . . .

The Land Reform Bill

The first section [of the bill] orders the confiscation of all the property belonging to the State governments, and the national government [of the Confederacy] which made war upon us, and which we have conquered. I presume no one is prepared to object to this unless it be those who condemned the conquest. To them I have nothing to say, except to hope that they will continue consistent in their love of the rebels; to show an exuberant humanity into which is merged and submerged all the exalted feelings of patriotism.

The second section requires the President to execute an existing law [the Confiscation Act of 1862, which authorized the president

---

A Man Must Earn

Lydia Maria Child, a prominent abolitionist and author from Massachusetts, favored the division of southern plantations and public lands to former slaves and poor whites, but she believed that the land should be sold rather than freely distributed. In her March 1864 letter to George W. Julian, chairman of the House Committee on Public Lands, Child explains her view.

I have observed with anxiety that large tracts of Southern confiscated lands were being bought by Northern capitalists. They ought to be mainly distributed among the emancipated slaves, and the poor whites who will consent to become loyal citizens of the U.S.; for the poor whites have been *almost* as much wronged by slave holding aristocrats, as the enslaved blacks have been. . . .

Experience and observation have taught me that men are generally injured by having property *given* to them. They don't prize it so highly, keep it so carefully, or improve it so diligently, as they do when they take some pains to obtain it. In various ways, it impairs the strength and dignity of character to receive *gifts*. Whosoever would be a *man* must *earn*. . . .

The *sale* of the public lands would not, as you say, *begin* to pay the national debt; yet, other things being equal, it would be of *some* importance as a help toward liquidating it. You truly remark that the wealth arising from the *cultivation* of the soil is what we must rely upon. But the sort of men who would *earn* their way to the possession of farms from the public lands would be the men most likely to *cultivate* them well, to keep them in their own hands, and gradually to increase their acres by new earnings.

---

to seize the property of rebels] which he is sworn to execute, but the performance of which oath is in abeyance. Certainly such law should be enforced or repealed; it is a mockery to allow it to stand on your statute-books and be not only not enforced, but violated every day by the executive government.

The third section furnishes a more convenient and speedy mode of adjudicating such forfeitures, and more consistent with the military conditions of the conquered States.

The fourth section provides first that out of the lands thus confiscated each liberated slave who is a male adult, or the head of a family, shall have assigned to him a homestead of forty acres of land (with $100 to build a dwelling), which shall be held for them by trustees during their pupilage. Let us consider whether this is a just and politic provision.

Whatever may be the fate of the rest of the bill I must earnestly pray that this may not be defeated. On its success, in my judgment, depends not only the happiness and respectability of the colored race, but their very existence. Homesteads to them are far more valuable than the immediate right of suffrage, though both are their due.

Four million persons have just been freed from a condition of dependence, wholly unacquainted with business transactions, kept systematically in ignorance of all their rights and of the common elements of education, without which none of any race are competent to earn an honest living, to guard against the frauds which will always be practiced on the ignorant, or to judge of the most judicious manner of applying their labor. But few of them are mechanics, and none of them skilled manufacturers. They must necessarily, therefore, be the servants and the victims of others unless they are made in some measure independent of their wiser neighbors. The guardianship of the Freedmen's Bureau, that benevolent institution, cannot be expected long to protect them. It encounters the hostility of the old slaveholders, whether in official or private station, because it deprives these dethroned tyrants of the luxury of despotism. In its nature it is not calculated for a permanent institution. Withdraw that protection and leave them a prey to the legislation and treatment of their former masters, and the evidence already furnished shows that they will soon become extinct, or be driven to defend themselves by civil war. Withhold from them all their rights, and leave them destitute of the means of earning a livelihood, the victims of the hatred or cupidity of the rebels whom they helped to conquer, and it seems probable that the war of races might ensue which the President feared would arise from kind treatment and the restoration of their rights. . . .

Make them independent of the old masters so that they may not

Dividing the Land

A freeborn Southerner of mixed blood, Francis L. Cardozo was educated in Great Britain and became one of the leading black politicians of the Reconstruction era. Speaking during the proceedings of the Constitutional Convention of South Carolina of 1868, Cardozo advocates compelling indebted plantation owners to sell their property to poor blacks and whites, thus breaking the monopoly the southern aristocracy has on the land.

One of the greatest bulwarks of slavery was the infernal plantation system, one man owning his thousand, another his twenty, and another fifty thousand acres of land. This is the only way by which we will break up that system, and I maintain that our freedom will be of no effect if we allow it to continue. What is the main cause of the prosperity of the North? It is because every man has his own farm and is free and independent. Let the lands of the South be similarly divided. I would not say for one moment they should be confiscated, but . . . now that slavery is destroyed, let the plantation system go with it. We will never have true freedom until we abolish the system of agriculture which existed in the Southern states. It is useless to have any schools while we maintain this stronghold of slavery as the agricultural system of the country. . . . I look upon it, therefore, as the natural result of the war that this system of large plantations, of no service to the owner or anybody else, should be abolished. . . .

In speaking against the landholders, and in taking this position I do not cherish one feeling of enmity against them as a class or individuals. But this question takes a larger range and is one in which the whole country is involved. I can never sacrifice the interests of nine or ten millions to the interests of three hundred thousand, more especially when the three hundred thousand initiated the war and were the very ones who established an infernal Negro code and want to keep their lands until better times. They do not want that a nigger or a Yankee shall ever own a foot of their land. Now is the time to take the advantage. Give them an opportunity, breathing time, and they will reorganize the same old system they had before the war.

be compelled to work for them upon unfair terms, which can only be done by giving them a small tract of land to cultivate for themselves, and you remove all this danger. You also elevate the character of the freedman. Nothing is so likely to make a man a good citizen as to make him a freeholder. Nothing will so multiply the productions of the South as to divide it into small farms. Nothing will make men so industrious and moral as to let them feel that they are above want and are the owners of the soil which they till. It will also be of service to the white inhabitants. They will have constantly among them industrious laborers, anxious to work for fair wages. How is it possible for them to cultivate their lands if these people were expelled? If [President Andrew Johnson] should lead or drive them into exile, or carry out the absurd idea of colonizing them, the South would become a barren waste. . . .

Bought by Toil

I do not speak of their fidelity and services in this bloody war. I put it on the mere score of lawful earnings. They and their ancestors have toiled, not for years, but for ages, without one farthing of recompense. They have earned for their masters this very land and much more. Will not he who denies them compensation now be accursed, for he is an unjust man? . . .

If the war had been between two regular Governments, both of which survived the war, the victor in the treaty of peace would require the vanquished to pay all such damages as well as all the expenses of the war. If neither had conquered the other they would probably be silent, and each bear his own loss. Congress is dictating the terms of peace. If she does not provide for these meritorious claimants she will be bound in honor to pay them out of the national Treasury. If she does not, individuals will be wronged and the nation dishonored. This bill is very merciful toward a cruel, outlawed belligerent, who, when their armies were dispersed, would gladly have compromised if their lives were saved. Those who will be affected by this bill will not exceed seventy thousand out of a population of six million whites, for this is a people of aristocrats and subjects; of a proud nobility and a cringing, poor peasantry. Those seventy thousand persons own about three hundred and ninety million acres of land out of the five hundred millions in the confederate States. This, together with the town property, cannot be worth less than $10,000,000,000. This estimate includes no man's property who was worth less than $10,000; nor does it include any personal property, which may perhaps swell it to $12,000,000,000. The fine proposed would be but one twentieth of their estates. Were ever such great malefactors so gently dealt with? It were well if all their large estates could be subdivided and sold in small tracts. No people will ever be republican in spirit and practice where a few own immense manors and the masses are landless. Small independent landholders are the support and guardians of republican liberty.

VIEWPOINT 4

"I see [neither] propriety nor justice in taking from the white people that which actually belongs to them and bestowing it upon any portion of the African race."

Southern Land Should Be Returned to the Owners

Burwell C. Ritter (1810-1880)

Established in March 1865, the Freedmen's Bureau was given responsibility for "the supervision and management of all abandoned lands" in the Confederate states. Among these lands were the Sea Islands off the Georgia coast and portions of South Carolina and Florida, which General William T. Sherman set aside for the exclusive settlement of blacks in his Special Field Order No. 15 of January 16, 1865. By June of 1865, approximately 40,000 blacks had settled on 400,000 acres of the region specified in Sherman's field order.

Congress initially intended that the Freedmen's Bureau would distribute forty acres of abandoned, confiscated, or public land to every family of freed slaves, which the bureau began to do in Louisiana, Tennessee, North Carolina, and Virginia. However, the bureau had only been authorized for a one-year existence. Early in 1866, the House of Representatives began debate on a Freedmen's Bureau Bill that would extend the life of the bureau and protect for three years the right of blacks to the lands designated in Sherman's order. Other sections of the proposed bill also provided that three million acres of public land in the South would be allocated to freed slaves and to white southern refugees who had been loyal to the Union.

Burwell C. Ritter, *Congressional Globe*, 39th Cong., 1st sess., February 3, 1866, pp. 635-36.

On February 3, 1866, Democratic Representative Burwell C. Ritter of Kentucky spoke to the House in opposition of the bill. Ritter maintains that Congress has no constitutional right to confiscate lands from its legal owners, many of whom were left destitute after the war. He also condemns the policy of distributing public land to blacks and questions the wisdom of using federal funds to purchase land, build schools and public facilities, and otherwise support the recently freed slaves. The intent of the bill, Ritter argues, is to create a black colony in the South and to drive out the white population.

Although the Freedmen's Bureau Bill was passed by Congress, it was vetoed by President Andrew Johnson. A reworked version of the bill, which did not include the land reform provisions, became law in July 1866; the confiscated lands were returned to the white owners.

The fourth section of [the Freedmen's Bureau] bill authorizes the President to reserve from sale or from settlement, for the use of freedmen and loyal refugees, unoccupied public lands in the States of Florida, Mississippi, Alabama, Louisiana, and Arkansas, not exceeding in all three million acres of good land. These lands are to be allotted and assigned to the freedmen and refugees in parcels not exceeding forty acres to each. These lands they are to have at such annual rent as may be agreed upon between the Commissioner [of the Freedmen's Bureau] and themselves. The rental shall be based upon a valuation of the land, to be ascertained in such manner as the Commissioner may, under the direction of the President, by regulation prescribe.

In the sixth section of this bill it is provided:

> That the Commissioner shall, under the direction of the President, procure in the name of the United States, by grant or purchase, such lands within the districts aforesaid as may be required for refugees and freedmen dependent on the Government for support; and he shall provide or cause to be erected suitable buildings for asylums and schools. But no such purchase shall be made, nor contract for the same entered into, nor other expense incurred, until after appropriations shall have been provided by Congress for such purposes. And no payments shall be made for lands purchased under this section, except for asylums and schools, from any moneys not specifically appropriated therefor. And the Commissioner shall cause such lands from time to time to be valued, allotted, assigned, and sold in manner and form provided in the fourth section of this act, at a price not less than the cost thereof to the United States.

Here, Mr. Speaker, we have, in my judgment, a development of the grant purposes and designs of those who introduced this bill. It is, sir, I have no doubt, to commence a colony in each one of the five States above named, which is ultimately to drive out the entire white population of those States and fill their places with the negro race. And whether this is the design or not, it is certain in my judgment to have this effect. And they could not have devised a more effectual scheme for that purpose. Sir, let us look at these provisions: in the first place they set apart the unoccupied public lands in those States for the use of the colored people. It is true they speak of loyal refugees; in this they may include white persons. But I presume that we all know that none of this class will be there.

Government Aid

These lands are now in a wild state; they are either in forests or prairie. What is the first thing to be done? Are the colored people to go there and make their own improvements at their own expense as the white people in this country have always had to do? No, sir, we are to be more kind and liberal to them. The Secretary of War is to be clothed with authority to erect shelters and furnish provision, clothing, medical attention, and, in a word, do everything that he may deem needful for temporary support. But, sir, they do not stop here; this is not enough; the Commissioner is authorized to purchase sites and buildings for schools and asylums, to be used by these people, but to be held as United States property. And not only this, the Commissioner under the direction of the President is to have power to purchase or rent such tracts of land in the several districts aforesaid as may be necessary to provide for the indigent refugees and freedmen dependent upon the Government for support. Sir, who can estimate the cost for all this? How much is it to cost to feed, clothe, and furnish medical aid, and etc., to these people until they can support themselves? Will they ever be in a condition to support themselves? How much is it to cost to purchase sites and buildings for schools and asylums? How many tracts of land will the Commissioner purchase under this authority? What is to be the size of the tracts? How much is he to pay per acre? How many farms will he rent, and what is he to pay for rent? Sir, these are important questions, the answers to which the people have a right to demand. But, sir, they will demand in vain; no living man can tell. And another still more important question, Mr. Speaker, is, how long is the Government to support these people? Will the white people who have to support the Government ever get done paying taxes to support the negroes? If this is not to continue always, why did not those who introduced this bill fix a time when all this was to stop?

Mr. Speaker, I have said that in my judgment, if this bill is

An Insidious Idea

From 1865 until 1871, Julius J. Fleming of Sumter, South Carolina, contributed a regular column to the Charleston Courier *under the pen name "Juhl." On January 29, 1866, Fleming condemns the apportioning of southern land among the freed slaves, warning that the result would be economically devastating.*

There is one great difficulty in the way of the country's hope and the freedmen's success: it is the idea which has been insidiously and sedulously instilled into the blacks that the government would give them lands and that each family should have its freehold possession—an idea which the military authorities have earnestly endeavored to remove, but which still pervades the mass and is cherished with a tenacity which nothing can overcome. To be an estated man is at present the height of the freedman's ambition—an ambition which Radical legislation seems disposed to gratify. If Congress persists in surrendering to them the Sea Islands and rice lands—the cream of the state—it will not only inflict irreparable injury upon individuals and the commonwealth to the full value of the estates involved, but it will by that one act give a galvanic shock to the entire labor system of the interior. It is yet an open question whether such a gift on the part of the government . . . would be a blessing to the recipients.

passed, that its effect would be to drive the white people all out of the States named, and substitute in their place the colored people. Sir, it is not to be expected that the two races will live contentedly where there are large numbers of the colored people living near to neighborhoods settled with white persons; experience has proved to many of us, that wherever large numbers of colored people live, that the white people living within five or ten miles of the place become sufferers to a very large extent. Now, sir, if this should be the case (as I have no doubt it will) in the States in which you propose to establish these people, the whites and blacks will disagree to such an extent that when people find that the colored people are permanently established they will be compelled, in self defense, to seek a home somewhere else. No doubt, Mr. Speaker, but that those who prepared this bill saw that the difficulties and disagreements to which I have just alluded would arise, and hence they require that military jurisdiction and protection shall be extended, so as to give safety in their movements; and if the white inhabitants become dissatisfied, the Commissioner is prepared with authority by this bill to buy them out and put the negroes upon the land. Who, then, can doubt as to what is to be the effect of this bill if it becomes a law? But, sir, it

158

may be said that the Commissioner is restrained or prohibited from purchasing or making contracts for these lands until Congress shall have made an appropriation to pay for them. Sir, if this bill is passed, I do not suppose that there will ever be much difficulty in getting Congress to make an appropriation, if it be recommended by the President and the Commissioner of this bureau. Sir, the necessity for purchasing these lands is admitted by those who vote for this measure; and if this is not so, why is it put in this bill? . . .

Black Settlements

Mr. Speaker, there is another portion of this very extraordinary bill to which I desire to ask the attention of this House. It is the fifth section of the bill, and reads as follows:

> That the occupants of land under Major General [William T.] Sherman's special field order, dated at Savannah, January 16, 1865, are hereby confirmed in their possession for the period of three years from the date of said order. And no person shall be disturbed in or ousted from said possession during said three years, unless a settlement shall be made with said occupant by the owner, satisfactory to the Commissioner of the Freedmen's Bureau.

Now, sir, I do not propose at this time to express any opinion in regard to the action of Major General Sherman upon that occasion. I only desire to say in regard to him that I regard him as one of the best military men known to this or any other age, a sound patriot and an able statesman. But, sir, I cannot see the propriety or the justice in singling out these people and bestowing upon them greater favors than upon any other colored people. Neither do I see the propriety nor justice in taking from the white people that which actually belongs to them and bestowing it upon any portion of the African race. Sir, I deny that Congress has the right thus to interfere with private property. The Constitution, which we have all taken an oath to support, expressly prohibits and forbids the taking of private property without just compensation. Sir, shall we now in time of peace disregard that Constitution and that oath for any purpose, much less to take property from white persons, who are, as I understand, the actual owners of the property, and give it to colored people or to any other race? For one, sir, I cannot do it. But, Mr. Speaker, suppose we have the right or authority under the Constitution to continue these people in possession of the lands referred to, would it be expedient, would it be better calculated to promote the interest of the Government than to allow the owners to take possession of their own lands? Sir, it is necessary in the present affairs of our country that the Government should afford all proper facilities to the people in or-

159

der that they may be enabled to assist in paying the immense debt now resting upon us. Do gentlemen suppose that these lands in the possession of the colored people will afford any revenue to this Government? If so, I must confess, sir, that they differ very greatly from myself. But, Mr. Speaker, there is one condition upon which this bill does agree that the owner may have his land, and that is that he shall first have a settlement with the occupant, and of course get his consent, and then make the arrangement satisfactory to the Commissioner of the Freedmen's Bureau. Sir, why is it, if these people are free and qualified to exercise the highest privileges that can be bestowed upon freemen, namely, the right of suffrage, why is it that they cannot be allowed the poor privilege to make a contract to give up to the owner property to which he has no right without having to obtain the consent of the Commissioner of this bureau? Sir, I do not covet such freedom as that, neither can I believe that where such supervision is necessary in order to protect the colored race that they are qualified to come in and take an equal stand by the side of the more intelligent, and participate in ruling this great nation by the exercise of the right of suffrage.

Mr. Speaker, there is another fact connected with this subject to which I desire to call the attention of this House, and that is the condition of the people who are the owners of these lands. I understand, sir, that perhaps the only property that they now own upon this earth is these lands. Many of these people are now old, and are tottering on the brink of the grave; many others, who are children, who are unable to do anything for a support, but who are as innocent, so far as the rebellion is concerned, as the child unborn; many others, females, who have no other means to depend upon for support except these lands. Sir, is it possible that gentlemen upon this floor can disregard the appeals that must be made by a knowledge of these facts, knowing these helpless people are now destitute? Sir, look at their condition. I imagine that I can almost hear the plaintive cries of these innocent children asking and beseeching their widowed mothers for bread or a morsel of something to eat. Yet that kind mother is unable to furnish that morsel, because all she owns has been taken by this Government and turned over to the colored people. Sir, I trust that that injustice will be continued no longer, but that these lands will be given back to their owners.

"How can a white man represent a colored constituency, if a colored man cannot do it?"

Blacks Are Capable of Holding Public Office

Henry McNeal Turner (1834-1915)

The son of free black parents in Columbia, South Carolina, Henry McNeal Turner was apprenticed to local plantation owners and worked alongside slaves. In the 1850s, Turner found better employment, obtained an education, and became an outspoken minister in the African Methodist Episcopal Church of South Carolina. Forced to leave the South by angry whites, Turner gained prominence in the black community of Washington, D.C. During the Civil War, he recruited black soldiers for the federal troops and became the first black chaplain in the United States Army.

Turner relocated to Georgia after the war, participating in the Reconstruction government. When Georgia was restored to the Union in July 1868, the state government's Democratic majority moved to expel twenty-seven black state congressmen because of their race. Turner was among the representatives who faced expulsion, and on September 3, 1868, he delivered a speech supporting the right of blacks to hold political office. Arguing that Georgia's reconstructed government was largely designed by black politicians, Turner insists that blacks have already proven themselves to be effective legislators. Furthermore, Turner states, black politicians are far more capable of accurately representing a black constituency than whites could possibly be.

Excerpted from Henry McNeal Turner's speech to the Georgia Legislature, September 3, 1868; later published as a pamphlet *On the Eligibility of Colored Members to Seats in the Georgia Legislature*. Reprinted in *Respect Black: The Writings of Henry McNeal Turner*, Edwin S. Redkey, ed., Arno Press, 1971.

Although the Georgia Democrats were initially successful in their attempt to expel Turner and his colleagues, the federal government pressured Georgia into readmitting the black members of the state government. Disillusioned by these experiences, Turner later became a leading advocate of black immigration to Africa.

Before proceeding to argue this question upon its intrinsic merits, I wish the Members of this House to understand the position that I take. I hold that I am a member of this body. Therefore, sir, I shall neither fawn nor cringe before any party, nor stoop to *beg* them for my rights. Some of my colored fellow-members, in the course of their remarks, took occasion to appeal to the *sympathies* of Members on the opposite side, and to eulogize their character for magnanimity. It reminds me very much, sir, of slaves begging under the lash. I am here to demand my rights, and to hurl thunderbolts at the men who would dare to cross the threshold of my manhood. There is an old aphorism which says, "Fight the Devil with fire," and if I should observe the rule in this instance, I wish gentlemen to understand that it is but fighting them with their own weapon.

The scene presented in this House, today, is one unparalleled in the history of the world. From this day, back to the day when God breathed the breath of life into Adam, no analogy for it can be found. Never, in the history of the world, has a man been arraigned before a body clothed with legislative, judicial or executive functions, charged with the offence of being of a darker hue than his fellow-men. I know that questions have been before the Courts of this country, and of other countries, involving topics not altogether dissimilar to that which is being discussed here today. But, sir, never, in all the history of the great nations of this world—never before—has a man been arraigned, charged, with an offence committed by the God of Heaven himself. Cases may be found where men have been deprived of their rights for crimes and misdemeanors; but it has remained for the State of Georgia, in the very heart of the nineteenth century, to call a man before the bar, and there charge him with an act for which he is no more responsible than for the head which he carries up on his shoulders. The Anglo-Saxon race, sir, is a most surprising one. No man has ever been more deceived in that race than I have been for the last three weeks. I was not aware that there was in the character of that race so much cowardice, or so much pusillanimity. The treachery which has been exhibited by gentlemen belonging to that race has shaken my confidence in it more than anything that has come under my observation from the day of my birth. . . .

Whose Legislature is this? Is it a white man's Legislature, or is it a black man's Legislature? Who voted for a Constitutional Convention, in obedience to the mandate of the Congress of the United States? Who first rallied around the standard of Reconstruction? Who set the ball of loyalty rolling in the State of Georgia? And whose voice was heard on the hills and in the valleys of this State? It was the voice of the brawny-armed negro, with the few humanitarian-hearted white men who came to our assistance. I claim the honor, sir, of having been the instrument of convincing hundreds—yea, thousands—of white men, that to reconstruct under the measures of the United States Congress was the safest and the best course for the interest of the State.

A Monopoly of Power

Let us look at some facts in connection with this matter. Did half the white men of Georgia vote for this Legislature? Did not the great bulk of them fight, with all their strength, the Constitution under which we are acting? And did they not fight against the organization of this Legislature? And further, sir, did they not *vote* against it? Yes, sir! And there are persons in this Legislature, today, who are ready to spit their poison in my face, while they themselves opposed, with all their power, the ratification of this Constitution. They question my right to a seat in this body, to represent the people whose legal votes elected me. This objection, sir, is an unheard of monopoly of power. No analogy can be found for it, except it be the case of a man who should go into my house, take possession of my wife and children, and then tell me to walk out. I stand very much in the position of a criminal before your bar, because I dare to be the exponent of the views of those who sent me here. Or, in other words, we are told that if black men want to speak, they must speak through white trumpets; if black men want their sentiments expressed, they must be adulterated and sent through white messengers, who will quibble, and equivocate, and evade, as rapidly as the pendulum of a clock. If this be not done, then the black men have committed an outrage, and their Representatives must be denied the right to represent their constituents.

The great question, sir, is this: Am I a man? If I am such, I claim the rights of a man. Am I not a man, because I happen to be of a darker hue than honorable gentlemen around me? Let me see whether I am or not. I want to convince the House, today, that I am entitled to my seat here. A certain gentleman has argued that the negro was a mere development similar to the orangutan or chimpanzee, but it so happens that, when a negro is examined,

A minister who was an articulate and dynamic speaker, Henry McNeal Turner defended the ability of blacks to serve in political offices.

physiologically, phrenologically and anatomically, and, I may say, physiognomically, he is found to be the same as persons of different color. I would like to ask any gentleman on this floor, where is the analogy? Do you find me a quadruped, or do you find me a man? Do you find three bones less in my back than in that of the white man? Do you find less organs in the brain? If you know nothing of this, I do; for I have helped to dissect fifty men, black and white, and I assert that by the time you take off the mucous pigment—the color of the skin—you cannot, to save your life, distinguish between the black man and the white. Am I a man? Have I a soul to save, as you have? Am I susceptible of eternal development, as you are? Can I learn all the arts and sciences that you can—has it ever been demonstrated in the history of the world? Have black men ever exhibited bravery, as white men have done? Have they ever been in the professions? Have they not as good articulative organs as you? Some people argue that there is a very close similarity between the larynx of the negro and that of the orangutan. Why, sir, there is not so much similarity between them as there is between the larynx of the man and that of the dog, and this fact I dare any Member of this House to dispute. God saw fit to vary everything in Nature. There are no two men alike—no two voices alike—no two trees alike. God has weaved and tissued variety and versatility throughout the boundless space of His creation. Because God saw fit to make some red, and some white, and some black, and some brown, are we to sit here in judgment upon what God has seen fit to do? As well might one play with the thunderbolts of heaven as with that creature that bears God's image—God's photograph. . . .

The negro is here charged with holding office. Why, sir, the negro never wanted office. I recollect that when we wanted candidates for the Constitutional Convention, we went from door to door in the "negro belt," and begged white men to run. Some promised to do so; and yet, on the very day of election, many of them *first* made known their determination not to comply with their promises. They told black men, everywhere, that they would rather see *them* run; and it was this encouragement of the white men that induced the colored man to place his name upon the ticket as a candidate for the Convention. In many instances, these white men voted for us. We did not want them, nor ask them, to do it. All we wanted them to do was, to stand still and allow us to walk up to the polls and deposit our ballots. They would not come here themselves, but would insist upon sending us. . . . Now, however, a change has come over the spirit of their dream. They want to turn the "nigger" out; and, to support their argument, they say that the black man is debarred from holding office by the Reconstruction measures of Congress. Let me tell them one thing for their information. Black men have held office, and are now holding office, under the United States Government. Andrew Johnson, President of the United States, in 1865, commissioned me as United States Chaplain, and I would have been Chaplain today, had I not resigned—not desiring to hold office any longer. Let the Democratic party, then, go to Mr. Johnson, and ask him why he commissioned a negro to that position? And if they inquire further, they will ascertain that black men have been commissioned as Lieutenants, Captains, Majors, Brevet Colonels, Surgeons, and other offices of trust and responsibility, under the United States Government. . . .

The honorable gentleman from Whitfield (Mr. Shumate), when arguing this question, a day or two ago, put forth the proposition that to be a Representative was not to be an officer—"it was a privilege that citizens had a right to enjoy." These are his words. It was not an office; it was a "privilege." Every gentleman here knows that he denied that to be a Representative was to be an officer. Now, he is recognized as a leader of the Democratic party in this House, and generally cooks victuals for them to eat; makes that remarkable declaration, and how are you, gentlemen on the other side of the House, to ignore that declaration? Are you going to expel me from this House, because I am an officer, when one of your great lights says that I am *not* an officer? If you deny my right—the right of my constituents to have representation here—because it is a "privilege," then, sir, I will show you that I have as many privileges as the whitest man on on this floor. If I am not permitted to occupy a seat here, for the purpose of representing my constituents, I want to know how white men can be permitted to do so? How can a white man represent a colored constituency, if a colored man cannot do it? The great argument is: "Oh, we have inherited" this, that and the other. Now, I want gentlemen to come down to cool, common sense. Is the created greater than the Creator? Is man greater than God? It is very

---

No Improper Advantage

Joseph H. Rainey, a former slave from South Carolina, served as a member of the South Carolina State Constitutional Convention in 1868 and was elected to the U.S. House of Representatives in 1870. In a speech delivered to the House on March 5, 1872, Rainey cites his experience as a member of the constitutional convention as an example of black politicians' competence and fairness.

I ask the country, I ask white men, I ask Democrats, I ask Republicans whether the Negroes have presumed to take improper advantage of the majority they hold in [South Carolina] by disregarding the interest of the minority? They have not. Our [constitutional] convention which met in 1868, and in which the Negroes were in a large majority, did not pass any proscriptive or disfranchising acts, but adopted a liberal constitution, securing alike equal rights to all citizens, white and black, male and female, as far as possible. Mark you, we did not discriminate, although we had a majority. Our constitution towers up in its majesty with provisions for the equal protection of all classes of citizens. Notwithstanding our majority there, we have never attempted to deprive any man in that State of the rights and immunities to which he is entitled under the Constitution of this Government. You cannot point me to a single act passed by our Legislature, at any time, which had a tendency to reflect upon or oppress any white citizen of South Carolina. You cannot show me one enactment by which the majority in our State have undertaken to crush the white men because the latter are in a minority.

strange, if a white man can occupy on this floor *a seat created by colored votes*, and a black man cannot do it. Why, gentlemen, it is the most short-sighted reasoning in the world. A man can see better than that with half an eye. . . .

A Political Slave

It is said that Congress never gave us the right to hold office. I want to know, sir, if the Reconstruction measures did not base their action on the ground that no distinction should be made on account of race, color, or previous condition! Was not that the grand fulcrum on which they rested? And did not every reconstructed State have to reconstruct on the idea that no discrimination, in any sense of the term, should be made? There is not a man here who will dare say, "No." If Congress has simply given me merely sufficient civil and political rights to make me a mere political slave for Democrats, or anybody else—giving them the opportunity of jumping on my back, in order to leap into political power—I do not thank Congress for it. Never, so help me, God, shall I be a political slave. I am not now speaking for those colored men who sit with me in this House, nor do I say that they endorse my sentiments [cries from the colored Members, "We do!"], but I am speaking simply and solely for myself. Congress, after assisting Mr. Lincoln to take me out of servile slavery, did not intend to put me and my race into *political* slavery. If they did, let them take away my ballot—I do not want it, and shall not have it. [Several colored Members: "Nor we!"] I don't want to be a mere tool of that sort. I have been a slave long enough already.

I tell you what I would be willing to do: I am willing that the question should be submitted to Congress for an explanation as to what was meant in the passage of these Reconstruction measures, and of the [Fourteenth] Constitutional Amendment. Let the Democratic party in this House pass a Resolution giving this subject that direction, and I shall be content. I dare you, gentlemen, to do it. Come up to the question openly, whether it meant that the negro might hold office, or whether it meant that he should merely have the right to vote. If you are honest men, you will do it. If, however, you will not do that, I would make another proposition: Call together, again, the Convention that framed the Constitution under which we are acting; let them take a vote upon the subject, and I am willing to abide their decision. . . .

But, Mr. Speaker, I do not regard this movement as a thrust at me. It is a thrust at the Bible—a thrust at the God of the Universe, for making a man and not finishing him; it is simply calling the Great Jehovah a fool. Why, sir, though we are not white, we have accomplished much. We have pioneered civilization here; we have built up your country; we have worked in your fields, and garnered your harvests, for two hundred and fifty years! And what do we ask of you in return? Do we ask you for compensation for the sweat our fathers bore for you—for the tears you have caused, and the hearts you have broken, and the lives you have curtailed, and the blood you have spilled? Do we ask retaliation? We ask it not. We are willing to let the dead past bury its dead; but we ask you, now, for our RIGHTS. You have all the elements of superiority upon your side; you have our money and your own; you have our education and your own; and you have our land and your own, too. We, who number hundreds of thousands in Georgia, including our wives and families, with not a foot of land to call our own—strangers in the land of our birth; without money, without education, without aid, without a roof to cover us while we live, nor sufficient clay to cover us when we die! It is extraordinary that a race such as yours, professing gallantry, and chivalry, and education, and superiority, living in a land where ringing chimes call child and sire to the Church of God—a land where Bibles are read and Gospel truths are spoken, and where courts of justice are presumed to exist; it is extraordinary, I say, that, with all these advantages on your side, you can make war upon the poor defenceless black man. You know we have no money, no railroads, no telegraphs, no advantages of any sort, and yet all manner of injustice is placed upon us. You know that the black people of this country acknowledge you as their superiors, by virtue of your education and advantages.

There was a Resolution passed here at the early part of this session stating that all persons who were in their seats were eligible thereto. What are gentlemen going to do, with that Resolution staring them in the face? Your children and my children will read that Resolution, and they will be astonished that persons, claiming to be men, with souls and consciences, should, contrary to the express provision of that Resolution, turn the colored man out of his seat in this Hall. . . .

You may expel us, gentlemen, but I firmly believe that you will some day repent it. The black man cannot protect a country, if the country doesn't protect him; and if, tomorrow, a war should arise, I would not raise a musket to defend a country where my manhood is denied. The fashionable way in Georgia, when hard work is to be done, is, for the white man to sit at his ease, while the black man does the work; but, sir, I will say this much to the colored men of Georgia, as, if I should be killed in this campaign, I may have no opportunity of telling them at any other time: Never lift a finger nor raise a hand in defence of Georgia, unless Georgia acknowledges that you are men, and invests you with the rights pertaining to manhood. Pay your taxes, however, obey all orders from your employers, take good counsel from friends, work faithfully, earn an honest living, and show, by your conduct, that you can be good citizens. . . .

Where have you ever heard of four millions of freemen being governed by laws, and yet have no hand in their making? Search the records of the world, and you will find no example. "Governments derive their just powers from the consent of the governed." How dare you to make laws by which to try me and my wife and children, and deny me a voice in the making of these laws? I know you can establish a monarchy, an autocracy, an oligarchy, or any other kind of an "ocracy" that you please; and that you can declare whom you please to be sovereign; but tell me, sir, how you can clothe me with more power than another, where all are sovereigns alike? How can you say you have a Republican form of Government, when you make such distinction and enact such proscriptive laws? . . .

Everlasting Shame

We are a persecuted people. Luther was persecuted; Galileo was persecuted; good men in all nations have been persecuted; but the persecutors have been handed down to posterity with shame and ignominy. If you pass this Bill, you will never get Congress to pardon or enfranchise another rebel in your lives. You are going to fix an everlasting disfranchisement upon Mr. [Robert A.] Toombs and the other leading men of Georgia. You may think you are doing yourselves honor by expelling us from this House; but when we go, we will . . . light a torch of truth that will never be extinguished—the impression that will run through the country, as people picture in their mind's eye these poor black men, in all parts of this Southern country, pleading for their rights. When you expel us, you make us forever your political foes, and you will never find a black man to vote a Democratic ticket again; for so help me God I will go through all the length and breadth of the land, where a man of my race is to be found, and advise him to beware of the Democratic party. Justice is the great doctrine taught in the Bible. God's Eternal Justice is founded upon Truth and the man who steps from Justice steps from Truth, and cannot make his principles to prevail.

VIEWPOINT 6

"It is the dregs of the population habilitated in the robes of their intelligent predecessors, and asserting over them the rule of ignorance and corruption."

Blacks Are Not Capable of Holding Public Office

James S. Pike (1811-1882)

Journalist James S. Pike, a Maine Republican and a longtime abolitionist, had supported emancipation throughout the Civil War. However, Pike was not an advocate of equal rights; during the war he had suggested that freed slaves be either deported from the United States or placed on a reservation. In 1873, the *New York Tribune* sent Pike on a reporting tour of South Carolina. In a series of newspaper articles, which were later published in the book *The Prostrate State*, Pike examined the condition of South Carolina's state government. Like many southern state governments during Reconstruction, South Carolina's legislature included a substantial number of black politicians. Most white Southerners were legally restricted from voting and holding political office due to their participation in the Confederacy, which enabled black voters to elect black leaders to office with little contest.

Pike depicts the black members of the South Carolina state government as uneducated and incompetent novices whose lack of experience in legislative matters hopelessly impedes the governmental process. Blacks are not in any way prepared for the responsibility of governing, Pike argues. Although Pike concedes that the black politicians' intentions are honest, he insists that they are able to gain majorities in government not through exper-

Excerpted from James S. Pike, *The Prostrate State*, chapter 1, New York, 1873. Reprinted in *Words That Made American History Since the Civil War*, Richard N. Current and John A. Garraty, eds., Little, Brown, 1965.

tise but through superiority in numbers. However, Pike contends, blacks will not be able to hold onto their political positions long, allowing southern whites to regain control of the state legislature. The description of black governments in *The Prostrate State* greatly influenced opinions in the North and garnered northern support for the restoration of white government in the South.

Columbia, the capital of South Carolina, is charmingly situated in the heart of the upland country, near the geographical centre of the State. It has broad, open streets, regularly laid out, and fine, shady residences in and about the town. . . .

Yesterday, about 4 P.M., the assembled wisdom of the State, whose achievements are illustrated on that theatre, issued forth from the State-House. About three-quarters of the crowd belonged to the African race. They were of every hue, from the light octoroon to the deep black. They were such a looking body of men as might pour out of a market-house or a court-house at random in any Southern State. Every negro type and physiognomy was here to be seen, from the genteel serving-man to the rough-hewn customer from the rice or cotton field. Their dress was as varied as their countenances. There was the second-hand black frock-coat of infirm gentility, glossy and threadbare. There were the stove-pipe hat of many ironings and departed styles. There were also to be seen a total disregard of the proprieties of costume in the coarse and dirty garments of the field; the stub-jackets and slouch hats of soiling labor. In some instances, rough woolen comforters embraced the neck and hid the absence of linen. Heavy brogans, and short, torn trousers, it was impossible to hide. The dusky tide flowed out into the littered and barren grounds, and, issuing through the coarse wooden fence of the inclosure, melted away into the street beyond. These were the legislators of South Carolina. . . .

"I tremble," wrote [Thomas] Jefferson, when depicting the character of Southern slavery, "I tremble when I reflect that God is just." But did any of that old band of Southern Revolutionary patriots who wrestled in their souls with the curse of slavery ever contemplate such a descent into barbarism as this spectacle implied and typified? "My God, look at this!" was the unbidden ejaculation of a low-country planter, clad in homespun, as he leaned over the rail inside the House, gazing excitedly upon the body in session. "This is the first time I have been here. I thought I knew what we were doing when we consented to emancipation.

I knew the negro, and I predicted much that has happened, but I never thought it would come to this. Let me go."

Here, then, is the outcome, the ripe, perfected fruit of the boasted civilization of the South, after two hundred years of experience. A white community, that had gradually risen from small beginnings, till it grew into wealth, culture, and refinement, and became accomplished in all the arts of civilization; that successfully asserted its resistance to a foreign tyranny by deeds of conspicuous valor, which achieved liberty and independence through the fire and tempest of civil war, and illustrated itself in the councils of the nation by orators and statesmen worthy of any age or nation—such a community is then reduced to this. It lies prostrate in the dust, ruled over by this strange conglomerate, gathered from the ranks of its own servile population. It is the spectacle of a society suddenly turned bottomside up. The wealth, the intelligence, the culture, the wisdom of the State, have broken through the crust of that social volcano on which they were contentedly reposing, and have sunk out of sight, consumed by the subterranean fires they had with such temerity braved and defied.

The New Government

In the place of this old aristocratic society stands the rude form of the most ignorant democracy that mankind ever saw, invested with the functions of government. It is the dregs of the population habilitated in the robes of their intelligent predecessors, and asserting over them the rule of ignorance and corruption, through the inexorable machinery of a majority of numbers. It is barbarism overwhelming civilization by physical force. It is the slave rioting in the halls of his master, and putting that master under his feet. And, though it is done without malice and without vengeance, it is nevertheless none the less completely and absolutely done. Let us approach nearer and take a closer view. We will enter the House of Representatives. Here sit one hundred and twenty-four members. Of these, twenty-three are white men, representing the remains of the old civilization. These are good-looking, substantial citizens. They are men of weight and standing in the communities they represent. They are all from the hill country. The frosts of sixty and seventy winters whiten the heads of some among them. There they sit, grim and silent. They feel themselves to be but loose stones, thrown in to partially obstruct a current they are powerless to resist. They say little and do little as the days go by. They simply watch the rising tide, and mark the progressive steps of the inundation. They hold their places reluctantly. They feel themselves to be in some sort martyrs, bound stoically to suffer in behalf of that still great element in the State whose prostrate fortunes are becoming the sport of an unpitying

Fate. Grouped in a corner of the commodious and well-furnished chamber, they stolidly survey the noisy riot that goes on in the great black Left and Centre, where the business and debates of the House are conducted, and where sit the strange and extraordinary guides of the fortunes of a once proud and haughty State. In this crucial trial of his pride, his manhood, his prejudices, his spirit, it must be said of the Southern Bourbon of the Legislature that he comports himself with a dignity, a reserve, and a decorum, that command admiration. He feels that the iron hand of Destiny is upon him. He is gloomy, disconsolate, hopeless. The gray heads of this generation openly profess that they look for no relief. They see no way of escape. The recovery of influence, of position, of control in the State, is felt by them to be impossible. They accept their position with a stoicism that promises no reward here or hereafter. They are the types of a conquered race. They staked all and lost all. Their lives remain, their property and their children do not. War, emancipation, and grinding taxation, have consumed them. Their struggle now is against complete confiscation. They endure, and wait for the night.

This dense negro crowd they confront do the debating, the squabbling, the law-making, and create all the clamor and disorder of the body. These twenty-three white men are but the observers, the enforced auditors of the dull and clumsy imitation of a deliberative body, whose appearance in their present capacity is at once a wonder and a shame to modern civilization.

Deducting the twenty-three members referred to, who comprise the entire strength of the opposition, we find one hundred and one remaining. Of this one hundred and one, ninety-four are colored, and seven are their white allies. Thus the blacks outnumber the whole body of whites in the House more than three to one. On the mere basis of numbers in the State the injustices of this disproportion is manifest, since the black population is relatively four to three of the whites. A just rectification of the disproportion, on the basis of population merely, would give fifty-four whites to seventy black members. And the line of race very nearly marks the line of hostile politics. As things stand, the body is almost literally a Black Parliament, and it is the only one on the face of the earth which is the representative of a white constituency and the professed exponent of an advanced type of modern civilization. But the reader will find almost any portraiture inadequate to give a vivid idea of the body, and enable him to comprehend the complete metamorphosis of the South Carolina Legislature, without observing its details. The Speaker is black, the Clerk is black, the door-keepers are black, the little pages are black, the chairman of the Ways and Means is black, and the chaplain is coal-black. At some of the desks sit colored men whose types it would be hard to find outside of Congo; whose costume, visages, attitudes, and expression, only befit the forecastle of a buccaneer. It must be remembered, also, that these men, with not more than half a dozen exceptions, have been themselves slaves, and that their ancestors were slaves for generations. Recollecting the report of the famous schooner Wanderer, fitted out by a Southern slave-holder twelve or fifteen years ago, in ostentatious defiance of the laws against the slave-trade, and whose owner and master boasted of having brought a cargo of slaves from Africa and safely landed them in South Carolina and Georgia, one thinks it must be true, and that some of these representatives are the very men then stolen from their African homes. If this be so, we will not now quarrel over their presence. It would be one of those extraordinary coincidences that would of itself almost seem to justify the belief of the direct interference of the hand of Providence in the affairs of men. . . .

Disorder in the House

One of the things that first strike a casual observer in this negro assembly is the fluency of debate, if the endless chatter that goes on there can be dignified with this term. The leading topics of discussion are all well understood by the members, as they are of a practical character, and appeal directly to the personal interests of every legislator, as well as to those of his constituents. When an appropriation bill is up to raise money to catch and punish the Ku-klux, they know exactly what it means. They feel it in their bones. So, too, with educational measures. The free school comes right home to them; then the business of arming and drilling the black militia. They are eager on this point. Sambo can talk on these topics and those of a kindred character, and their endless ramifications, day in and day out. There is no end to his gush and babble. The intellectual level is that of a bevy of fresh converts at a negro camp-meeting. Of course this kind of talk can be extended indefinitely. It is the doggerel of debate, and not beyond the reach of the lowest parts. Then the negro is imitative in the extreme. He can copy like a parrot or a monkey, and he is always ready for a trial of his skill. He believes he can do any thing, and never loses a chance to try, and is just as ready to be laughed at for his failure as applauded for his success. He is more vivacious than the white, and, being more volatile and good-natured, he is correspondingly more irrepressible. His misuse of language in his imitations is at times ludicrous beyond measure. He notoriously loves a joke or an anecdote, and will burst into a broad guffaw on the smallest provocation. He breaks out into an incoherent harangue on the floor just as easily, and being without practice, discipline, or experience, and wholly oblivious of Lindley Murray, or any other restraint on composition, he will go on repeating himself, dancing as it were to the music of his own voice, forever. He will speak half a dozen times on one question, and every time say the same things without knowing it. He answers completely to the description of a stupid speaker in Parliament, given by Lord Derby on one occasion. It was said of him that he did not know what he was going to say when he got up; he did not know what he was saying while he was speaking, and he did not know what he had said when he sat down.

This cartoon by Thomas Nast, entitled "Colored Rule in a Reconstructed (?) State," appeared in Harper's Weekly *on March 14, 1875. The caption reads, "The members call each other thieves, liars, rascals, and cowards."*

North Wind Picture Archives

But the old stagers admit that the colored brethren have a wonderful aptness at legislative proceedings. They are "quick as lightning" at detecting points of order, and they certainly make incessant and extraordinary use of their knowledge. No one is allowed to talk five minutes without interruption, and one interruption is the signal for another and another, until the original speaker is smothered under an avalanche of them. Forty questions of privilege will be raised in a day. At times, nothing goes on but alternating questions of order and of privilege. The inefficient colored friend who sits in the Speaker's chair cannot suppress this extraordinary element of the debate. Some of the blackest members exhibit a pertinacity of intrusion in raising these points of order and questions of privilege that few white men can equal. Their struggles to get the floor, their bellowings and physical contortions, baffle description. The Speaker's hammer plays a perpetual tattoo all to no purpose. The talking and the interruptions from all quarters go on with the utmost license. Every one esteems himself as good as his neighbor, and puts in his oar, apparently as often for love of riot and confusion as for any thing else. It is easy to imagine what are his ideas of propriety and dignity among a crowd of his own color, and these are illustrated without reserve. The Speaker orders a member whom he has discovered to be particularly unruly to take his seat. The member obeys, and with the same motion that he sits down, throws his feet on to his desk, hiding himself from the Speaker by the soles of his boots. In an instant he appears again on the floor. After a few experiences of this sort, the Speaker threatens, in a laugh, to call "the gemman" to order. This is considered a capital joke, and a guffaw follows. The laugh goes round, and then the peanuts are cracked and munched faster than ever; one hand being employed in fortifying the inner man with this nutriment of universal use, while the other enforces the views of the orator. This laughing propensity of the sable crowd is a great cause of disorder. They laugh as hens cackle—one begins and all follow.

Good Intentions

But underneath all this shocking burlesque upon legislative proceedings, we must not forget that there is something very real to this uncouth and untutored multitude. It is not all sham, nor all burlesque. They have a genuine interest and a genuine earnestness in the business of the assembly which we are bound to recognize and respect, unless we would be accounted shallow critics. They have an earnest purpose, born of a conviction that their position and condition are not fully assured, which lends a sort of dignity to their proceedings. The barbarous, animated jargon in which they so often indulge is on occasion seen to be so transparently sincere and weighty in their own minds that sympathy supplants disgust. The whole thing is a wonderful novelty to them as well as to observers. Seven years ago these men were raising corn and cotton under the whip of the overseer. To-day they are raising points of order and questions of privilege. They find they can raise one as well as the other. They prefer the latter. It is easier, and better paid. Then, it is the evidence of an accomplished result. It means escape and defense from old oppressors. It means liberty. It means the destruction of prison-walls only too real to them. It is the sunshine of their lives. It is their day of jubilee. It is their long-promised vision of the Lord God Almighty.

Shall we, then, be too critical over the spectacle? Perhaps we might more wisely wonder that they can do so well in so short a time. The barbarians overran Rome. The dark ages followed. But then the day finally broke, and civilization followed. The days were long and weary; but they came to an end at last. Now we have the printing-press, the railroad, the telegraph; and these denote an utter revolution in the affairs of mankind. Years may now accomplish what it formerly took ages to achieve. Under the new lights and influences shall not the black man speedily emerge? Who knows? We may fear, but we may hope. Nothing in our day is impossible. Take the contested supposition that South Carolina is to be Africanized. We have a Federal Union of great and growing States. It is incontestably white at the centre. We know it to possess vital powers. It is well abreast of all modern progress in ideas and improvements. Its influence is all-pervading. How can a State of the Union escape it? South Carolina alone, if left to herself, might fall into midnight darkness. Can she do it while she remains an integral part of the nation?

But will South Carolina be Africanized? That depends. Let us hear the judgment of an intelligent foreigner who has long lived in the South, and who was here when the war began. He does not believe it. White people from abroad are drifting in, bad as things are. Under freedom the blacks do not multiply as in slavery. The pickaninnies die off from want of care. Some blacks are coming in from North Carolina and Virginia, but others are going off farther South. The white young men who were growing into manhood did not seem inclined to leave their homes and migrate to foreign parts. There was an exodus after the war, but it has stopped, and many have come back. The old slave-holders still hold their lands. The negroes were poor and unable to buy, even if the land-owners would sell. This was a powerful impediment to the development of the negro into a controlling force in the State. His whole power was in his numbers. The present disproportion of four blacks to three whites in the State he believed was already decreasing. The whites seemed likely to more than hold their own, while the blacks would fall off. Cumulative voting would encourage the growth and add to the political power of the whites in the Legislature, where they were at present over-slaughed.

VIEWPOINT 7

"The right of a citizen to associate exclusively with those . . . whom he recognizes as his peers, is an individual liberty, and no Government can prostrate it to his inferiors."

Segregation Should Be Maintained

Henry Davis McHenry (1826-1890)

First submitted by Senator Charles Sumner in 1870, the second Civil Rights Bill was intended as a supplement to the Civil Rights Act of 1866. The provisions of the proposed bill strictly banned the segregation of blacks in public facilities and transportation. Henry Davis McHenry, Democratic representative from Kentucky, delivered a speech in opposition to the bill on April 13, 1872.

To allow blacks onto streetcars, in restaurants, and in public schools, McHenry argues, would force social associations with blacks onto unwilling whites. Choosing whom to associate with is an individual right over which the government should have no control, McHenry maintains. Private businesses also have the right to discriminate, he asserts, when it is in their best interests to do so. Listing the penalties for discrimination that would be authorized by the Civil Rights Bill, McHenry insists that the bill actually gives special treatment to blacks while allowing discrimination against whites to go unpunished. Blacks have already obtained full political rights, McHenry contends; any rights of social equality must be granted by public opinion and sentiment, not mandated by law.

Henry Davis McHenry, *Congressional Globe*, 42nd Cong., 2nd sess., April 13, 1872, pp. 633-35.

[W]hatsoever of personal privilege or individual right appertains to man, the local laws and courts as enforced in the States are far better adapted to enforce that privilege and maintain that right than any remedy we can devise and execute through the instrumentality of the Federal Government.

Everything that is really a right in this bill is already secured by State laws to the negro as well as the white man. He has the right to travel upon land and water; no one is forbidden to entertain him or to amuse him, and his right of education and burial are not denied him; but it is a far different thing when the law prescribes who shall do these things for him and the manner in which they are to be done. That is a matter of contract, in which the law has no right to interfere. Who shall restrict my right to keep a house of entertainment for such persons only as I see proper to entertain? Shall the law forbid the black man from opening a house of amusement for the black people alone; or the white man from establishing schools for the education of white children; or laying off cemeteries for the exclusive burial of their own race? This bill undertakes to compel every innkeeper to extend to the negro the full and equal enjoyment of every accommodation, advantage, facility, or privilege furnished by him to other guests. It gives the negro the right to demand the best bed, to occupy the best room, and to eat at the same table with the most favored guest, and to receive the same attention in every respect.

If a man sees proper to associate with negroes, to eat at the same table, ride on the same seat with them in cars, or sees proper to send his children to the same schools with them, and place himself upon the same level with them in any regard, I would not abridge his right to do so; but that is a very different thing from compulsory social equality and association with those whose company is distasteful to him. Under this law, if your wife should be traveling alone, any negro man who happened to be traveling in the same car has a right to seat himself by her side, and if the conductor or any one else should interfere for her protection they render themselves amendable to heavy penalties—penalties so heavy that no conductor would interfere to protect the most refined lady from such intrusion if there were a vacant seat by her side and the filthiest negro should see proper to occupy it. No man can afford to hold the place of a conductor and incur the heavy penalties of this bill by protecting a lady under the circumstances; and the result will be that she must submit to this degradation forced on her by the Congress of the United States.

If a man is in the habit of receiving travelers in his house, and furnishing them food and lodging for a compensation, he thereby becomes an innkeeper; a boarding-house keeper, who receives transient guests, is an innkeeper. It is not required that a sign shall be over the door or a license obtained to make an inn, and consequently not only the hotels in the cities, but the village inns and country taverns are included in this bill; and the negro can stop at the inn or tavern where the wife and daughters of the landlord wait on the table and demand entertainment, which must be given him, or severe penalties will fall upon the household, and there is no escape from them unless the man submits to the equality or quits his occupation. It will not do to take down his sign and surrender up his license. If he continues to receive and charge transient customers, he is an innkeeper under the law, and is embraced in this bill.

Legislating Private Business

Sir, hotels and inns are private property. The owners have no exclusive privilege or right to keep entertainment for the public. Any man can do it; and the State does nothing for him that it does not do for any other private citizen. He needs no special protection, nor is any special privilege given him. The entertainment he gives is a matter of contract between him and his guest, and the State has no interest in it, and no right to interfere between them, except to enforce the contract as it does in all other affairs. Then, upon what principle do we pretend to interfere and compel the innkeeper to receive guests distasteful to him? We levy specific taxes upon him, it is true; but I do not see that he has any exclusive right, privilege, or immunity granted him. He levies no toll upon the public, nor is he exempt from the duties and responsibilities which belong to other citizens. He simply gives a consideration for what he receives, as do men of all avocations of life, and he should be exempt from legislation which interferes with his individual rights. Hotels in this country have always discriminated as to the class of persons who they entertain. And they will continue to do it, even when this bill is passed.

Sir, let a poor, meanly-dressed white man, however worthy, if his appearance is such as to indicate that he moves in a sphere below that of the other guests, call at the Arlington or Metropolitan, and he would be refused entertainment, and would have no redress; but when the well-dressed negro with money in his pocket shall call and demand entertainment, notwithstanding his presence would be much more objectionable to those guests, the landlord cannot refuse him, because a special law has been passed for his benefit, and he is the representative of a race who are the wards and pets of the Federal Government.

The negro has the right to set up and keep an inn wherever and whenever he chooses, as they have the right to set themselves up in every other business; and they do have their boarding-houses, and in every city and town they will find those of their own race and color who are ready and willing to accommodate them with lodging and board; and the owners and proprietors of such houses do not want white guests, and would consider it a hardship if they were compelled to entertain them; and I would vote against a law compelling them to do so as a violation of their personal liberty. No doubt that in traveling they frequently suffer some inconvenience; but it is not for the law to furnish them conveniences at the expense of other people's rights; and if we are to consider the question of inconvenience, what shall be said of that of the white man whom we propose to compel to do subservience to the negro, and who is required to receive him in his parlor, entertain him at his table, and lodge him in his bed, or give up an occupation that he has followed all his life? Sir, it is a tyranny such as would not be imposed on its subjects by the most monarchical Government on the face of the earth.

The bill also undertakes to regulate the "benevolent institutions incorporated by national and State authority." Free Masons, Odd Fellows, Good Templars, and many other secret societies are benevolent institutions, and are in most instances incorporated by "national or State authority." Their rules, I believe, generally

Advising Patience

Albion Tourgée, a northern carpetbagger living in North Carolina, was a dedicated advocate of black rights. However, in his letter of May 11, 1874, Tourgée expressed concern that the second Civil Rights Bill was premature and ill-advised.

The worst thing will be the Civil Rights Bill. . . . I have no use for those who prescribe for diseases without knowing their nature—[Senator Charles] Sumner knew no more of the actual condition of the colored man here than he realized his condition on the Gold Coast [of Africa]. . . . The most important thing in the world is to let the South forget the negro for a bit:—let him acquire property, stability and self-respect; let as many as possible be educated; in short let the race itself get used to freedom self-dependence and proper self assertion; and then let this bill come little by little if necessary.—Of course, if it becomes law, it will be constantly avoided—No man can frame a statue which some other cannot avoid. . . . It is just pure folly and results from what I have so long claimed, that the people of the North and our Legislators, will not study the people of the South—reasonably. They will not remember that a prejudice 250 years old (at least) should only be legislated against when *positively harmful*, and should always be let alone when it only conflicts with good doctrine—fine theory.

181

require a unanimous vote of all the members to admit new men to their fellowship. Suppose a negro puts in his petition to become a member of one of these societies where social equality and fraternity is the basis of their organization, would not some one vote against him? In my State not a white ball would be found in the box. Then all the members are to be indicted, and if it shall be determined that the applicant was refused membership on account of his color or race, all are to suffer the severe penalties of this bill. The individual liberty of these men is violated, and their rights are taken from them by a despotism which is as unjust as it is iniquitous.

The asylums and alms-houses are "benevolent institutions, incorporated by national or State authority," and the poor unfortunate white men and women whom age and imbecility have rendered beneficiaries of such institutions, can only receive these charities by submitting to the social equality of the negro. I would not prevent such charities from being extended to the negroes. I want provision made for them when they become old and helpless, but I would keep up a distinction between the races even in their misery and poverty.

Prejudice Is a Right

This is my feeling, and it is the feeling of those whom I represent. You may call it prejudice if you please, but it is a prejudice that will cling to the present generation, and will not be yielded up by the men now living; and all your laws, all your penalties, will not eradicate it. A prejudice is a right which belongs to a man as much as his love and partiality, and you cannot control it by law, and all your efforts in that direction only tend to increase it. The law can only prevent prejudice from interfering with the legal rights of others; but social prejudice is a social liberty that the law has no right to disturb. Whether it is a prejudice against the negro or a partiality for the whites, it is based upon a manifest and acknowledged superiority of class and race. I certainly have no sort of hostility to the negroes. I want them protected in all their just rights. But I do claim for my race a superiority over them in intelligence, morality, and in all the virtues of true manhood, and I can never consent to have it dragged down to their level; and it is in this view that I speak and protest against the great wrong and outrage this bill attempts against the white people.

The bill does not stop at the alms-house or the theater, but it goes to the school-house and the grave-yard, and forces this equality upon the little children at school and upon their parents under the sod. When a man's spirit shall have left this world his body becomes the dust of the earth, and there is no superiority. With him it is equality with all. But kind hearts and loving hands will mark his grave, not for any good to him, but to keep alive in the memories of those living his virtues, and his kindred and friends love to linger around his grave and feel that the spot is sacred, and reserve to themselves places by his side, when one day they must join him. But this reservation cannot be, for this law declares that the privilege of the negro to be buried there shall not be denied.

The rich man can educate his children in private schools, and this law will be no great hardship upon him; but the poor man's child must look to the common schools or go without education, and this bill forces that child to sit on the same seat with the negro, and to be raised up in fellowship with him. I believe, sir, that in my State the people will abandon the common-school system rather than submit to this unjust and unconstitutional regulation which is forced upon them by a fanaticism which heeds neither the liberty of the people nor the rights of the States.

This bill has not been debated. Gentlemen on the other side [Republicans] do not wish to discuss it. They well know that it cannot be defended under the Constitution, and hence for party purposes they silently cast their votes for it. All power belongs to the States, except such as has been delegated to the Federal Government, and there must be an authority found in the Constitution for all that we do here, and no advocate of this bill can point to a single clause in that instrument which can authorize or empower us to interfere with the schools in the States, which are supported not by any aid, nor maintained by any authority or permission, direct or indirect, derived from the Federal Government. We cannot force a State to establish a system of general education, and when she does establish it, it is an unwarranted interference if we assume to control or regulate it in any way.

It would not be right for a State to tax negroes to educate the whites unless they had the privilege of the schools, and in every State where they are so taxed they have that privilege. In my State we do not tax them for school purposes, nor have we undertaken to educate them, and we do not propose to be forced to do so by despotic laws. For many years we had no common-school system at all, and it is only of recent date that our system has become efficient, and after we have paid the enormous taxes imposed on us for the Federal Government, and the taxes to support our State government and educate the white children, it is unreasonable to ask us to tax ourselves further to educate the negroes who pay no tax, comparatively speaking.

By this bill when a negro is excepted and excluded "from the full and equal enjoyment of any accommodation, advantage, facility, or privilege furnished by innkeepers, by common carriers, by owners of theaters," he has a remedy not given to the white man when the same "accommodation, advantage, facility, and privilege" are denied him. No remedy is by the bill given the white man for the denial of these rights; but when a negro is excepted or excluded from them he has a remedy in the Federal courts, and the amount of his damages is fixed by the law at $500, with full costs, and this remedy is not only against the innkeeper and owner of the steamboat, trustee, or commissioner, but is against any person aiding and inciting him to deny their rights; and not only this civil remedy is given to the negro, but the defendant is deemed to have committed a misdemeanor, and upon conviction thereof is to be fined from $500 to $1,000, or imprisonment not less than thirty days nor more than one year.

Sir, any member of this House, if he happens to be one of the white members, can be kicked out of any hotel in this city or set ashore from any steamboat on the Potomac, or excluded from the theater, and no such remedy is given to him either by existing law or by this bill; and not only these remedies are given, but the same jurisdiction and powers are conferred, and the same duties enjoined, upon the courts and officers of the United States in the execution of this bill as are conferred in sections three, four, five, seven, and ten of the civil rights act [of 1866], and said sections are here again reënacted and made part of this bill.

By the provisions of those sections the district attorney, marshal, and commissioner appointed by Federal courts, the officers and agents of the Freedmen's Bureau, and every other officer who may be specially empowered by the President of the United States, are specially authorized and required at the expense of the United States to institute proceedings against all and every person who violates the provisions of this act, and if they shall fail to institute and prosecute such proceedings required by the bill, shall for every offense forfeit and pay the sum of $500 to the party aggrieved, and also be deemed guilty of a misdemeanor, and fined from $1,000 to $5,000.

The district courts are to have jurisdiction exclusive of the State courts for all offenses under this act. Penalties of $1,000 are imposed on marshals and deputy marshals for failure to execute the civil rights law. Extra commissioners are to be appointed, so as to afford a speedy and convenient means for the arrest and examination of persons charged with a violation of this act, and said commissioners are authorized and empowered to appoint one or more suitable persons in each county to execute any warrant or process, and they may call out the *posse comitatus* of the county or summon the Army and Navy of the United States or the militia to assist them in the performance of their duty.

It has never occurred that such extraordinary remedies have been given by Congress for the protection of any white man in his rights. To be a negro is to belong to the favored class.

All these remedies are given against trustees, commissioners, superintendents, teachers, and other officers of common schools and other public institutions of learning authorized by law, and against trustees and officers of cemetery associations and benevolent institutions. No such penalty is imposed against a trustee or commissioner for excluding a white child from the public schools, and the poor, decrepit old white man or woman would look in vain for such facilities to admit them to the alms-house. The object of this bill is to abolish distinctions on account of "race, color, or previous condition of servitude," but it in fact makes a discrimination against the white man on account of his color.

But, sir, the crowning infamy of this bill is to be found in the fourth section, which disregards the statutory regulations of the States and forces the negro in the jury-box, where, with his ignorance and prejudice, he is made the arbiter of the life, liberty, and property of the white man. Can any State right be more manifest than that of regulating her own courts and the forms of trial as between her own citizens? The Federal Government has no concern in it whatever; she cannot even prescribe to a State whether it will be governed by the common or civil law. She can only guaranty to them a republican form of government and provide that the Constitution of the United States, and laws made in pursuance thereof, shall be paramount and held sacred by the State courts, and this she only has the right to control through her judiciary department.

In my State the law requires the following qualifications for jurymen:

> No person shall be a competent juryman for the trial of criminal, penal, or civil cases in the circuit court unless he be a free white citizen, at least twenty-one years of age, a house-keeper, likewise sober, temperate, discreet, and of good demeanor.

And the jury commissioners are sworn—

> That they will not knowingly select any man as a juryman whom they believe to be unfit and not qualified.

Now, did my State have the right to make this qualification for her jurymen? If she had the right to say that they should be twenty-one years of age, and housekeepers, and that they should be sober and discreet, and of good demeanor, she had the right to say that they should be white. If it is a citizen's right to be a juryman, surely a man does not lose his right by not being a housekeeper or by being indiscreet, intemperate, and not of good demeanor. Then, if my State had the right to make these qualifications for her jurymen and compel her officers to swear to observe those qualifications in the selection of them, how can Congress repeal or modify or amend that law or in any way change the qualification as prescribed by the State? The Federal Government can prescribe the qualification of jurymen in her own courts, and whatever may be said of the policy of admitting negroes as jurors in those courts, the right and power of Congress to do it is not denied; but when we attempt to exercise that power in State courts we interfere where we have no authority.

The fifth section of this bill is short, but more comprehensive than all else that is in it, and is as follows:

That every discrimination against any citizen on account of color, by the use of the word "white" in any law, statute, ordinance, or regulation, is hereby repealed and annulled.

In this is asserted the power of Congress to repeal State laws, municipal ordinances, and corporate regulations, and takes from States the power to prescribe the qualifications of their own officers, and makes the negro eligible to all State offices, and I presume is intended, and will have the effect, to repeal the statutes in force in all the States preventing the intermarriage of whites and blacks. Except as to the penalties provided in the previous sections of the bill, this will cover all that is embraced in them. Its scope and intent is to establish perfect equality, legal and social. No distinction of race is to be tolerated. The African is not elevated, but the Anglo-Saxon is brought down to the same level with him. . . .

The amendments to the Constitution have gone to the full extent of giving to the negro political rights. His freedom and citizenship, rights of property and protection, and right of franchise are recognized in all the States; and now it is intended to give him social rights enforced by law, and to secure this the liberty of the white man is made subservient to it. Sir, equality is one thing and liberty is another. The right of a citizen to associate exclusively with those who are congenial to him, and whom he recognizes as his peers, is an individual liberty, and no Government can prostrate it to his inferiors under the specious pretext of "equality before the law."

VIEWPOINT 8

"The solution . . . is to enact such laws and prescribe such penalties for their violation as will prevent any person from discriminating against another in public places on account of color."

Segregation Should Be Abolished

James T. Rapier (1837-1883)

Born in Alabama, James T. Rapier was the son of a black mother and a white father. His father arranged for private tutors in Alabama and then sent Rapier to study law at universities in Canada and Scotland. After the Civil War, Rapier returned to Alabama and participated in state government, including the 1867 State Constitutional Convention. In 1872, Rapier was elected to the U.S. House of Representatives, where he repeatedly campaigned for civil rights.

On June 9, 1874, Rapier delivered the following speech in support of the second Civil Rights Bill, which prohibited racial discrimination in public schools, theaters, hotels, jury selection, churches, cemeteries, and public transportation. Rapier cites his own experiences with racial discrimination and those of other prominent black politicians, such as Francis L. Cardozo. Pointing out the absurdity of denying blacks the same public services that their taxes pay for, Rapier argues that equal access to those services should be protected by law. Segregation and racial discrimination create a caste system, Rapier contends, similar to those in Europe and India—a system that is unacceptable in a republic based on tenets of equality.

Minus the public school provisions, the Civil Rights Bill became law in 1875.

James T. Rapier, *Congressional Record*, 43rd Cong., 1st sess., June 9, 1874, pp. 4782-86.

Mr. Speaker, I had hoped there would be no protracted discussion on the civil-rights bill. It has been debated all over the country for the last seven years; twice it has done duty in our national political campaigns; and in every minor election during that time it has been pressed into service for the purpose of intimidating the weak white men who are inclined to support the republican ticket. I was certain until now that most persons were acquainted with its provisions, that they understood its meaning; therefore it was no longer to them the monster it had been depicted, that was to break down all social barriers, and compel one man to recognize another socially, whether agreeable to him or not.

I must confess it is somewhat embarrassing for a colored man to urge the passage of this bill, because if he exhibit an earnestness in the matter and express a desire for its immediate passage, straight-way he is charged with a desire for social equality, as explained by the demagogue and understood by the ignorant white man. But then it is just as embarrassing for him not to do so, for, if he remain silent while the struggle is being carried on around, and for him, he is liable to be charged with a want of interest in a matter that concerns him more than any one else, which is enough to make his friends desert his cause. So in steering away from Scylla I may run upon Charybdis. But the anomalous, and I may add the supremely ridiculous, position of the negro at this time, in this country, compel me to say something. Here his condition is without a comparison, parallel alone to itself. Just think that the law recognizes my right upon this floor as a law-maker, but that there is no law to secure to me any accommodations whatever while traveling here to discharge my duties as a Representative of a large and wealthy constituency. Here I am the peer of the proudest, but on a steamboat or car I am not equal to the most degraded. Is not this most anomalous and ridiculous? . . .

Half Slave, Half Free

I wish to say in justice to myself that no one regrets more than I do the necessity that compels one to the manner born to come in these Halls with hat in hand (so to speak) to ask at the hands of his political peers the same public rights they enjoy. And I shall feel ashamed for my country if there be any foreigners present, who have been lured to our shores by the popular but untruthful declaration that this land is the asylum of the oppressed, to hear a member of the highest legislative body in the world declare from his place, upon his responsibility as a Representative, that notwithstanding his political position he has no civil rights that another class is bound to respect. Here a foreigner can learn what

188

he cannot learn in any other country, that it is possible for a man to be half free and half slave, or, in other words, he will see that it is possible for a man to enjoy political rights while he is denied civil ones; here he will see a man legislating for a free people, while his own chains of civil slavery hang about him, and are far more galling than any the foreigner left behind him; here he will see what is not to be seen elsewhere, that position is no mantle of protection in our "land of the free and home of the brave"; for I am subjected to far more outrages and indignities in coming to and going from this capital in discharge of my public duties than any criminal in the country providing he be white. Instead of my position shielding me from insult, it too often invites it.

Let me cite a case. Not many months ago Mr. [Francis L.] Cardozo, treasurer of the State of South Carolina, was on his way home from the West. His route lay through Atlanta. There he made request for a sleeping-berth. Not only was he refused this, but was denied a seat in a first-class carriage, and the parties went so far as to threaten to take his life because he insisted upon his rights as a traveler. He was compelled, a most elegant and accomplished gentleman, to take a seat in a dirty smoking-car, along with the traveling rabble, or else be left, to the detriment of his public duties.

I affirm, without the fear of contradiction, that any white ex-convict (I care not what may have been his crime, nor whether the hair on the shaven side of his head has had time to grow out or not) may start with me to-day to Montgomery [Alabama], that all the way down he will be treated as a gentleman, while I will be treated as the convict. He will be allowed a berth in a sleeping-car with all its comforts, while I will be forced into a dirty, rough box with the drunkards, apple-sellers, railroad hands, and next to any dead that may be in transit, regardless of how far decomposition may have progressed. Sentinels are placed at the doors of the better coaches, with positive instructions to keep persons of color out; and I must do them the justice to say that they guard these sacred portals with a vigilance that would have done credit to the flaming swords at the gates of Eden. Tender, pure, intelligent young ladies are forced to travel in this way if they are guilty of the crime of color, the only unpardonable sin known in our Christian and Bible lands, where sinning against the Holy Ghost (whatever that may be) sinks into insignificance when compared with the sin of color. If from any cause we are compelled to lay over, the best bed in the hotel is his if he can pay for it, while I am invariably turned away, hungry and cold, to stand around the railway station until the departure of the next train, it matters not how long, thereby endangering my health, while my life and property are at the mercy of any highwayman who may wish to murder and rob me.

And I state without the fear of being gainsaid . . . that there is not an inn between Washington [D.C.] and Montgomery, a distance of more than a thousand miles, that will accommodate me to a bed or meal. Now, then, is there a man upon this floor who is so heartless, whose breast is so void of the better feelings, as to say that this brutal custom needs no regulation? I hold that it does and that Congress is the body to regulate it. Authority for its action is found not only in the fourteenth amendment to the Constitution, but by virtue of that amendment (which makes all persons born here citizens), authority is found in article 4, section 2 of the Federal Constitution, which declares in positive language "that the citizens of each State shall have the same rights as the citizens of the several States." Let me read Mr. [Frederick Charles] Brightly's comment upon this clause; he is considered good authority, I believe. In describing the several rights he says they may be all comprehended under the following general heads: "Protection by the Government; the enjoyment of life and liberty, with the right to acquire and possess property of every kind, and to pursue and obtain happiness and safety; the right of a citizen of one State to pass through or to reside in any other State for purposes of trade, agriculture, professional pursuits, or otherwise."

Rights Under the Constitution

It is very clear that the right of locomotion without hindrance and everything pertaining thereto is embraced in this clause; and every lawyer knows if any white man in ante bellum times had been refused first-class passage in a steamboat or car, who was free from any contagious disease, and was compelled to go on deck of a boat or into a baggage-car, and any accident had happened to him while he occupied that place, a lawsuit would have followed and damages would have been given by any jury to the plaintiff; and whether any accident had happened or not in the case I have referred to, a suit would have been brought for a denial of rights, and no one doubts what would have been the verdict. White men had rights then that common carriers were compelled to respect, and I demand the same for the colored men now.

Mr. Speaker, whether this deduction from the clause of the Constitution just read was applicable to the negro prior to the adoption of the several late amendments to our organic law is not now a question, but that it does apply to him in his new relations no intelligent man will dispute. Therefore I come to the national, instead of going to the local Legislatures for relief, as has been suggested, because the grievance is national and not local; because Congress is the law-making power of the General Government, whose duty it is to see that there be no unjust and odious discriminations made between its citizens. I look to the Government in the place of the several States, because it claims my first allegiance, exacts at my hands strict obedience to its laws, and because it promises in the implied contract between every citizen and the Government to protect my life and property. I have fulfilled my part of the contract to the extent I have been called upon, and I demand that the Government, through Congress do likewise. Every day my life and property are exposed, are left to the mercy of others, and will be so as long as every hotel-keeper, railroad conductor, and steamboat captain can refuse me with impunity the accommodations common to other travelers. I hold further, if the Government cannot secure to a citizen his guaran-

---

We Do Not Intend to Wait

In May 1867, the Alabama Colored Convention met in Mobile to discuss equal rights and segregation. The "Address of the Colored Convention to the People of Alabama," drafted by the members of the convention, was published in the Montgomery Daily State Sentinel *on May 21, 1867.*

There are some good people who are always preaching patience and procrastination. They would have us wait a few months, years, or generations, until the whites voluntarily give us our rights, but we do not intend to wait one day longer than we are absolutely compelled to. Look at our demands, and then at theirs. We ask of them simply that they surrender unreasonable and unreasoning prejudice; that they cease imitating dog in the manger; that they consent to allow others as well as themselves to prosper and be happy. But they would have us pay for what we do not get; tramp through the broiling sun or pelting rain, or stand upon a platform, while empty seats mockingly invite us to rest our wearied limbs; our sick must suffer or submit to indignity; we must put up with inconvenience of every kind; and the virtuous aspirations of our children must be continually checked by the knowledge that no matter how upright their conduct, they will be looked on as less worthy of respect than the lowest wretch on earth who wears a white skin. We ask you—only while in public, however—to surrender your prejudices,—nothing but prejudices; and you ask us to sacrifice our personal comfort, health, pecuniary interests, self-respect, and the future prospects of our children. The men who make such requests must suppose us devoid of spirit and of brains, but they will find themselves mistaken. Solemnly and distinctly, we again say to you, men of Alabama, that we will not submit voluntarily to such infamous discrimination, and if you will insist upon tramping on the rights and outraging the feelings of those who are so soon to pass judgment upon you, then upon your own heads will rest the responsibility for the effect of your course.

teed rights it ought not to call upon him to perform the same duties that are performed by another class of citizens who are in the free and full enjoyment of every civil and political right.

Sir, I submit that I am degraded as long as I am denied the public privileges common to other men, and that the members of this House are correspondingly degraded by recognizing my political equality while I occupy such a humiliating position. What a singular attitude for law-makers of this great nation to assume: rather come down to me than allow me to go up to them. Sir, did you ever reflect that this is the only Christian country where poor, finite man is held responsible for the crimes of the infinite God whom you profess to worship? But it is; I am held to answer for the crime of color, when I was not consulted in the matter. Had I been consulted, and my future fully described, I think I should have objected to being born in this gospel land. The excuse offered for all this inhuman treatment is that they consider the negro inferior to the white man, intellectually and morally. This reason might have been offered and probably accepted as truth some years ago, but no one now believes him incapable of a high order of culture, except someone who is himself below the average of mankind in natural endowments. This is not the reason, as I shall show before I have done.

Sir, there is a cowardly propensity in the human heart that delights in oppressing somebody else, and in the gratification of this base desire we always select a victim that can be outraged with safety. As a general thing the Jew has been the subject in most parts of the world; but here the negro is the most available for this purpose; for this reason in part he was seized upon, and not because he is naturally inferior to anyone else. Instead of his enemies believing him to be incapable of a high order of mental culture, they have shown that they believe the reverse to be true, by taking the most elaborate pains to prevent his development. And the smaller the caliber of the white man the more frantically has he fought to prevent the intellectual and moral progress of the negro, for the simple but good reason that he has most to fear from such a result. He does not wish to see the negro approach the high moral standard of a man and gentleman. . . .

A Question of Manhood

Mr. Speaker, nothing short of a complete acknowledgment of my manhood will satisfy me. I have no compromises to make, and shall unwillingly accept any. If I were to say that I would be content with less than any other member upon this floor I would forfeit whatever respect anyone here might entertain for me, and would thereby furnish the best possible evidence that I do not and cannot appreciate the rights of a freeman. Just what I am charged with by my political enemies. I cannot willingly accept anything less than my full measure of rights as a man, because I am unwilling to present myself as a candidate for the brand of inferiority, which will be as plain and lasting as the mark of Cain. If I am to be thus branded, the country must do it against my solemn protest. . . .

After all, this question resolves itself to this: either I am a man or I am not a man. If one, I am entitled to all the rights, privileges, and immunities common to any other class in this country; if not a man, I have no right to vote, no right to a seat here; if no right to vote, then 20 percent of the members on this floor have no right here, but, on the contrary, hold their seats in violation of law. If the negro has no right to vote, then one-eighth of your Senate consists of members who have no shadow of a claim to the places they occupy; and if no right to a vote, a half-dozen governors in the South figure as usurpers.

This is the legitimate conclusion of the argument, that the negro is not a man and is not entitled to all the public rights common to other men, and you cannot escape it. But when I press my claims I am asked, 'Is it good policy?" My answer is, "Policy is out of the question; it has nothing to do with it; that you can have no policy in dealing with your citizens; that there must be one law for all; that in this case justice is the only standard to be used, and you can no more divide justice than you can divide Deity." On the other hand, I am told that I must respect the prejudices of others. Now, sir, no one respects reasonable and intelligent prejudices more than I. I respect religious prejudices, for example; these I can comprehend. But how can I have respect for the prejudices that prompt a man to turn up his nose at the males of a certain race, while at the same time he has a fondness for the females of the same race to the extent of cohabitation? Out of four poor unfortunate colored women who from poverty were forced to go to the lying-in branch of the Freedmen's Hospital here in the District last year three gave birth to children whose fathers were white men, and I venture to say that if they were members of this body, would vote against the civil-rights bill. Do you, can you wonder at my want of respect for this kind of prejudice? To make me feel uncomfortable appears to be the highest ambition of many white men. It is to them a positive luxury, which they seek to indulge at every opportunity.

I have never sought to compel anyone, white or black, to associate with me, and never shall; nor do I wish to be compelled to associate with anyone. If a man does not wish to ride with me in the street-car I shall not object to his hiring a private conveyance; if he does not wish to ride with me from here to Baltimore, who shall complain if he charters a special train? For a man to carry out his prejudices in this way would be manly, and would leave no cause for complaint, but to crowd me out of the usual conveyance into an uncomfortable place with persons for whose manners I have a dislike, whose language is not fit for ears polite, is decidedly unmanly and cannot be submitted to tamely by any one who has a particle of self-respect.

Sir, this whole thing grows out of a desire to establish a system of "caste," an anti-republican principle, in our free country. In Europe they have princes, dukes, lords, etc., in contradistinction to the middle classes and peasants. Further East they have the brahmans or priests, who rank above the sudras or laborers. In those countries distinctions are based upon blood and position. Every one there understands the custom and no one complains. They, poor innocent creatures, pity our condition, look down upon us with a kind of royal compassion, because they think we have no tangible lines of distinction, and therefore speak of our society as being vulgar. But let not our friends beyond the seas lay the flattering unction to their souls that we are without distinctive lines; that we have no nobility; for we are blessed with both. Our distinction is color (which would necessarily exclude the brahmans), and our lines are much broader than anything they know of. Here a drunken white man is not only equal to a drunken negro (as would be the case anywhere else), but superior to the most sober and orderly one; here an ignorant white man is not only the equal of an unlettered negro, but is superior to the most cultivated; here our nobility cohabit with our female peasants, and then throw up their hands in holy horror when a male of the same class enters a restaurant to get a meal, and if he insist upon being accommodated our scion of royalty will leave and go to the arms of his colored mistress and there pour out his soul's complaint, tell her of the impudence of the "damned nigger" incoming to a table where a white man was sitting. . . .

Mr. Speaker, though there is not a line in this bill the democracy approve of, yet they made the most noise about the school clause. Dispatches are freely sent over the wires as to what will be done with the common-school system in the several Southern States in the event this bill becomes a law. I am not surprised at this, but, on the other hand, I looked for it. Now what is the force of that school clause? It simply provides that all the children in every State where there is a school system supported in whole or in part by general taxation shall have equal advantages of school privileges. So that if perfect and ample accommodations are not made convenient for all the children, then any child has the right to go to any school where they do exist. And that is all there is in this school clause. . . .

Mr. Speaker, to call this land the asylum of the oppressed is a

194

misnomer, for upon all sides I am treated as a pariah. I hold that the solution of this whole matter is to enact such laws and prescribe such penalties for their violation as will prevent any person from discriminating against another in public places on account of color. No one asks, no one seeks the passage of a law that will interfere with anyone's private affairs. But I do ask the enactment of a law to secure me in the enjoyment of public privileges. But when I ask this I am told that I must wait for public opinion; that it is a matter that cannot be forced by law. While I admit that public opinion is a power, and in many cases is a law of itself, yet I cannot lose sight of the fact that both statute law and the law of necessity manufacture public opinion. I remember, it was unpopular to enlist negro soldiers in our late war, and after they enlisted it was equally unpopular to have them fight in the same battles; but when it became a necessity in both cases public opinion soon came around to that point. No white father objected to the negro's becoming food for powder if thereby his son would be saved. No white woman objected to the negro marching in the same ranks and fighting in the same battles if by that her husband could escape burial in our savannas and return to her and her little ones.

Suppose there had been no reconstruction acts nor amendments to the Constitution, when would public opinion in the South have suggested the propriety of giving me the ballot? Unaided by law when would public opinion have prompted the Administration to appoint members of my race to represent this Government at foreign courts? It is said by some well-meaning men that the colored man has now every right under the common law; in reply I wish to say that that kind of law commands very little respect when applied to the rights of colored men in my portion of the country; the only law that we have any regard for is uncommon law of the most positive character. And I repeat, if you will place upon your statute-books laws that will protect me in my rights, that public opinion will speedily follow.

CHAPTER 5

The End of Reconstruction

Chapter Preface

The presidential election of November 1876 sparked a new crisis between the North and the South, one that many feared would lead to another Civil War. The race between Republican candidate Rutherford B. Hayes and Democratic candidate Samuel J. Tilden had been very close, but the first election results gave Tilden a majority of 250,000 in the popular vote. However, Louisiana, Florida, and South Carolina had each returned not one but two sets of results—one supporting Tilden and the other Hayes. Until Congress could decide which of the two sets of votes to admit, the electoral vote was in dispute. Tilden only needed one more electoral vote to win, whereas Hayes, who was lagging behind, needed all the disputed electoral votes. As Congress entered a prolonged partisan debate over the proper procedure for determining the new president, the cry "Tilden or blood!" echoed ominously throughout the South. At the same time, though, Hayes and his supporters devised what would become the Compromise of 1877, in which they agreed to end federal interference in southern affairs in exchange for southern acceptance of Hayes's presidency. Congress finally established a fifteen-member election committee, consisting of eight Republicans and seven Democrats, to vote on the validity of the electoral returns. During February 1877, the committee members (who consistently voted eight to seven, along party lines) gave Hayes the disputed electoral votes.

Most historians now refer to the Compromise of 1877 and the collapse of the Radical Reconstruction governments in the South that followed as the end of Reconstruction. The people of the time, however, spoke of the compromise as signaling a new kind of reconstruction policy, one in which the southern states would continue the process on their own accord. For over a decade, the South had experienced "presidential reconstruction" under Abraham Lincoln and Andrew Johnson, "military reconstruction" according to the dictates of the Reconstruction Acts, and "Radical Reconstruction" as engineered by the Radical Republicans. Now, ran the common wisdom, came the time for "home rule," in which the individual states—not the federal government—would determine how reconstruction should progress.

Hayes's new plan was often referred to as "peaceful reconstruction," indicating that federal troops would no longer be sent into southern states to regulate reconstruction. According to general opinion, the South—liberated from the military occupation that had served as a constant reminder of its defeat in the Civil War—would finally return to its status as a free and equal member of the Union.

In part, the widespread approval of Hayes's plan reflected Americans' growing disillusionment with the progress of Radical Reconstruction and their increasing reluctance to use military intervention in the South. Despite federal attempts to keep the peace, the southern states periodically erupted in violence—usually directed against blacks and Republicans—throughout Radical Reconstruction. The North eventually became inured to constant accounts of election violence, Klan atrocities, and race riots. It seemed to many Northerners that the federal government had responded repeatedly to southern problems with military power, yet the violence continually worsened. On September 13, 1875, commenting on yet another violent disturbance in Mississippi, President Ulysses S. Grant summed up the national feeling: "The whole public are tired out with these annual autumnal outbreaks in the South . . . [and] the great majority are ready now to condemn any interference on the part of the Government." Northerners were also preoccupied with economic troubles that had begun with the depression of 1873 and were resentful of the expense of military deployment in the South. By 1877, Northerners were more than ready to let Southerners deal with their own problems.

Another major factor in the acceptance of Hayes's policy was that, by 1876, Radical Republicanism had significantly declined in power. Over the past few years, Democrats had regained control of most state governments in the South, and in the 1874 national elections Democrats had obtained a majority in the U.S. House of Representatives for the first time since 1860. Never a Radical himself, President Grant had given less support to Radical causes during his second term and had become more hesitant to intervene in the South—a presidential policy that Hayes would embrace. Throughout Reconstruction, southern blacks had been a bulwark of Radical Republicanism, but accelerating violence in the South had essentially neutralized blacks' political power.

Though Hayes entered into the Compromise of 1877 with the best of intentions—and with the assurance of southern leaders that blacks would be treated equitably—the compromise marked the end of blacks' legal advancements during this era. Over the next three decades, southern legislatures would pass measures designed to effectively disfranchise blacks and to legally enforce racial segregation. The U.S. Supreme Court would uphold these laws while declaring the Enforcement Acts and the Civil Rights Act of 1875 unconstitutional. Yet Reconstruction did not end without protest—from both blacks and whites. The viewpoints in this chapter illustrate the debates that arose from the end of Reconstruction.

VIEWPOINT 1

"We do not calculate wisely regarding human impulses, nor the power of kindness over the hearts of men, if the result [of peaceful Reconstruction] does not prove satisfactory."

The Compromise of 1877 Will Help Reconstruction

John Mercer Langston (1829-1897)

John Mercer Langston was born a slave in Virginia and was emancipated after the death of his father/owner. After graduating from Oberlin College in Ohio, Langston became the first black elected to public office in the United States when he received a post as a town clerk in 1855. He held a variety of civic and political offices, including one term as a U.S. senator, and was a dean at Howard University in Washington, D.C. The following viewpoint contains excerpts from "The Other Phase of Reconstruction," a speech Langston delivered in Jersey City, New Jersey, on April 17, 1877, concerning the Compromise of 1877.

The results of the 1876 presidential election between Rutherford B. Hayes, a Republican, and Samuel J. Tilden, a Democrat, had been hotly contested. Early in 1877, a special election committee decided the election in favor of Hayes, but southern Democrats conceded Hayes's election largely because Hayes agreed to withdraw the remaining federal troops from the South and stop federal interference in southern state governments. This compromise was promoted as a new phase of southern reconstruction, one that would be attained by peaceful means rather than military compulsion.

In his speech, Langston asserts that the Compromise of 1877 will further the process of reconstruction by allowing Southerners

Excerpted from "The Other Phase of Reconstruction," a speech by John Mercer Langston addressed to the people of Jersey City, N.J., April 17, 1877. Reprinted in *Negro Orators and Their Orations*, Carter G. Woodson, ed., Association for the Study of Negro Life and History, 1925.

more control over their governments and institutions. Attitudes in the South toward secession and civil rights have greatly improved, Langston argues, and Southerners can now be trusted to "build anew upon sounder principles." The new amendments to the Constitution and the civil rights legislation passed by Congress during Radical Reconstruction, Langston maintains, will serve as sufficient protection of the rights and safety of southern blacks.

The thoughtful and patriotic American, animated by other than partisan and sectional considerations and feelings, turns with delight from the contemplation of the belligerent to the pacific phase of reconstruction.

Four years of bloody contest, characterized by all the evils attendant in the most aggravated form upon a civil strife of gigantic proportions; and twelve years of effort at reconciliation and readjustment, marked by displays of cruel, unrestrained fury, controlled only by military power, brings us, in all earnestness of soul, to inquire: "Is there no method by which the problem of reconstruction may be satisfactorily solved in some peaceful manner?". . .

Following the revolution, which has just been wrought in the South, breaking up institutions, changing the system of labor, necessitating the remodeling of law and legislation, the establishment of other and better educational organizations, the submission of the political and the religious opinion of the people to a new crucial test, the deposing of many old, and the advancement of other leaders, the condition of the public mind, now upon inquiry, the best, the most gifted and learned, seeking knowledge, makes this the time preëminently to speak and be heard. The public address, the considerate editorial, the pamphlet or book, in which are discussed, with wisdom and moderation, the problems of Reconcilement and Pacification, the material and moral welfare of the South, its just local self-government, will be read, and their sentiments considered and diffused to the good of all the people. This is the hour for its performance, and this is the work which should be done for the South. The truth and the light should be given the people of this section. . . .

But will Pacific Reconstruction prove injurious to the colored citizen? I believe not. I believe it will prove to him, as to all other residents of the South, an inestimable blessing. Of all others thus located, he is most ill prepared for a continuance of political strife, so costly of time, industry, the fruits of toil, personal safety, life, liberty, and pursuit of happiness. Reconciliation—the peace, the rest, the opportunity and blessings which come of this, he needs. And if he is to gain positive footing as a citizen of character, means, and influence where he lives, this he must have. With harmony and good neighborhood existing between him and the white classes, his life, under the 13th, 14th, and 15th Amendments of the Constitution of the United States and the laws passed in pursuance thereof, with his liberty and rights duly protected, as emergency may require, by the State or Federal Government, will prove, it may be, at times rugged and hard, but on the whole, successful and profitable. Relieved from too pressing and absorbing political excitement, he will cultivate industry more thoroughly and advantageously, locate his family, educate his children, accumulate wealth, and improve himself in all those things which pertain to dignified life.

THE NEW POLICY TRAIN. -
Conductor Hayes—"All aboard, Mr. Packard! We want to take all you Carpetbaggers in one tr..."

Culver Pictures

In this 1877 cartoon, President Rutherford B. Hayes is depicted as a railroad conductor escorting carpetbaggers Stephen B. Packard and Daniel H. Chamberlain back to the North. Packard and Chamberlain were the Republican candidates in disputed gubernatorial elections in Louisiana and South Carolina, respectively; Hayes chose to support their Democratic rivals.

He will become, in this way, a valuable and influential member of society, respected and honored, it may be, by his neighbors and fellow-citizens. He will become, indeed, interested in all matters which concern the State in which he lives, and like his fellow-citizens, by voice and vote, advance and conserve the welfare of the community. He will become self-reliant and self-supporting; no longer a pariah, but a man and citizen in fact. Having passed thus his life in honest industry and noble endeavor, winning honors, official and other, no distinctions made against him on account of his color—distinctions offensive and harassing—he spends his declining years in the midst of a happy family, his children respected, as they show themselves honest, honorable and worthy. Is this condition possible? May we justly contemplate this as the promise of Peaceful Reconstruction to the former slave? God grant that it may be so!

I will not pass, I will not treat as a thing of small account, the hatred, intense and seemingly implacable, exhibited since the war by the dominant class of the South against the enfranchised colored citizen. The intensity and the implacability of this feeling cannot be denied, and this fact we must not fail to appreciate. In an amicable readjustment, however, and under the milder sway of truth and justice, law and liberty, it is to be hoped that the condition of things indicated will be established, and an intelligent and permanent friendship secured between these classes.

Several important circumstances, now existing facts, must contribute directly and largely to the accomplishment of this result. The improved condition of the colored people, their advancement in education, property, and social character, in their knowledge of their rights as well as their courage to assert earnestly their claim thereto; the presence and residence of many Northern white men in the South, with their broad and liberal education, their knowledge and appreciation of the beautiful and ennobling lessons of Christian civilization, their value of manhood and the best methods of developing and fostering its noblest qualities, their energy, their industry, their thrift, their progress, their love of liberty, equal rights, and free institutions; the influence of the native-Union white man of the South, his brave assertion of loyal sentiments, and his fearless maintenance of the doctrines of our amended Constitution and the equal rights of all, as therein enunciated, must all aid in producing and sustaining such state of society. . . .

Besides, the South had not accepted as the basis of political action, prior to the war, those great and fundamental principles which distinguished the American Revolution. The principles of the Declaration, the doctrines of the Constitution, the sentiments of the wisest and best statesmanship of the country, were generally treated as "glittering generalities," void of practical significance. But now they profess to accept all these; and no one is found to advocate the re-enslavement of the Negro, or to oppose Universal Suffrage. Freedom and popular government are accepted and established facts. Everybody admits the utter absurdity and impracticability of secession, and yields a cordial and supreme allegiance to the General Government. . . .

Radical Reconstruction Has Failed

The importance, the magnitude, and difficulty, as well as the necessity, of Reconstruction by peaceful means will be conceded.

And however we may regret it, it will be conceded that the method heretofore pursued proves by no means satisfactory in its results. Whether this failure is owing to the unhandsome and obnoxious conduct of political adventurers; the unnecessary and too constant political excitement and agitation of the people, the injudicious and oppressive acts of Republican legislatures and officials, the former composed, frequently, largely of ignorant, unqualified, and impecunious persons, white and black, and the latter frequently not only incompetent, but offensive and exasperating in their conduct; the too frequent interference by the National Government in State affairs with the Army, seemingly for party purposes; the general bad temper and purpose of the native dominant white class—whatever the cause, as to the failure of the former method, there is but one opinion. The failure is a fact, and some new and, if possible, better method must be tried. This, the welfare of those immediately concerned, as well as the general good of the country in all its material and moral interests, requires.

We must remember, however, in dealing with this subject, that there is to be no compromise, no surrender of principle, no betrayal of plighted faith. And there need not be; for with us it is not a question of new principles and measures; it is simply a matter of administration, or policy involving the mode of applying the principles and measures, already accepted and fixed in the Constitution and the laws.

The present [Hayes] Administration, in its efforts at pacification in dealing with States, classes, races and individuals, proposes, as one must believe, to stand on the law, as now written and determined, insisting upon the cordial recognition of the equal rights of all citizens, the practical guarantee of their protection in such rights, the establishment and maintenance of such condition of good order and peace as to encourage immigration, the introduction of capital, and the advancement of labor, as well as the inauguration of such local self-governments as in all their departments and acts shall be harmonious with the altered status of the former slave, the new provisions of the Constitution, and the enactment of the State and General Government passed in accordance therewith. Occupying such position, and insisting upon such conditions as precedent and indispensable, the good omens of its initial efforts promise a happy success. The acceptance of these conditions as precedent and indispensable, constitutes the only correct and sure test of the willingness and the fitness of the dominant white classes of the South, for properly considering and appreciating efforts for the permanent pacification of that section. Did such condition of public feeling exist, discoverable in the acts and utterances of the leading and influential men of the South, in their treatment of the classes and persons differing with them in political sentiments and party relations, in the solution and determination of those questions, material, educational and political, which more especially affect the newly enfranchised people, we might wisely give ourselves no further anxiety with regard to this subject, resting assured that the general management of it by the Government would improve and sustain it.

The New Southern Policy

In his inaugural address of March 5, 1877, President Rutherford B. Hayes expresses his intention to restore home rule to the South, officially ending federal reconstruction. Because white southern leaders had sworn, as part of the Compromise of 1877, to support the equal rights of blacks once home rule was established, Hayes believed that the work of reconstruction would be continued by southern state governments.

The evils which afflict the Southern States can only be removed or remedied by the united and harmonious efforts of both races, actuated by motives of mutual sympathy and regard; and while in duty bound and fully determined to protect the rights of all by every constitutional means at the disposal of my Administration, I am sincerely anxious to use every legitimate influence in favor of honest and efficient local *self*-government as the true resource of those States for the promotion of the contentment and prosperity of their citizens. In the effort I shall make to accomplish this purpose I ask the cordial cooperation of all who cherish an interest in the welfare of the country, trusting that party ties and the prejudice of race will be freely surrendered in behalf of the great purpose to be accomplished....

Let me assure my countrymen of the Southern States that it is my earnest desire to regard and promote their truest interests—the interests of the white and of the colored people both and equally—and to put forth my best efforts in behalf of a civil policy which will forever wipe out in our political affairs the color line and the distinction between North and South, to the end that we may have not merely a united North or a united South, but a united country.

Our anxieties, our fears come of the fact, that too little such public feeling is now discernible; and that it is to be created and fostered largely by agencies and influences brought to bear mainly from without, and through the instrumentality of the Government, upon those who are to be reconciled and made obedient, law-abiding subjects of the State. The thing to be done, then, is to manifest in bold and decisive manner, such impartial and patriotic disposition and purpose, with reference to the management of the Southern problem, as to convince all concerned of the sincerity and wisdom of the pacific yet positive intentions of the Government and country with regard to their case. In this way, win their confidence, if possible, and secure an earnest and hearty response to such beneficent purposes. We do not calculate wisely regarding human impulses, nor the power of kindness over the hearts of men, if the result does not prove satisfactory.

Restoration of Ex-Rebels

The acts, expressive of such disposition and purpose—whether by the appointment of a distinguished former Rebel [David M. Key], to the Cabinet, and prominent Southern men of the same class to conspicuous official positions, are matters of detail, which may be very properly, under the law and the admonitions of public opinion, entrusted to the President. It must be insisted, however, as both wise and just, that, in the distribution of official patronage, Republicans, especially native Whites and Blacks of the South, shall not be neglected, and that the recognition accorded them shall be of equal dignity and responsibility with that accorded the other class. For in this way the aristocratic feeling . . . , the hatred of the Negro, and the political repellency existing between the classes, will be the more speedily corrected and removed. It must also be insisted, where no such domestic violence as that described in the Constitution exists in a State, although there exist therein dispute as to the fact and legality of one of two governments, that the Federal army shall not be used to interfere therewith; but decision as to the dispute shall be made under the law in accordance with the mode and methods provided thereby. Thus an exciting, irritating, and exasperating cause is removed, and Government and people remitted to the established methods of the law. The experience, the habits of thought and feeling of Americans, ill prepare them for tolerating the use of the army in the settlement of political differences; and in the presence of any such real or supposed condition of things, permanent peace is impossible in any section of our country.

The pleasing contemplation of the people of the South, engaging in the wise and profitable cultivation of all the industries, agricultural and other, peculiar to and remunerative in that section; human life and human rights, without regard to class or color, properly valued and protected; just local self-government established; the vexed and trying question of reconstruction settled; the union of our States and the Government no longer endangered by any exciting sectional dispute, but adjusted upon enduring principles of justice, law, and liberty, excites in our minds the deepest feelings of hope, the profoundest purpose to do all that is practicable to secure such consummation, so devoutly to be wished.

VIEWPOINT 2

"In these days of voluntary Reconstruction [the Freedman] is virtually freed by the consent of his master, but the master retaining the exclusive right to define the bounds of his freedom."

The Compromise of 1877 Will Harm Reconstruction

George Washington Cable (1844-1925)

George Washington Cable was born in New Orleans and served as a Confederate soldier in the Civil War. After the war, he worked as a reporter for a New Orleans newspaper and published short stories about Louisiana life in *Scribner's Monthly* magazine, gradually gaining renown as one of the foremost southern writers of his time. In the 1880s, Cable published several novels and collections of essays in which he broke sharply with prevailing southern views of the Civil War, reconstruction, and civil rights. Cable was greatly concerned with social injustice toward blacks and was critical of the policy of peaceful reconstruction instituted after the Compromise of 1877.

In an essay that first appeared in the magazine *Century* in January 1885, Cable insists that southern control over reconstruction will result in destroying much of what has been accomplished. In particular, Cable contends, peaceful reconstruction will prove harmful to the ex-slaves, who still need protection from white Southerners. Although blacks possess their full rights as citizens under federal laws, Cable argues, their rights are systematically negated by the actions and attitudes of white Southerners. Dur-

George Washington Cable, "The Freedman's Case in Equity," *Century*, January 1885. Reprinted in *The Struggle for Racial Equality*, Henry Steele Commager, ed., Harper & Row, 1967.

ing 1885, this essay and others by Cable were collected in a book entitled *The Silent South*. The book was met with such hostility in the South that Cable moved to Massachusetts, where he continued to write and lecture on civil rights for blacks and conditions in the South.

The greatest social problem before the American people today is, as it has been for a hundred years, the presence among us of the Negro.

No comparable entanglement was ever drawn round itself by any other modern nation with so serene a disregard of its ultimate issue, or with a more distinct national responsibility. The African slave was brought here by cruel force, and with everybody's consent except his own. Everywhere the practice was favored as a measure of common aggrandizement. When a few men and women protested, they were mobbed in the public interest, with the public consent. There rests, therefore, a moral responsibility on the whole nation never to lose sight of the results of African-American slavery until they cease to work mischief and injustice. . . .

Old Prejudices

The old alien relation might have given way if we could only, while letting that pass, have held fast by the other old ideas. But they were all bound together. See our embarrassment. For more than a hundred years we had made these sentiments the absolute essentials to our self-respect. And yet if we clung to them, how could we meet the Freedman on equal terms in the political field? Even to lead would not compensate us; for the fundamental profession of American politics is that the leader is servant to his followers. It was too much. The ex-master and ex-slave—the quarterdeck and the forecastle, as it were—could not come together. But neither could the American mind tolerate a continuance of martial law. The agonies of Reconstruction followed.

The vote, after all, was a secondary point, and the robbery and bribery on one side, and whipping and killing on the other were but huge accidents of the situation. The two main questions were really these: on the Freedman's side, how to establish republican state government under the same recognition of his rights that the rest of Christendom accorded him; and on the former master's side, how to get back to the old semblance of republican state government, and—allowing that the Freedman was *de facto* a voter—still to maintain a purely arbitrary superiority of all whites over all blacks, and a purely arbitrary equality of all blacks among themselves as an alien, menial, and dangerous class.

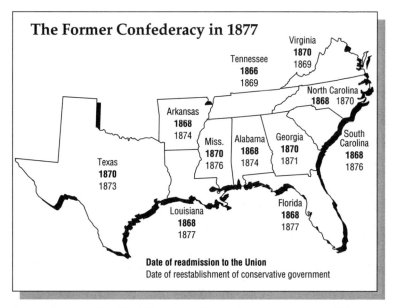

In many respects, President Hayes's southern policy was simply an official validation of a process that was already taking place. As shown by the map, by 1877 all of the former Confederacy had been readmitted to the Union and most of the southern states had already reinstated conservative governments.

Exceptionally here and there some one in the master caste did throw off the old and accept the new ideas, and, if he would allow it, was instantly claimed as a leader by the newly liberated thousands around him. But just as promptly the old master race branded him also an alien reprobate, and in ninety-nine cases out of a hundred, if he had not already done so, he soon began to confirm by his actions the brand on his cheek. However, we need give no history here of the dreadful episode of Reconstruction. Under an experimentative truce its issues rest today upon the pledge of the wiser leaders of the master class: Let us but remove the hireling demagogue, and we will see to it that the Freedman is accorded a practical, complete, and cordial recognition of his equality with the white man before the law. As far as there has been any understanding at all, it is not that the originally desired ends of Reconstruction have been abandoned, but that the men of North and South have agreed upon a new, gentle, and peaceable method for reaching them; that, without change as to the ends in view, compulsory Reconstruction has been set aside and a voluntary Reconstruction is on trial.

It is the fashion to say we paused to let the "feelings engendered by the war" pass away, and that they are passing. But let not these truths lead us into error. The sentiments we have been analyzing, and upon which we saw the old compulsory Reconstruction go hard aground—these are not the "feelings engendered by the war." We must disentangle them from the "feelings engendered by the war," and by Reconstruction. They are older than either. But for them slavery would have perished of itself, and emancipation and Reconstruction been peaceful revolutions.

Indeed, as between master and slave, the "feelings engendered by the war" are too trivial, or at least were too short-lived, to demand our present notice. One relation and feeling the war destroyed: the patriarchal tie and its often really tender and benevolent sentiment of dependence and protection. When the slave became a Freedman, the sentiment of alienism became for the first time complete. The abandonment of this relation was not one-sided; the slave, even before the master, renounced it. Countless times, since Reconstruction began, the master has tried, in what he believed to be everybody's interest, to play on that old sentiment. But he found it a harp without strings. The Freedman could not formulate, but he could see, all our old ideas of autocracy and subserviency, of master and menial, of an arbitrarily fixed class to guide and rule, and another to be guided and ruled. He rejected the overture. The old master, his well-meant condescensions slighted, turned away estranged, and justified himself in passively withholding that simpler protection without patronage which any one American citizen, however exalted, owes to any other, however humble. Could the Freedman in the bitterest of those days have consented to throw himself upon just that one old relation, he could have found a physical security for himself and his house such as could not, after years of effort, be given him by constitutional amendments, Congress, United States marshals, regiments of regulars, and ships of war. But he could not; the very nobility of the civilization that had held him in slavery had made him too much a man to go back to that shelter; and by his manly neglect to do so he has proved to us who once ruled over him that, be his relative standing among the races of men what it may, he is worthy to be free.

To be a free man is his [the Negro's] still distant goal. Twice he has been a Freedman. In the days of compulsory Reconstruction he was freed in the presence of his master by that master's victorious foe. In these days of voluntary Reconstruction he is virtually freed by the consent of his master, but the master retaining the exclusive right to define the bounds of his freedom. Many everywhere have taken up the idea that this state of affairs is the end to be desired and the end actually sought in Reconstruction as handed over to the state. I do not charge such folly to the best intelligence of any American community; but I cannot ignore my own knowledge that the average thought of some regions rises to no better idea of the issue. The belief is all too common that the nation, having aimed at a wrong result and missed, has left us of the Southern states to get now such other result as we think best. I say this belief is not universal. There are those among us who see that America has no room for a state of society which makes its lower classes harmless by abridging their liberties, or, as one of the favored class lately said to me, has "got 'em so they don't

---

Abandoning Lawful Government

As with the presidential election, the results of the 1876 South Carolina gubernatorial race were disputed. President Rutherford B. Hayes supported the Democratic candidate (former Confederate general Wade Hampton) and refused to recognize the claim of Republican candidate and former governor Daniel H. Chamberlain. Returning to the North, Chamberlain criticized the president's southern policy in his speech of July 4, 1877.

What is [President Hayes's] Southern policy? In point of physical or external fact, it consists in withdrawing the military forces of the United States from the points in South Carolina and Louisiana where they had been previously stationed for the protection and support of the lawful Governments of those States.

In point of immediate, foreseen, and intended consequence, it consists in the overthrow and destruction of those State Governments, and the substitution in their stead of certain other organizations called State Governments.

In point of actual present results, it consists in the abandonment of Southern Republicans, and especially the colored race, to the control and rule not only of the Democratic party, but of that class at the South which regarded slavery as a Divine Institution, which waged four years of destructive war for its perpetuation, which steadily opposed citizenship and suffrage for the negro—in a word, a class whose traditions, principles, and history are opposed to every step and feature of what Republicans call our national progress since 1860.

In point of general political and moral significance it consists in the proclamation to the country and the world that the will of the majority of the voters of a State, lawfully and regularly expressed, is no longer the ruling power in our States, and that the constitutional guaranty to every State in this Union of a republican form of government and of protection against domestic violence, is henceforth ineffectual and worthless.

give no trouble." There is a growing number who see that the one thing we cannot afford to tolerate at large is a class of people less than citizens; and that every interest in the land demands that the Freedman be free to become in all things, as far as his own personal gifts will lift and sustain him, the same sort of American citizen he would be if, with the same intellectual and moral caliber, he were white.

Thus we reach the ultimate question of fact. Are the Freedman's liberties suffering any real abridgement? The answer is easy. The letter of the laws, with a few exceptions, recognizes him as entitled to every right of an American citizen; and to some it may seem unimportant that there is scarcely one public relation of life in the South where he is not arbitrarily and unlawfully compelled to hold toward the white man the attitude of an alien, a menial, and a probable reprobate, by reason of his race and color. One of the marvels of future history will be that it was counted a small matter, by a majority of our nation, for six millions of people within it, made by its own decree a component part of it, to be subjected to a system of oppression so rank that nothing could make it seem small except the fact that they had already been ground under it for a century and a half.

Examine it. It proffers to the Freedman a certain security of life and property, and then holds the respect of the community, that dearest of earthly boons, beyond his attainment. It gives him certain guarantees against thieves and robbers, and then holds him under the unearned contumely of the mass of good men and women. It acknowledges in constitutions and statutes his title to an American's freedom and aspirations, and then in daily practice heaps upon him in every public place the most odious distinctions, without giving ear to the humblest plea concerning mental or moral character. It spurns his ambition, tramples upon his languishing self-respect, and indignantly refuses to let him either buy with money, or earn by any excellence of inner life or outward behavior, the most momentary immunity from these public indignities even for his wife and daughters. Need we cram these pages with facts in evidence, as if these were charges denied and requiring to be proven? They are simply the present avowed and defended state of affairs peeled of its exteriors. . . .

Turning the Tables

Suppose, for a moment, the tables turned. Suppose the courts of our Southern states, while changing no laws requiring the impaneling of jurymen without distinction as to race, etc., should suddenly begin to draw their thousands of jurymen all black, and well-nigh every one of them counting, not only himself, but all his race, better than any white man. Assuming that their average

211

of intelligence and morals should be not below that of jurymen as now drawn, would a white man, for all that, choose to be tried in one of those courts? Would he suspect nothing? Could one persuade him that his chances of even justice were all they should be, or all they would be were the court not evading the law in order to sustain an outrageous distinction against him because of the accidents of his birth? Yet only read white man for black man, and black man for white man, and that—I speak as an eyewitness—has been the practice for years, and is still so today; an actual emasculation, in the case of six million people both as plaintiff and defendant, of the right of trial by jury.

In this and other practices the outrage falls upon the Freedman. Does it stop there? Far from it. It is the first premise of American principles that whatever elevates the lower stratum of the people lifts all the rest, and whatever holds it down holds all down. For twenty years, therefore, the nation has been working to elevate the Freedman. It counts this one of the great necessities of the hour. It has poured out its wealth publicly and privately for this purpose. It is confidently hoped that it will soon bestow a royal gift of millions for the reduction of the illiteracy so largely shared by the blacks. Our Southern states are, and for twenty years have been, taxing themselves for the same end. The private charities alone of the other states have given twenty millions in the same good cause. Their colored seminaries, colleges, and normal schools dot our whole Southern country, and furnish our public colored schools with a large part of their teachers. All this and much more has been or is being done in order that, for the good of himself and everybody else in the land, the colored man may be elevated as quickly as possible from all the debasements of slavery and semi-slavery to the full stature and integrity of citizenship. And it is in the face of all this that the adherent of the old regime stands in the way to every public privilege and place—steamer landing, railway platform, theater, concert hall, art display, public library, public school, courthouse, church, everything—flourishing the hot branding iron of ignominious distinctions. He forbids the Freedman to go into the water until *he* is satisfied that he knows how to swim and, for fear he should learn, hangs millstones about his neck. This is what we are told is a small matter that will settle itself. Yes, like a roosting curse, until the outraged intelligence of the South lifts its indignant protest against this stupid firing into our own ranks.

VIEWPOINT 3

"In anything like a normal condition of things the South is the best place for the Negro. Nowhere else is there for him a promise of a happier future."

Blacks Should Stay in the South

Frederick Douglass (1817-1895)

Between 1879 and 1881, approximately 55,000 blacks left the South to move to Kansas and other western states. This migration became known as the Exodus (referring to the biblical exodus of the Israelites from Egypt), and the migrants were called Exodusters.

At the beginning of the Exodus in the spring of 1879, Frederick Douglass was the marshal of the District of Columbia and the most prominent black leader in the United States. Douglass first spoke against the migration in May 1879 and was soundly criticized by those who supported the Exodus. Soon thereafter, Douglass was given the opportunity to defend his position by the American Social Science Association, which asked Douglass to deliver a speech on the Exodus at its annual general meeting at Saratoga, New York, on September 12, 1879. However, once Douglass learned that his appearance would include a debate with Richard T. Greener, a strong supporter of the Exodus movement, he canceled his appearance. The speech that Douglass had prepared was read at the meeting by Professor Francis Wayland and later published in the *Journal of Social Science* in May 1880.

In this speech, Douglass admits that conditions in the South are intolerable, but he calls on the federal government to remedy the situation and protect black citizens in their own homes. Warning against financially unsound decisions, Douglass argues that the freed slaves are better off remaining in the South with whatever

Excerpted from Frederick Douglass, "The Negro Exodus from the Gulf States," *Journal of Social Science* 11 (May 1880):1-21.

gains they have made rather than selling their assets in order to finance risky ventures in unknown territory. He also contends that a large-scale migration will decimate black political majorities in the South, leaving little chance for blacks or those sympathetic to blacks to regain control of the southern states.

The Negro, long deemed to be too indolent and stupid to discover and adopt any rational measure to secure and defend his rights as a man, may now be congratulated upon the telling contradiction which he has recently and strikingly given to this withering disparagement and reproach. He has discovered and adopted a measure which may assist very materially in the solution of some of the vital problems involved in his sudden elevation from slavery to freedom, and from chattelhood to manhood and citizenship. . . . He has not chosen to copy the example of his would-be enslavers. It is to his credit that he has steadily refused to resort to those extreme measures of repression and retaliation to which the cruel wrongs he has suffered might have tempted a less docile and forgiving race. . . .

On the contrary, he has adopted a simple, lawful and peaceable measure. It is emigration—the quiet withdrawal of his valuable bones and muscles from a condition of things which he considers no longer tolerable. Innocent as this remedy is for the manifold ills, which he has thus far borne with marvellous patience, fortitude, and forbearance, it is none the less significant and effective. Nothing has occurred since the abolition of slavery, which has excited a deeper interest among thoughtful men in all sections of the country, than has this Exodus. In the simple fact that a few thousand freedmen have deliberately laid down the shovel and the hoe, quitted the sugar and cotton fields of Mississippi and Louisiana, and sought homes in Kansas, and that thousands more are seriously meditating upon following their example, the sober thinking minds of the South have discovered a new and startling peril to the welfare and civilization of that section of our country. Already apprehension and alarm have led to noisy and frantic efforts on the part of the South to arrest and put an end to what it considers a ruinous evil. . . .

We have the story of the emigrants themselves, and if any can reveal the true cause of this Exodus they can. They have spoken, and their story is before the country. It is a sad story, disgraceful and scandalous to our age and country. Much of their testimony has been given under the solemnity of an oath. They tell us with great unanimity that they are very badly treated at the South. The land owners, planters, and the old master-class generally, deal unfairly with them, having had their labor for nothing when they were slaves. These men, now they are free, endeavor by various devices to get it for next to nothing; work as hard, faithfully and constantly as they may, live as plainly and as sparingly as they may, they are no better off at the end of the year than at the beginning. They say that they are the dupes and victims of cunning and fraud in signing contracts which they cannot read and cannot fully understand; that they are compelled to trade at stores owned in whole or in part by their employers, and that they are paid with orders and not with money. They say that they have to pay double the value of nearly everything they buy; that they are compelled to pay a rental of ten dollars a year for an acre of ground that will not bring thirty dollars under the hammer; that land owners are in league to prevent land-owning by Negroes; that when they work the land on shares they barely make a living; that outside the towns and cities no provision is made for education, and, ground down as they are, they cannot themselves employ teachers to instruct their children; that they are not only the victims of fraud and cunning, but of violence and intimidation; that from their very poverty the temples of justice are not open to them; that the jury box is virtually closed; that the murder of a black man by a white man is followed by no conviction or punishment. They say further, that a crime for which a white man goes free a black man is severely punished; that impunity and encouragement are given by the wealthy and respectable classes to men of the baser sort who delight in midnight raids upon the defenceless; that their ignorance of letters has put them at the mercy of men bent upon making their freedom a greater evil to them than was their slavery; that the law is the refuge of crime rather than of innocence; that even the old slave driver's whip has reappeared, and the inhuman and disgusting spectacle of the chain-gang is beginning to be seen; that the government of every Southern State is now in the hands of the old slave oligarchy, and that both departments of the National Government soon will be in the same hands. They believe that when the government, State and National, shall be in the control of the old masters of the South, they will find means for reducing the freedmen to a condition analogous to slavery. They despair of any change for the better, declaring that everything is waxing worse for the Negro, and that his only means of safety is to leave the South. . . .

Objections to the Exodus

Without abating one jot of our horror and indignation at the outrages committed in some parts of the Southern States against the Negro, we cannot but regard the present agitation of an African Exodus from the South as ill-timed, and in some respects hurtful. We stand today at the beginning of a grand and beneficent reaction. There is a growing recognition of the duty and obligation of the American people to guard, protect and defend the personal and political rights of all the people of the States; to uphold the principles upon which rebellion was suppressed, slavery abolished, and the country saved from dismemberment and ruin. We see and feel today, as we have not seen and felt before, that the time for conciliation, and trusting to the honor of the late rebels and slaveholders, has past. . . .

Frederick Douglass fought for civil rights but opposed mass migration from the South.

At a time like this, so full of hope and courage, it is unfortunate that a cry of despair should be raised in behalf of the colored people of the South; unfortunate that men are going over the country begging in the name of the poor colored man of the South, and telling the people that the Government has no power to enforce the Constitution and Laws in that section, and that there is no hope for the poor Negro, but to plant him in the new soil of Kansas and Nebraska. These men do the colored people of the South a real damage. They give their enemies an advantage in the argument for their manhood and freedom. They assume the inability of the colored people of the South to take care of themselves. The country will be told of the hundreds who go to Kansas, but not of the thousands who stay in Mississippi and Louisiana. They will be told of the destitute who require material aid, but not of the multitude who are bravely sustaining themselves where they are. In Georgia the Negroes are paying taxes upon six millions of dollars; in Louisiana upon forty or fifty millions, and upon unascertained sums elsewhere in the Southern States. Why should a people who have made such progress in the course of a few years now be humiliated and scandalized by Exodus agents, begging money to remove them from their home; especially at a time when every indication favors the position that the wrongs and hardships which they suffer are soon to be redressed?

Besides the objections thus stated, it is manifest that the public and noisy advocacy of a general stampede of the colored people from the South to the North, is necessarily an abandonment of the great and paramount principle of protection to person and property in every State of the Union. It is an evasion of a solemn obligation and duty. The business of this nation is to protect its citizens where they are, not to transport them where they will not need protection. The best that can be said of this exodus in this respect is that it is an attempt to climb up some other than the right way; it is an expedient, a half-way measure, and tends to weaken in the public mind a sense of the absolute right, power and duty of the Government, inasmuch as it concedes, by implication at least, that on the soil of the South, the law of the land cannot command obedience; the ballot box cannot be kept pure; peaceable elections cannot be held; the Constitution cannot be enforced; and the lives and liberties of loyal and peaceable citizens cannot be protected. It is a surrender, a premature, disheartening surrender, since it would make freedom and free institutions depend upon migration rather than protection; by flight, rather than by right; by going into a strange land, rather than by staying in one's own. It leaves the whole question of equal rights on the soil of the South open and still to be settled, with the moral influence of Exodus against us; since it is a confession of the utter impracticability of equal rights and equal protection in any State, where those rights may be struck down by violence.

It does not appear that the friends of freedom should spend either time or talent in furtherance of this Exodus as a desirable measure either for the North or the South; for the blacks of the South or the whites of the North. If the people of this country cannot be protected in every State of this Union, the Government of the United States is shorn of its rightful dignity and power; the late rebellion has triumphed; the sovereignty of the nation is an empty name, and the power and authority in individual States is greater than the power and authority of the United States.

While necessity often compels men to migrate; to leave their old homes and seek new ones; to sever old ties and create new ones; to do this the necessity should be obvious and imperative. It should be a last resort and only adopted after carefully considering what is against the measure as well as what is in favor of it. There are prodigal sons everywhere, who are ready to demand the portion of goods that would fall to them and betake themselves to a strange country. Something is ever lost in the process of migration, and much is sacrificed at home for what is gained abroad. A world of wisdom is in the saying of Mr. [Ralph Waldo] Emerson, "that those who made Rome worth going to stayed there." Three moves from house to house are said to be worse than a fire. That a rolling stone gathers no moss has passed into the world's wisdom. The colored people of the South, just beginning to accumulate a little property, and to lay the foundation of families, should not be in haste to sell that little and be off to the banks of the Mississippi. The habit of roaming from place to place in pursuit of better conditions of existence is by no means a good one. A man should never leave his home for a new one till he has earnestly endeavored to make his immediate surroundings accord with his wishes. The time and energy expended in wandering about from place to place, if employed in making him comfortable where he is, will, in nine cases out of ten, prove the best investment. No people ever did much for themselves or for the world, without the sense and inspiration of native land; of a fixed home; of familiar neighborhood, and common associations. The fact of being to the manor born has an elevating power upon the mind and heart of a man. It is a more cheerful thing to be able to say, "I was born here and know all the people," than to say, "I am a stranger here and know none of the people." It cannot be doubted, that in so far as this Exodus tends to promote restlessness in the colored people of the South, to unsettle their feeling of home and to sacrifice positive advantages where they are, for fancied ones in Kansas or elsewhere, it is an evil. Some have sold their little homes at a sacrifice, their chickens, mules and pigs, to follow the Exodus. Let it be understood that you are going, and you advertise the fact that your mule has lost half his value—for your staying with him makes half his value. Let the colored people of Georgia offer their six millions worth of property for sale, with the purpose to leave Georgia, and they will not realize half its value. Land is not worth much where there are no people to occupy it, and a mule is not worth much where there is no one to use it.

It may safely be asserted that, whether advocated and commended to favor on the ground that it will increase the political power of the Republican party, and thus help to make a solid North against a solid South; or upon the ground that it will increase the power and influence of the colored people as a political element, and enable them the better to protect their rights, and ensure their moral and social elevation, the Exodus will prove a disappointment, a mistake and a failure; because, as to strengthening the Republican party, the emigrants will go only to those States where the Republican party is strong and solid enough already without their votes; and in respect to the other part of the argument, it will fail, because it takes colored voters from a section of the country where they are sufficiently numerous to elect some of their number to places of honor and profit, and places them in a country where their proportion to other classes will be so small as not to be recognized as a political element, or entitled to be represented by one of themselves; and further, because, go where they will, they must, for a time, inevitably carry with them poverty, ignorance and other repulsive incidents inherited from their former conditions as slaves; a circumstance which is about as likely to make votes for Democrats as for Republicans, and to raise up bitter prejudices against them, as to raise up friends for them. No people can be much respected in this country, where all are eligible to office, that cannot point to any one of their class in an honorable, responsible position. In sending a few men to Congress, the Negroes of the South have done much to dispel prejudice and raise themselves in the estimation of the country and the world. By staying where they are, they may be able to send abler, better and more effective representatives of their race to Congress, than it was possible for them to send at first, because of their want of education, and their recent liberation from bondage. In the South the Negro has at least the possibility of power; in the North he has no such possibility, and it is for him to say how well he can afford to part with this possible power.

But another argument in favor of this emigration is, that having a numerical superiority in Mississippi, Louisiana and South Carolina, and thereby possessing the ability to choose some of their own number to represent them in the state and nation, they are necessarily brought into antagonism with the white race, and invite the very political persecution of which they complain. So they are told that the best remedy for this persecution is to surrender the right and advantage given them by the Constitution and the Government, of electing men of color to office. They are not to overcome prejudice and persecution where it is, but to go where it is not; not to stand where they are, and demand the full constitutional protection which the Government is solemnly bound to give, but to go where the protection of the Government is not needed. Plainly enough this is an evasion of a solemn obligation and duty, an attempt to climb up some other way; a half-way measure, a makeshift, a miserable substitution of expediency for right. For an egg, it gives the Negro a stone. The dissemination of this doctrine by the agents of emigration cannot but do the cause of equal rights much harm. It lets the public mind down from the high ground of a great national duty to a miserable compromise, in which wrong surrenders nothing, and right everything. The South is not to repent its crimes, and submit to the Constitution in common with all other parts of the country, but such repentance and submission is to be conveniently made unnecessary by removing the temptation to commit violations of the Law and the Constitution. Men may be pardoned for refusing their assent to a measure supported upon a principle so unsound, subversive and pernicious. The nation should be held steadily to the high and paramount principle, that allegiance and protection are inseparable; that this Government is solemnly bound to protect and defend the lives and liberties of all its citizens, of whatever race or color, or of whatever political or religious opinion, and to do this in every State and territory within the American Union. . . .

Not only is the South the best locality for the Negro on the ground of his political powers and possibilities, but it is best for him as a field of labor. He is there, as he is nowhere else, an absolute necessity. He has a monopoly of the labor market. His labor is

---

I Have Got Nowhere to Go

Often attempting to relocate with little cash and few resources, many Exodusters found themselves in dire straits. Sarah Smith wrote for help to her former employer, a plantation owner who paid for her railroad fare home. This letter and others like it were publicized in southern newspapers in an attempt to discourage black migration.

Mr. S. I. Wooten
Sir: Putnam Co., Indiana, January 5, 1880
I am now in Ind[iana] in the worst fixt I ever was in in all the days of my life. I am out of cloes, and I have not got no where to go and no house to stay in day or night and no boddy wount let me in with them and I have not got nothing to eat and nothing to dow to get not a cents worth for myself nor my children to eat. No boddy wount implore a woman that have childdran and no husband. Brother Allen would let me stay with him but the man that he lives with dont want him to take no orther famly with him and I am a sufren here. Please send me some money to get back with to your plantation and I will work with you till you say you are pa[i]d and never will leave again.
                          Mrs. Sarah Smith

the only labor which can successfully offer itself for sale in that market. This, with a little wisdom and firmness, will enable him to sell his labor there on terms more favorable to himself than he can elsewhere. As there are no competitors or substitutes, he can demand living prices with the certainty that the demand will be complied with. Exodus would deprive him of this advantage. It would take him from a country where the land owners and planters must have his labor, or allow their fields to go untilled and their purses unsupplied with cash; to a country where the land owners are able and proud to do their own work, and do not need to hire hands except for limited periods at certain seasons of the year. The effect of this will be to send the Negro to the towns and cities to compete with white labor. With what result, let the past tell. They will be crowded into lanes and alleys, cellars and garrets, poorly provided with the necessaries of life, and will gradually die out. The Negro . . . is preeminently a Southern man. He is so both in constitution and habits, in body as well as mind. He will not only take with him to the North, Southern modes of labor, but Southern modes of life. The careless and improvident habits of the South cannot be set aside in a generation. If they are adhered to in the North, in the fierce winds and snows of Kansas and Nebraska, the emigration must be large to keep up their numbers. It would appear, therefore, that neither the laws of politics, labor nor climate favor this Exodus. It does not conform to the laws of healthy emigration which proceeds not from South to North, not from heat to cold, but from East to West, and in climates to which the emigrants are more or less adapted and accustomed.

As an assertion of power by a people hitherto held in bitter contempt; as an emphatic and stinging protest against high-handed, greedy and shameless injustice to the weak and defenceless; as a means of opening the blind eyes of oppressors to their folly and peril, the Exodus has done valuable service. Whether it has accomplished all of which it is capable in this particular direction for the present, is a question which may well be considered. With a moderate degree of intelligent leadership among the laboring class at the South, properly handling the justice of their cause, and wisely using the Exodus example, they can easily exact better terms for their labor than ever before. Exodus is medicine, not food; it is for disease, not health; it is not to be taken from choice, but necessity. In anything like a normal condition of things the South is the best place for the Negro. Nowhere else is there for him a promise of a happier future. Let him stay there if he can, and save both the South and himself to civilization. While, however, it may be the highest wisdom under the circumstances for the freedmen to stay where they are, no encouragement should be given to any measures of coercion to keep them there. The

American people are bound, if they are or can be bound to anything, to keep the North gate of the South open to black and white, and to all the people. . . . Woe to the oppressed and destitute of all countries and races if the rich and powerful are to decide when and where they shall go or stay. The deserving hired man gets his wages increased when he can tell his employer that he can get better wages elsewhere. And when all hope is gone from the hearts of the laboring classes of the old world, they can come across the sea to the new. If they could not do that their crushed hearts would break under increasing burdens. The right to emigrate is one of the most useful and precious of all rights. But not only to the oppressed, to the oppressor also, is the free use of this right necessary. To attempt to keep these freedmen in the South, who are spirited enough to undertake the risks and hardships of emigration, would involve great possible danger to all concerned. . . .

It will not be wise for the Southern slaveholders and their successors to shape their policy upon the presumption that the Negro's cowardice or forbearance has no limit. The fever of freedom is already in the Negro's blood. He is not just what he was fourteen years ago. To forcibly dam up the stream of emigration would be a measure of extreme madness as well as oppression. It would be exposing the heart of the oppressor to the pistol and dagger, and his home to fire and pillage. The cry of "Land and Liberty," the watchword of the Nihilistic party in Russia, has a music in it sweet to the ear of all oppressed peoples, and well it shall be for the landholders of the South if they shall learn wisdom in time and adopt such a course of just treatment towards the landless laborers of the South in the future as shall make this popular watchword uncontagious and unknown among their laborers, and further stampede to the North wholly unknown, indescribable and impossible.

VIEWPOINT 4

"This emigration will benefit the Negro, who is now too much inclined to stay where he is put. At the South he never knows his own possibilities."

Blacks Should Leave the South

Richard Theodore Greener (1844-1922)

Richard Theodore Greener was born and educated in the North; in 1870, he became the first black to graduate from Harvard with a Bachelor of Arts degree. Greener held positions as a professor at black universities in both the North and the South, and in 1879 he became dean of the law school of Howard University in Washington, D.C.

Perhaps the most outspoken critic of Frederick Douglass's opposition to the migration (Exodus) of southern blacks to the western states, Greener was scheduled to debate Douglass on the topic at the annual meeting of the American Social Science Association on September 12, 1879. Although Douglass canceled his appearance three days before the conference, his essay criticizing the migration was read to the audience. Afterward, Greener delivered a speech in which he defended the Exodus movement and countered each of Douglass's arguments against it.

Greener points out that migration has been a common occurrence throughout the history of all races, and he reminds his audience that before emancipation many runaway slaves (of whom Douglass was one) left the South in order to better their situation. Conditions in the South are so severe, Greener argues, that the possible risks of migrating are nothing compared to the certain hardships of remaining in the South. Greener further advocates the establishment of fund-raising organizations to aid the Exodusters and prevent fraud.

Excerpted from Richard Theodore Greener, "The Emigration of Colored Citizens from the Southern States," *Journal of Social Science* 11 (May 1880):22-35.

In the mid-1880s, Greener began a law practice and became active in politics, later serving as American consul to Bombay, India, and Vladivostok, Russia.

The land question is no new one; at the present time there are difficulties in England, Ireland, Scotland, and India with regard to this tenure of land; and when we come to study them, we find many cases analogous to those in America. There are remarkable coincidences and wonderful similarities of conditions, complaints and demands, which show conclusively that injustice and wrong, and disregard of rights and abuses of privilege are not confined to any one country, race or class. As a rule, capital takes advantage of the needs of labor. Landlords in every country oppress tenants, and sometimes disregard the welfare of the humbler agricultural laborer. The race in power lords it over the humbler; and if any change takes place from such normal condition, it only comes after a fierce outbreak of pent-up passion, or smouldering fires of wrong; or because some bold champion of the people rises to denounce oppression and demand redress. It has been fourteen years since the Confederacy collapsed, and eleven years since reconstruction. The South has now had for three years home rule, "Autonomy"; and yet, instead of the renewed prosperity, harmony of races, and absence of political violence and lawlessness, which we were promised, we find demoralized credit, shameless repudiation, and organized lawlessness—rendering the condition of the Negro tenant class worse than at any period since slavery. So deplorable and abject indeed is it that expatriation and escape to Liberia [in Africa], or the West, seems the only hope, as it is the continued dream of the Negroes, old and young, in the six Southern States. We are accustomed to blame the Southern whites for the ultimate and approximate causes of this sad state of affairs. They are deeply responsible. I do not hesitate to place upon their shoulders all they deserve; but the North is not wholly innocent. We legislate for the interests of four million blacks just freed from bondage, demoralized by four years of war, and for two million rebellious whites, landless, hopeless, thankful at that time, even if their lives were spared, and we ignore all the precedents of history—the West Indies, Ireland, Russia and Germany. We threw the Negro without anything, the carpet-bagger with his musket, the ex-Confederate disarmed, pell-mell together, and told them to work out the problem.

After the war it was difficult to purchase land because the old master was not disposed to sell. With the downfall of reconstruction a new lease of life was given to Southern barbarity and lawlessness. As usual, the Negro was the principal sufferer. Negro representation went first; next the educational system, which the carpet-bagger had brought to the South, was crippled by insufficient appropriations. Majorities were overcome by shot-gun intimidation, or secretly by the tissue ballot. Radical office-holders were forced to resign, robbed of their property by "due process of law," and driven North. The jury-box and representation the Negro was forced to give up; but after enduring all this, he found himself charged exorbitantly for the most necessary articles of food. His land was rented to him at fabulous prices. His cabin was likely to be raided at any time, whenever capricious lust, or a dreadful thirst for blood was roused. He saw his crop dwindling day by day; he saw himself growing poorer and getting into debt; his labor squandered between exacting landlords and rapacious store-keepers. It was then the Negro resolved to give up the fruitless contest so long and hopelessly waged, and try his fortune in the great West, of which he had heard and read so much during the past ten years. . . .

Benefits of the Exodus

This emigration will benefit the Negro, who is now too much inclined to stay where he is put. At the South he never knows his own possibilities. Then again, the South is a wretched place for any people to develop in, and this is especially true of the Negro; because, like all subject races, he imitates the life about him. The Negro at the South is in a demoralized condition, and no jury will convict for political offences committed against him. . . . District attorneys are appointed at the recommendation of known rebels and sympathizers and assassins. Of course, they will not do their duty; hence, the Negro dares not look for justice in the courts— once proudly called the palladium of English liberty. The use of the military power to enforce any right is repudiated at the North. . . . I need not enumerate the demoralizing features of Southern life, the reckless disregard for human life, the lack of thrift, drinking customs, gaming, horse-racing, etc. The Negro needs contact with all that is healthful and developing in modern civilization, and by emigration the Negro will learn to love thrift, and unlearn many bad habits and improvident notions acquired from preceding generations.

The exclusive devotion of the Negro to the culture of cotton and rice is demoralizing to him. They drag women and children into the field, with no commissioner of labor to look out for outraged childhood and impaired maternity. I do not expect this argument to find favor with those who think the Negro has no other future before him than to cultivate sugar, cotton and rice. On the politico-economic side a partial Exodus will benefit those who remain, by raising the wage fund, increasing the demand, and insuring better treatment to those who are left. . . .

This 1879 illustration by James H. Moser depicts the wharves at Vicksburg, Mississippi, where migrating blacks wait for their northern-bound boats to arrive.

At present the Negro stands in the way of his own advancement, by reason of political fidelity, and the very excess of population, not diminished since the war, and yet not so systematically diffused and employed. Even Senator [Matthew C.] Butler, of South Carolina, says: "We have too much cheap Negro labor in the South." As to wages, the average Negro can earn higher wages and live more comfortably at the North, even if confined to humble employments, than he can at the South. When we add such trifles as protection, school privileges, free suffrage and Christian influences, we transcend the limits of legitimate comparison. . . .

I assume that the predominance of the Negro in politics at the South is gone for a generation at least. The South will not have it and the North has exhibited no very marked disposition to enforce it. If it be ever desirable again, let it come when the children of the present black colonists go back to the mother land, improved in all that makes good citizens by a sojourn in the West.

There are few opponents of the Exodus. Most of them are only negative objectors. The only class positively objecting is the planting class. At Vicksburg, and in Washington County (Miss.), they objected vehemently and loudly. Foreign labor, they say, would cost money. Not one planter in ten is able to make further outlay. During the change of laborers, even, they would go to rack and ruin. The Negro is the only one who can do their work. To go now will ruin the cotton crop, and, hence, affect the North as well as the South.

No one disputes the right of the Negro to go West, now that he is free. We accord to all men the right to improve their condition by change of residence or employment. Nearly all of the objectors, white and black, have grave doubts as to our ability to stand this severe Northern climate. They fear we may not find work adapted to our limited peculiar powers; may not meet with kind friends and genial sympathy. We must endure privations and meet with ostracism at the North. Mechanics will not work with Negroes. The Negro remembers Slavery, Black Codes, Ku-Klux, . . . and says: "My relatives and friends who have gone North since the war tell a different story. They have held no offices, but they are free. They sleep in peace at night; what they earn is paid them, if not, they can appeal to the courts. They vote without fear of the shot-gun, and their children go to school. It is true the Northern people do not love us so well as you did, and hence the intermixture of races is not so promiscuous there as here. This we shall try to endure, if we go North, with patience and Christian resignation. We have never heard of the people at the North paying in ten, twenty-five and fifty cent scrip, payable four years hence, nor charging $2.00 a plug for tobacco, and $2.50 for witnessing a contract. While we may not have so much social equality as with you, we shall have more political equality and man to man justice. You charge $15.00 and $25.00 per acre for worn-out land; we can buy better in Kansas and Nebraska at $2.50 an acre. We had rather die free at the North than live as paupers and pariahs here, only nominally free. You thought Kansas not too cold for us in 1854-5; we are not afraid to try it now."

An Honest Reply

The most important opponent of the Exodus is Marshal Frederick Douglass, my distinguished antagonist in this discussion, who, I sincerely regret, is not here to lend to his able and ingenious argument the magic of his presence and the influence of his eloquent voice. The greatest Negro whom America has produced, having suffered all that our race could endure, and having been elevated higher than any other Negro, he cannot lack sympathy with any movement which concerns his race, and hence, any objection coming from him challenges attention, and demands to be answered. Age, long service, and a naturally keen and analytic mind would presume a soundness of view on almost any topic of national importance or race interest. It is, therefore, with the highest regard for the honesty of Mr. Douglass's views that I venture to reply to some of his objections. . . .

Mr. Douglass's arguments, as I have been able to find them in speeches, resolutions, and the paper just read, are briefly these:

1. Emigration is not the proper nor permanent remedy.

2. The Government ought to protect colored citizens at the South; to encourage emigration gives the government a chance to shirk its duty; while the advocates of the measure leave Equal Rights, Protection and Allegiance open questions.

3. The colored race should be warned against a nomadic life and habits of wandering.

4. African emigration and migration to the West are analogous; the failure of the one is prophetic of the other.

5. The Negro now is potentially able to elect some members of his race at the South to Congress; this is impossible at the North.

6. At the South he has a monopoly of the supply of labor; at the West he would not have it. At the South, land owners must have laborers or starve; Western land owners are independent. . . .

To these objections first, it may be said, no favorer of migration claims it as the sole, proper or only permanent remedy for the aggravated relation of landlord and tenant at the South. It is approved of as one remedy, thus far the most salutary, in stopping lawlessness and exactions. The reciprocity of allegiance and protection is granted; but it is asked, "How can the United States Government protect its black citizens while the fallacy of State rights and undefinable 'home rule' or 'autonomy,' prevent interference?". . . With us, neither Government nor courts may interfere with contracts, either to enforce the terms or insure justice, when the local sentiment is opposed. The Government does not protect the Negro because it finds itself powerless to do so. As a general rule, the Negro may well be warned against a wandering life; but in the present instance such advice is gratuitous.

The failure of the analogy drawn between African colonization and migration to the West may be stated in this way; the one was worked up by slave-owners in the interest of slavery; this one springs spontaneously, according to Mr. Douglass's view, from the class considering itself aggrieved; one led out of the country to a comparative wilderness; the other directs to better land and larger opportunities here at home. The one took the Negro to contend with barbarism. This places him under more civilizing influences than he has ever enjoyed, involving no change of allegiance nor serious differences of climate. If the colored people are "potentially" able to elect one of their own race to Congress, they cannot now make that potentiality possible. Emigration surely cannot lessen the potentiality, since the emigrants will remain citizens. I am inclined to think it will not diminish the probability. If I remember correctly, Massachusetts first elected colored men to her General Court [legislature]; Ohio has nominated one, and Illinois has a colored representative.

Mr. Douglass is rather misleading and fails again in his analogy, when he infers that the Negro must go West as a civilizer or not go at all. He goes out from the house of bondage up from the land of Egypt, directed, I am inclined to think, by the same mighty hand which pointed out the way to Israel. . . .

When Mr. Douglass grants in his paper that if the half is true of what the Negro suffers, the Exodus is justified,—he grants all that any advocate of it asks. It is from causes, which he condemns, denounces, deplores and considers disgraceful, that we say, "emigrate, and if you can, better your condition."

The Exodus is complained of as a "policy." We might answer, it is a result, not a policy in the ordinary sense, although, as a safe check to certain ulterior causes, we might well commend it to oppressed people anywhere as a measure of policy.

Misery

We are told, aphoristically, that the Negro's labor made him free, and therefore, it can make him "free, comfortable, and independent." The assumed fact is not exactly clear, and the conclusion is scarcely warranted by the Negro's statements of his condition, according to Mr. Douglass. . . .

In short, Mr. Douglass grants the Negro's misery, but tells him to wait, his present state is "exceptional and transient," his rights "will revive, survive and flourish"; but the poor frightened, half-starved Negroes, crouching along the Mississippi, fear this will not happen until they have literally passed over. Mr. Douglass is not willing to have Congress nor capitalists help these houseless wanderers, to whom we gave nothing when we freed them. We did better than that by fugitives forty years ago, and I see no good reason why Northern philanthropy should close its hand and ears now to a cry which is as despairing as that which rang from Ireland in 1848 [the potato famine], or from the yellow fever sufferers, a twelvemonth ago. We see capital employed to build better houses for the poor, to transport young children to the West; why shall we not try to help those who are trying as best they may to help themselves? The statement that Massachusetts was once Mississippi, is a favorite one of Mr. Douglass, and has been reiterated so often as to lead the unwary to believe that the Marshal of the District of Columbia thinks it true. I am more inclined to ascribe it to the orator's love of antithesis; so incorrect, so unjust, and for Frederick Douglass, so unkind would such a remark be.

To say to the emigrants, "Better stay than go," is analogous to

229

saying "Be ye warmed and filled, notwithstanding ye give not those things which are needful for the body." Nor do proverbs add protection to the one argument any more than food and raiment to the other.

Better Living

Roseline Cunningham was a black teacher in Mississippi. In 1879, she wrote the governor of Kansas, John D. St. John, to inquire about relocating to his state.

Governor John D. St. John   Clay County, Mississippi
Respected sir: June 18, 1879
I write a few lines to you for information about our emigrating to your state next fall. We are hard working people but can not reap the benefit of our labor. I went to the State of Ohio in 1877 [and] found there is better living in a grain fruits and stock growing state than in a cotton growing one. Rev. Ephraim Strong my brother served in united states army three years during the war of 1861 and was honorable discharged at its close desired me to write to you for information. We wants to know if we can get any assistance from the government or any society to emigrate to Kansas. We have seen some papers from there and feel if we could get there we could make a better support.
I have been teaching public schools in the districts ever since they began in Miss[issippi] in 1871. When the republican laws rule the state I made right good support at it but since the democratic power has got in we can scarcely board and clothes ourselves. All the people in district I taught are wanting to emigrate to Kansas this fall if they can get assistance from any quarter. If I can get information from you that I can get in any business or a support and get assistance to get there my brother father and husband and I am coming. [A] great many desired me to Write to Kansas for information. I see . . . that you have a freedmen aid society thinking perhaps we could get assistance from it. Please answer our letter and let us know if you can aid us. By doing so you will [aid us] and a great many more and we will be grateful in our hearts. Your humble obedient and grateful Servant
Roseline Cunningham

The Exodus may be a failure and a mistake, but whether it is or not, it has no connection with the power of the Republican party, or the retention of political power by the Negro. Both may be benefited, and it may fail; both may be injured by it, and it may nevertheless succeed. This is a specimen *non sequitur*, very familiar in arguments against the present migration.
We are assured that there will be misery and want resulting from

this "ill-timed" movement. Doubtless there will be; every movement having in it the elements of good, has brought some hardship. . . . The crucial test, however, is whether there will be more misery and want by migrating than by remaining; we think not. . . .

The western lands are waiting for settlers, and are being rapidly filled up by Swedes, Norwegians, Mennonites, Icelanders and Poles, why should not the Negro participate? Six hundred thousand acres of public land have been taken up since June 30, 1878; 50,000 families have gone westward under the homestead law, exclusive of those who have small sums to invest. Why shall we debar the Negro? Irish Catholics have raised a fund of $100,000 to assist their poor from the large cities. The Hebrews have also an excellent association for the same purpose. These aid societies hold meetings and solicit funds. No one denounces them or impugns the motives of their advocates. What will benefit Irish, Hebrew, Swede, and Norwegian, cannot be decidedly injurious to the colored race alone. . . .

Emigration is no new thing. . . . It began in 1840 and has kept up ever since. You may remember some of the old pictures of the emigrant with bundle on his shoulder [i.e., runaway slaves]. He went alone formerly, and was often taken back at the Government's expense; now he takes his family, and cannot be taken back against his will. In Kansas there are now five or six colonies, some of them established since 1870; Baxter Springs, Nicodemus, Morton City, and Singleton. The reports from all are favorable. The people are said to be thrifty, intelligent and willing to work. All are paying for their land by instalments, at prices from $1.25 to $6.00 per acre. If, dissatisfied with Kansas, they wish to "move on," no one interferes with them. Mississippi, in spite of her Constitution, which says, "No citizen shall be prevented from emigrating on any pretence whatever," attempts to keep them back by libelling the steamboats for carrying excessive numbers. The Negroes are also detained by writs gotten up on spurious charges. In short, the Southern landlord now demands more than the lord paramount in the middle ages; the tenant must be a permanent fixture to the land. Georgia and South Carolina . . . sell idle vagrants, or farm them out to service in gangs, as their prejudice dictates.

We are told it is a political scheme. To insure success as a political movement, 60,000 colored voters should be distributed in certain States before November, 1879, the end of the period allowed for legal residence. If the Exodus were promoted by politicians, we should find 20,000 Negroes going to Pennsylvania, 20,000 to New Jersey, 10,000 at least to New York, the same number for Indiana, and a spare 5,000 for Connecticut. This could not be done under $2,000,000, even had it begun six months ago. Thus far at the North, not $20,000 has been raised to help the refugees, notwithstanding $100,000,000 would not be idly spent to help the Negro and end this vexed question. It is estimated that 15,000 have gone West within eight months; 150 leave New Orleans each week. All are not going to Kansas. Many are wisely pushing farther North. As a class, they differ from the West India Negroes after their emancipation. The Southern Negro did not relapse into barbarism; he manifests a disposition and an adaptability to work. That he is industrious is shown by the immense cotton crop, just reported as contributing to the exportable products of the nation, $189,000,000 per annum.

No view of the movement would be complete which did not notice the relation of the colored people of the country to this flight from oppression. The first stage is passed, the appeal to white philanthropists. My notion is the second is here, the appeal to ourselves. We must organize societies, contribute our dimes, and form a network of communication between the South and every principal point North and West. We should raise $200,000 to form a company; we should have a National Executive Committee, and have agents to buy land, procure cheap transportation, disseminate accurate information, and see to it that they are neither deluded nor defrauded. Such an organization, working through our churches and benevolent societies, would do more to develop our race than all the philanthropic measures designed to aid us since the war.

Growth of the Exodus

The little rill has started on its course toward the great sea of humanity. It moves slowly on by virtue of the eternal law of gravitation, which leads peoples and individuals toward peace, protection and happiness. Today it is a slender thread and makes way with difficulty amid the rocks and tangled growth; but it has already burst through serious impediments, showing itself possessed of a mighty current. It started in Mississippi, but it is even now being rapidly fed by other rills and streams from the territory through which it flows. Believing that it comes from God, and feeling convinced that it bears only blessings in its course for that race so long tossed, so ill-treated, so sadly misunderstood, I greet its tiny line, and almost see in the near future its magnificent broad bosom, bearing proudly onward, until at last, like the travel-worn and battle-scarred Greeks of old, there bursts upon its sight the sea, the broad sea of universal freedom and protection.

VIEWPOINT 5

"When a man has emerged from slavery . . . there must be some stage . . . when he takes the rank of a mere citizen, and ceases to be the special favorite of the laws."

The Civil Rights Act of 1875 Is Unconstitutional

Joseph P. Bradley (1813-1892)

A Republican lawyer from New Jersey, Joseph P. Bradley was appointed as an associate justice of the Supreme Court in 1870 by President Ulysses S. Grant. Bradley played a significant role in the Compromise of 1877; as the last appointee to the commission that decided the result of the disputed election, Bradley entered several tie-breaking votes in favor of Rutherford B. Hayes.

In 1883, the Supreme Court heard several suits alleging violations of the Civil Rights Act of 1875, which prohibited racial discrimination in hotels, restaurants, theaters, and public transportation. After consideration of the cases, the Court declared the first two sections of the Civil Rights Act of 1875 unconstitutional on the grounds that the provisions were not authorized by either the Thirteenth or Fourteenth Amendments. Bradley explained the judgment of the Court in the majority opinion, which was handed down on October 15, 1883. The Thirteenth and Fourteenth Amendments, Bradley concedes, do give the federal government the power to protect all individuals from federal and state infringement of their civil rights. However, he argues, the amendments do not give the federal government jurisdiction over discrimination committed by private individuals or organizations. Rather, it is the state governments that hold this jurisdiction, Bradley concludes. This judgment set the tone for later Supreme Court decisions that upheld and extended the policy of racial segregation.

Excerpted from the majority opinion in *Declaring the Unconstitutionality of Section 1 and 2 of the Civil Rights Act of March 1, 1875, as Applied to the Several States*, 109 U.S. (1883).

These cases are all founded on the first and second sections of the act of Congress known as the Civil Rights Act, passed March 1st, 1875, entitled "An act to protect all citizens in their civil and legal rights." (18 Stat. 335.) Two of the cases, those against Stanley and Nichols, are indictments for denying to persons of color the accommodations and privileges of an inn or hotel, two of them, those against Ryan and Singleton, are, one an information, the other an indictment, for denying to individuals the privileges and accommodations of a theatre. . . . The case of Robinson and wife against the Memphis & Charleston R.R. Company was an action brought in the Circuit Court of the United States for the Western District of Tennessee, to recover the penalty of five hundred dollars given by the second section of the act; and the gravamen was the refusal by the conductor of the railroad company to allow the wife to ride in the ladies' car, for the reason, as stated in one of the counts, that she was a person of African descent. . . .

It is obvious that the primary and important question in all the cases, is the constitutionality of the law: for if the law is unconstitutional none of the prosecutions can stand. . . .

The Civil Rights Act

The essence of the law is, not to declare broadly that all persons shall be entitled to the full and equal enjoyment of the accommodations, advantages, facilities, and privileges of inns, public conveyances, and theatres; but that such enjoyment shall not be subject to any conditions applicable only to citizens of a particular race or color, or who had been in a previous condition of servitude. In other words, it is the purpose of the law to declare that, in the enjoyment of the accommodations and privileges of inns, public conveyances, theatres, and other places of public amusement, no distinction shall be made between citizens of different race or color, or between those who have, and those who have not, been slaves. Its effect is to declare, that in all inns, public conveyances, and places of amusement, colored citizens, whether formerly slaves or not, and citizens of other races, shall have the same accommodations and privileges in all inns, public conveyances, and places of amusement as are enjoyed by white citizens; and *vice versa*. The second section makes it a penal offence in any person to deny to any citizen of any race or color, regardless of previous servitude, any of the accommodations or privileges mentioned in the first section.

Has Congress constitutional power to make such a law? Of course, no one will contend that the power to pass it was contained in the Constitution before the adoption of the last three amendments. The power is sought, first, in the Fourteenth Amendment, and the views and arguments of distinguished Senators, advanced whilst the law was under consideration, claiming authority to pass it by virtue of that amendment, are the principal arguments adduced in favor of the power. We have carefully considered those arguments, as was due to the eminent ability of those who put them forward, and have felt, in all its force, the weight of authority which always invests a law that Congress deems itself competent to pass. But the responsibility of an independent judgment is now thrown upon this court; and we are bound to exercise it according to the best lights we have.

The Civil Rights Act of 1875

The first two sections of the Civil Rights Act of 1875 banned racial discrimination in public establishments and set penalties for any violation of its provisions.

Be it enacted by the Senate and House of Representatives of the United States of America in Congress assembled, That all persons within the jurisdiction of the United States shall be entitled to the full and equal enjoyment of the accommodations, advantages, facilities, and privileges of inns, public conveyances on land or water, theaters, and other places of public amusement; subject only to the conditions and limitations established by law, and applicable alike to citizens of every race and color, regardless of any previous condition of servitude.

SEC. 2. That any person who shall violate the foregoing section by denying to any citizen, except for reasons by law applicable to citizens of every race and color, and regardless of any previous condition of servitude, the full enjoyment of any of the accommodations, advantages, facilities, or privileges in said section enumerated, or by aiding or inciting such denial, shall, for every such offense, forfeit and pay the sum of five hundred dollars to the person aggrieved thereby, to be recovered in an action of debt, with full costs; and shall also, for every such offense, be deemed guilty of a misdemeanor, and, upon conviction thereof, shall be fined not less than five hundred nor more than one thousand dollars, or shall be imprisoned not less than thirty days nor more than one year.

The first section of the Fourteenth Amendment (which is the one relied on), after declaring who shall be citizens of the United States, and of the several states, is prohibitory in its character, and prohibitory upon the states. It declares that "no state shall make or enforce any law which shall abridge the privileges or immunities of citizens of the United States; nor shall any state deprive any person of life, liberty or property without due process of law;

nor deny to any person within its jurisdiction the equal protection of the laws." It is state action of a particular character that is prohibited. Individual rights is not the subject-matter of the amendment. It has a deeper and broader scope. It nullifies and makes void all state legislation, and state action of every kind, which impairs the privileges and immunities of citizens of the United States, or which injures them in life, liberty or property without due process of law, or which denies to any of them the equal protection of the laws. It not only does this, but, in order that the national will, thus declared, may not he a mere *brutum fulmen* [futile display], the last section of the amendment invests Congress with power to enforce it by appropriate legislation. To enforce what? To enforce the prohibition. To adopt appropriate legislation for correcting the effects of such prohibited state laws and state acts, and thus to render them effectually null, void and innocuous. This is the legislative power conferred upon Congress and this is the whole of it. It does not invest Congress with power to legislate upon subjects which are within the domain of state legislation; but to provide modes of relief against state legislation, or state action, of the kind referred to. It does not authorize Congress to create a code of municipal law for the regulation of private rights; but to provide modes of redress against the operation of state laws, and the action of state officers, executive or judicial, when these are subversive of the fundamental rights specified in the amendment. Positive rights and privileges are undoubtedly secured by the Fourteenth Amendment; but they are secured by way of prohibition against state laws and state proceedings affecting those rights and privileges, and by power given to Congress to legislate for the purpose of carrying such prohibition into effect: and such legislation must necessarily be predicated upon such supposed state laws or state proceedings, and be directed to the correction of their operation and effect. . . .

And so in the present case, until some state law has been passed, or some state action through its officers or agents has been taken, adverse to the rights of citizens sought to be protected by the Fourteenth Amendment, no legislation of the United States under said amendment, nor any proceedings under such legislation, can be called into activity: for the prohibitions of the amendment are against state laws and acts done under state authority. Of course, legislation may, and should be, provided in advance to meet the exigency when it arises; but it should be adapted to the mischief and wrong which the amendment was intended to provide against; and that is, state laws, or state action of some kind, adverse to the rights of the citizen secured by the amendment. Such legislation cannot properly cover the whole domain of rights appertaining to life, liberty and property, defining them and providing for their vindication. That would be to establish a code of municipal law regulative of all private rights between man and man in society. It would be to make Congress take the place of the state legislatures, and to supersede them. It is absurd to affirm that, because the rights of life, liberty and property (which include all civil rights that men have), are by the amendment sought to be protected against invasion on the part of the state without due process of law, Congress may therefore provide due process of law for their vindication in every case; and that, because the denial by a state to any persons, of the equal protection of the laws, is prohibited by the amendment, therefore Congress may establish laws for their equal protection. In fine, the legislation which Congress is authorized to adopt in this behalf is not general legislation upon the rights of the citizen, but corrective legislation—that is, such as may be necessary and proper for counteracting such laws as the states may adopt or enforce, and which, by the amendment, they are prohibited from making or enforcing, or such acts and proceedings as the states may commit or take, and which, by the amendment, they are prohibited from committing or taking. . . .

An inspection of the law shows that it makes no reference whatever to any supposed or apprehended violation of the Fourteenth Amendment on the part of the states. It is not predicated on any such view. It proceeds *ex directo* [directly] to declare that certain acts committed by individuals shall be deemed offences, and shall be prosecuted and punished by proceedings in the courts of the United States. It does not profess to be corrective of any constitutional wrong committed by the states; it does not make its operation to depend upon any such wrong committed. It applies equally to cases arising in states which have the justest laws respecting the personal rights of citizens, and whose authorities are ever ready to enforce such laws, as to those which arise in states that may have violated the prohibition of the amendment. In other words, it steps into the domain of local jurisprudence, and lays down rules for the conduct of individuals in society towards each other, and imposes sanctions for the enforcement of those rules, without referring in any manner to any supposed action of the state or its authorities.

Limits

If this legislation is appropriate for enforcing the prohibitions of the amendment, it is difficult to see where it is to stop. Why may not Congress with equal show of authority enact a code of laws for the enforcement and vindication of all rights of life, liberty, and property? If it is supposable that the states may deprive persons of life, liberty, and property without due process of law (and the amendment itself does suppose this), why should not Congress proceed at once to prescribe due process of law for the protection of every one of these fundamental rights in every possible case, as well as to prescribe equal privileges in inns, public conveyances, and theatres? The truth is, that the implication of a power to legislate in this manner is based upon the assumption that if the states are forbidden to legislate or act in a particular way on a particular subject, and power is conferred upon Congress to enforce the prohibition, this gives Congress power to legislate generally upon that subject, and not merely power to provide modes of redress against such state legislation or action. The assumption is certainly unsound. It is repugnant to the Tenth Amendment of the Constitution, which declares that powers not delegated to the United States by the Constitution, nor prohibited by it to the states, are reserved to the states respectively or to the people. . . .

In this connection it is proper to state that civil rights, such as are guaranteed by the Constitution against State aggression, cannot be impaired by the wrongful acts of individuals, unsupported by state authority in the shape of laws, customs, or judicial or executive proceedings. The wrongful act of an individual, unsupported by any such authority, is simply a private wrong, or a crime of that individual; an invasion of the rights of the injured party, it is true, whether they affect his person, his property, or his reputation; but if not sanctioned in some way by the State, or not done under State authority, his rights remain in full force, and may presumably be vindicated by resort to the laws of the State for redress. An individual cannot deprive a man of his right to vote, to hold property, to buy and to sell, to sue in the courts, or to be a witness or a juror; he may, by force or fraud, interfere with the enjoyment of the right in a particular case; he may commit an assault against the person, or commit murder, or use ruffian violence at the polls, or slander the good name of a fellow citizen; but, unless protected in these wrongful acts by some shield of state law or State authority, he cannot destroy or injure the right; he will only render himself amenable to satisfaction or punishment; and amenable therefor to the laws of the State where the wrongful acts are committed. Hence, in all those cases where the Constitution seeks to protect the rights of the citizen against discriminative and unjust laws of the State by prohibiting such laws, it is not individual offences, but abrogation and denial of rights, which it denounces, and for which it clothes the Congress with power to provide a remedy. This abrogation and denial of rights, for which the States alone were or could be responsible, was the great seminal and fundamental wrong which was intended to be remedied. And the remedy to be provided must necessarily be predicated upon that wrong. It must assume that in the cases pro-

Separate but Equal

After the Supreme Court ruled the Civil Rights Act of 1875 unconstitutional, southern states began to establish a system of segregation. This July 9, 1890, editorial from the New Orleans Times Democrat *advocates a bill that would establish segregated public transportation. Although at the time of this editorial the bill had failed to pass the Louisiana Senate, it was reconsidered and became law within the month.*

The bill providing separate cars for white and colored people failed to pass the [Louisiana State] Senate yesterday in consequence of a lack of three votes. This is greatly to be regretted. . . .

The Southern whites, in no spirit of hostility to the negroes, have insisted that the two races shall live separate and distinct from each other in all things, with separate schools, separate hotels and separate cars. They would rise to-morrow against the proposition to educate the white and black children together; and they resist any intercourse in theatre, hotel or elsewhere that will bring the race into anything like social intercourse. The quarter of a century that has passed since the war has not diminished in the slightest degree the determination of the whites to prevent any such dangerous doctrine as social equality, even in the mildest form. . . .

It is not proposed to refuse the negroes any right to which they are entitled. They are to have the same kind of cars, but separate ones. The man who believes that the white race should be kept pure from African taint will vote against that commingling of the races inevitable in a "mixed car" and which must have bad results.

The matter comes up again before the Senate. Let it consider well over it and do as the Legislatures of Texas, Mississippi and other Southern States have done.

vided for, the evil or wrong actually committed rests upon some State law or State authority for its excuse and perpetration. . . .

If the principles of interpretation which we have laid down are correct, as we deem them to be, . . . it is clear that the law in question cannot be sustained by any grant of legislative power made to Congress by the Fourteenth Amendment. That amendment prohibits the States from denying to any person the equal protection of the laws, and declares that Congress shall have power to enforce, by appropriate legislation, the provisions of the amendment. The law in question, without any reference to adverse State legislation on the subject, declares that all persons shall be entitled to equal accommodations and privileges of inns, public conveyances, and places of public amusement, and imposes a penalty upon any individual who shall deny to any citizen such equal accommodations and privileges. This is not corrective legislation; it is primary and direct; it takes immediate and absolute possession of the subject of the right of admission to inns, public conveyances, and places of amusement. It supersedes and displaces State legislation on the same subject, or only allows it permissive force. It ignores such legislation, and assumes that the matter is one that belongs to the domain of national regulation. Whether it would not have been a more effective protection of the rights of citizens to have clothed Congress with plenary power over the whole subject, is not now the question. What we have to decide is, whether such plenary power has been conferred upon Congress by the Fourteenth Amendment; and, in our judgment, it has not. . . .

The Thirteenth Amendment

[T]he power of Congress to adopt direct and primary, as distinguished from corrective legislation on the subject in hand, is sought, in the second place, from the Thirteenth Amendment, which abolishes slavery. This amendment declares "that neither slavery, nor involuntary servitude, except as a punishment for crime, whereof the party shall have been duly convicted, shall exist within the United States, or any place subject to their jurisdiction;" and it gives Congress power to enforce the amendment by appropriate legislation.

This amendment, as well as the Fourteenth, is undoubtedly self-executing without any ancillary legislation, so far as its terms are applicable to any existing state of circumstances. By its own unaided force and effect it abolished slavery, and established universal freedom. Still, legislation may be necessary and proper to meet all the various cases and circumstances to be affected by it, and to prescribe proper modes of redress for its violation in letter or spirit. And such legislation may be primary and direct in its character; for the amendment is not a mere prohibition of State laws establishing or upholding slavery, but an absolute declaration that slavery or involuntary servitude shall not exist in any part of the United States.

It is true, that slavery cannot exist without law, any more than property in lands and goods can exist without law: and, therefore, the Thirteenth Amendment may be regarded as nullifying all State laws which establish or uphold slavery. But it has a reflex character also, establishing and decreeing universal civil and political freedom throughout the United States; and it is assumed, that the power vested in Congress to enforce the article by appropriate legislation, clothes Congress with power to pass all laws necessary and proper for abolishing all badges and incidents of slavery in the United States: and upon this assumption it is claimed, that this is sufficient authority for declaring by law that all persons shall have equal accommodations and privileges in all inns, public conveyances, and places of public amusement; the argument being, that the denial of such equal accommodations and privileges is, in itself, a subjection to a species of servitude within the meaning of the amendment. Conceding the major proposition to be true, that Congress has a right to enact all necessary and proper laws for the obliteration and prevention of slavery with all its badges and incidents, is the minor proposition also true, that the denial to any person of admission to the accommodations and privileges of an inn, a public conveyance, or a theatre, does subject that person to any form of servitude, or tend to fasten upon him any badge of slavery? If it does not, then power to pass the law is not found in the Thirteenth Amendment. . . .

[I]s there any similarity between such servitudes and a denial by the owner of an inn, a public conveyance, or a theatre, of its accommodations and privileges to an individual, even though the denial be founded on the race or color of that individual? Where does any slavery or servitude, or badge of either, arise from such an act of denial? Whether it might not be a denial of a right which if sanctioned by the State law, would be obnoxious to the prohibitions of the Fourteenth Amendment, is another question. But what has it to do with the question of slavery?

It may be that by the black code (as it was called), in the times when slavery prevailed, the proprietors of inns and public conveyances were forbidden to receive persons of the African race, because it might assist slaves to escape from the control of their masters. This was merely a means of preventing such escapes, and was no part of the servitude itself. A law of that kind could not have any such object now, however justly it might be deemed an invasion of the party's legal right as a citizen, and amenable to the prohibitions of the Fourteenth Amendment. . . .

We must not forget that the province and scope of the Thirteenth and Fourteenth Amendments are different; the former simply abolished slavery: the latter prohibited the states from abridging the privileges or immunities of citizens of the United States, from depriving them of life, liberty, or property without due process of law, and from denying to any the equal protection of the laws. The amendments are different, and the powers of Congress under them are different. What Congress has power to do under one, it may not have power to do under the other. Under the Thirteenth Amendment, it has only to do with slavery and its incidents. Under the Fourteenth Amendment, it has power to counteract and render nugatory all state laws and proceedings which have the effect to abridge any of the privileges or immunities of citizens of the United States, or to deprive them of life, liberty, or property, without due process of law, or to deny to any of them the equal protection of the laws. Under the Thirteenth Amendment, the legislation, so far as necessary or proper to eradicate all forms and incidents of slavery and involuntary servitude, may be direct and primary, operating upon the acts of individuals, whether sanctioned by state legislation or not; under the Fourteenth, as we have already shown, it must necessarily be, and can only be, corrective in its character, addressed to counteract and afford relief against state regulations or proceedings.

Servitude

The only question under the present head, therefore, is, whether the refusal to any persons of the accommodations of an inn, or a public conveyance, or a place of public amusement, by an individual, and without any sanction or support from any state law or regulation, does inflict upon such persons any manner of servitude, or form of slavery, as those terms are understood in this country? Many wrongs may be obnoxious to the prohibitions of the Fourteenth Amendment, which are not, in any just sense, incidents or elements of slavery. Such, for example, would be the taking of private property without due process of law; or allowing persons who have committed certain crimes (horse stealing, for example), to be seized and hung by the *posse comitatus* without regular trial; or denying to any person, or class of persons, the right to pursue any peaceful avocations allowed to others. What is called class legislation would belong to this category, and would be obnoxious to the prohibitions of the Fourteenth Amendment, but would not necessarily be so to the Thirteenth, when not involving the idea of any subjection of one man to another. The Thirteenth Amendment has respect, not to distinctions of race, or class, or color, but to slavery. The Fourteenth Amendment extends its protection to races and classes, and prohibits any state legislation which has the effect of denying to any race or class, or to any individual, the equal protection of the laws.

Now, conceding, for the sake of the argument, that the admission to an inn, a public conveyance, or a place of public amusement, on equal terms with all other citizens, is the right of every man and all classes of men, is it any more than one of those rights which the states by the Fourteenth Amendment are forbidden to deny to any person? And is the Constitution violated until the denial of the right has some state sanction or authority? Can the act of a mere individual, the owner of the inn, the public conveyance or place of amusement, refusing the accommodation, be justly regarded as imposing any badge of slavery or servitude upon the applicant, or only as inflicting an ordinary civil injury, properly cognizable by the laws of the state, and presumably subject to redress by those laws until the contrary appears?

After giving to these questions all the consideration which their importance demands, we are forced to the conclusion that such an act of refusal has nothing to do with slavery or involuntary servitude, and that if it is violative of any right of the party, his redress is to be sought under the laws of the state; or if those laws are adverse to his rights and do not protect him, his remedy will be found in the corrective legislation which Congress has adopted, or may adopt, for counteracting the effect of state laws, or state action, prohibited by the Fourteenth Amendment. It would be running the slavery argument into the ground to make it apply to every act of discrimination which a person may see fit to make as to the guests he will entertain, or as to the people he will take into his coach or cab or car, or admit to his concert or theatre, or deal with in other matters of intercourse or business. Innkeepers and public carriers, by the laws of all the states, so far as we are aware, are bound, to the extent of their facilities, to furnish proper accommodation to all unobjectionable persons who in good faith apply for them. If the laws themselves make any unjust discrimination, amenable to the prohibitions of the Fourteenth Amendment, Congress has full power to afford a remedy under that amendment and in accordance with it.

When a man has emerged from slavery, and by the aid of beneficent legislation has shaken off the inseparable concomitants of that state, there must be some stage in the progress of his elevation when he takes the rank of a mere citizen, and ceases to be the special favorite of the laws, and when his rights as a citizen, or a man, are to be protected in the ordinary modes by which other men's rights are protected. There were thousands of free colored people in this country before the abolition of slavery, enjoying all the essential rights of life, liberty and property, the same as white citizens; yet no one, at that time, thought that it was any invasion of their personal status as freemen because they were not admitted to all the privileges enjoyed by white citizens, or because they were subjected to discriminations in the enjoyment of accommodations in inns, public conveyances and places of amusement. Mere discriminations on account of race or color were not regarded as badges of slavery. If, since that time the enjoyment of equal rights in all the respects has become established by constitutional enactment, it is not by force of the Thirteenth Amendment, (which merely abolishes slavery,) but by force of the Fourteenth and Fifteenth Amendments.

On the whole we are of opinion that no countenance of authority for the passage of the law in question can be found in either the Thirteenth or Fourteenth Amendment of the Constitution; and no other ground of authority for its passage being suggested, it must necessarily be declared void, at least so far as its operation in the several States is concerned.

"It is . . . scarcely just to say that the colored race has been the special favorite of the laws. The statute of 1875 . . . is for the benefit of citizens of every race and color."

The Civil Rights Act of 1875 Is Constitutional

John Marshall Harlan (1833-1911)

John Marshall Harlan, a lawyer from Kentucky, fought in the Union Army during the Civil War, but he supported slavery and opposed the Emancipation Proclamation. During 1864, Harlan campaigned against the Thirteenth Amendment and the reelection of President Abraham Lincoln. In the 1870s, however, Harlan became dedicated to civil rights, in part because of his dismay over the widespread violence against southern blacks. Appointed to the U.S. Supreme Court by President Rutherford B. Hayes in 1877, Harlan was often the only liberal voice in the Court during his 34-year tenure.

The following viewpoint contains excerpts from Harlan's October 15, 1883, dissent in the Civil Rights cases, in which he supports the constitutionality of the Civil Rights Act of 1875. Harlan maintains that the Thirteenth and Fourteenth Amendments do grant Congress the power to protect citizens against the deprivation of their civil rights because of their race, even when those rights are infringed upon by a single individual. While Harlan acknowledges that innkeepers, theater owners, and the like have the right to refuse patrons who might be unruly or otherwise unacceptable, he insists that no one has the right to deny service to a person on the basis of race or color. Although the Supreme Court ruling held during his lifetime, Harlan's arguments in this dissent and others provided the basis for much of the civil rights reform enacted in the 1960s.

Excerpted from the dissenting opinion in *Declaring the Unconstitutionality of Section 1 and 2 of the Civil Rights Act of March 1, 1875, as Applied to the Several States*, 109 U.S. (1883).

The opinion in these cases proceeds, it seems to me, upon grounds entirely too narrow and artificial. I cannot resist the conclusion that the substance and spirit of the recent amendments of the Constitution have been sacrificed by a subtle and ingenious verbal criticism. "It is not the words of the law but the internal sense of it that makes the law: the letter of the law is the body; the sense and reason of the law is the soul." Constitutional provisions, adopted in the interest of liberty, and for the purpose of securing, through national legislation, if need be, rights inhering in a state of freedom, and belonging to American citizenship, have been so construed as to defeat the ends the people desired to accomplish, which they attempted to accomplish, and which they supposed they had accomplished by changes in their fundamental law. By this I do not mean that the determination of these cases should have been materially controlled by considerations of mere expediency or policy. I mean only, in this form, to express an earnest conviction that the court has departed from the familiar rule requiring, in the interpretation of constitutional provisions, that full effect be given to the intent with which they were adopted.

Discrimination

The purpose of the first section of the act of Congress of March 1, 1875, was to prevent *race* discrimination in respect of the accommodations and facilities of inns, public conveyances, and places of public amusement. It does not assume to define the general conditions and limitations under which inns, public conveyances, and places of public amusement may be conducted, but only declares that such conditions and limitations, whatever they may be, shall not be applied so as to work a discrimination solely because of race, color, or previous condition of servitude. The second section provides a penalty against any one denying, or aiding or inciting the denial, to any citizen, of that equality of right given by the first section, except for reasons by law applicable to citizens of every race or color and regardless of any previous condition of servitude.

There seems to be no substantial difference between my brethren and myself as to the purpose of Congress; for, they say that the essence of the law is, not to declare broadly that all persons shall be entitled to the full and equal enjoyment of the accommodations, advantages, facilities, and privileges of inns, public conveyances, and theatres; but that such enjoyment shall not be subject to conditions applicable only to citizens of a particular race or color, or who had been in a previous condition of servitude. The effect of the statute, the court says, is, that colored citizens, whether formerly slaves or not, and citizens of other races, shall have the same accommodations and privileges in all inns, public conveyances, and places of amusement as are enjoyed by white persons; and *vice versa*.

The court adjudges, I think erroneously, that Congress is without power, under either the Thirteenth or Fourteenth Amendment, to establish such regulations, and that the first and second sections of the statute are, in all their parts, unconstitutional and void. . . .

Agitate for Our Rights

On October 22, 1883, in Washington, D.C., the Civil Rights Mass Meeting adopted resolutions in response to the Supreme Court's decision that invalidated the Civil Rights Act of 1875.

Whereas, The Supreme Court of the United States has solemnly declared its opinion that the Congressional Enactment known as the Civil Rights Law, of February 27, 1875, is not in accordance with the United States Constitution, and is consequently inoperative as a measure for the protection of the Negro in his manhood rights; and whereas, the customs and traditions of many of the States in the Union are inimical to the Negro as a man and a citizen, and he finds neither in the common law nor in the sentiments of his white fellow citizen that full protection which he has earned by his loyalty and devotion to the Nation in its hour of extreme peril; and whereas, it is our duty as good, law abiding citizens, to respect the decisions of the Courts as to the validity of the laws upon which they are called to pass judgment, therefore, be it

Resolved, That words of indignation or disrespect aimed at the Supreme Court of the United States would not only be useless as a means for securing our main object—namely, the protection due to our manhood and citizenship—but, on the contrary, would tend to alienate our friends and all who have faith in the honesty and integrity of that august and learned tribunal. . . .

Resolved, That we invite the co-operation of all good men and women in securing such legislation as may be necessary to complete our freedom, and that we advise the immediate organization of civil rights associations through the country, through which proper agitation and earnest work for our cause may be inaugurated and carried out.

The Thirteenth Amendment, it is conceded, did something more than to prohibit slavery as an *institution*, resting upon distinctions of race, and upheld by positive law. My brethren admit that it established and decreed universal *civil freedom* throughout the United States. But did the freedom thus established involve nothing more than exemption from actual slavery? Was nothing more intended than to forbid one man from owning another as property? Was it the purpose of the nation simply to destroy the institution, and then remit the race, theretofore held in bondage, to the several States for such protection, in their civil rights, necessarily growing out of freedom, as those States, in their discretion, might choose to provide? Were the States against whose protest the institution was destroyed, to be left free, so far as national interference was concerned, to make or allow discriminations against that race, as such, in the enjoyment of those fundamental rights which by universal concession, inhere in a state of freedom? . . .

That there are burdens and disabilities which constitute badges of slavery and servitude, and that the power to enforce by appropriate legislation the Thirteenth Amendment may be exerted by legislation of a direct and primary character, for the eradication, not simply of the institution, but of its badges and incidents, are propositions which ought to be deemed indisputable. They lie at the foundation of the Civil Rights Act of 1866. Whether that act was authorized by the Thirteenth Amendment alone, without the support which it subsequently received from the Fourteenth Amendment, after the adoption of which it was re-enacted with some additions, my brethren do not consider it necessary to inquire. But I submit, with all respect to them, that its constitutionality is conclusively shown by their opinion. They admit, as I have said, that the Thirteenth Amendment established freedom; that there are burdens and disabilities, the necessary incidents of slavery, which constitute its substance and visible form; that Congress, by the act of 1866, passed in view of the Thirteenth Amendment, before the Fourteenth was adopted, undertook to remove certain burdens and disabilities, the necessary incidents of slavery, and to secure to all citizens of every race and color, and without regard to previous servitude, those fundamental rights which are the essence of civil freedom, namely, the same right to make and enforce contracts, to sue, be parties, give evidence, and to inherit, purchase, lease, sell, and convey property as is enjoyed by white citizens; that under the Thirteenth Amendment, Congress has to do with slavery and its incidents; and that legislation, so far as necessary or proper to eradicate all forms and incidents of slavery and involuntary servitude, may be direct and primary, operating upon the acts of individuals, whether sanctioned by State legislation or not. . . . Congress, therefore, under its express power to enforce that amendment, by appropriate legislation, may enact laws to protect that people against the deprivation, *because of their race,* of any civil rights granted to other freemen in the same State; and such legislation may be of a direct and primary character, operating upon States, their officers and agents, and, also, upon, at least, such individuals and corporations as exercise public functions and wield power and authority under the State. . . .

Universal Freedom

Congress has not, in these matters, entered the domain of State control and supervision. It does not, as I have said, assume to prescribe the general conditions and limitations under which inns, public conveyances, and places of public amusement, shall be conducted or managed. It simply declares, in effect, that since the nation has established universal freedom in this country, for all time, there shall be no discrimination, based merely upon race or color, in respect of the accommodations and advantages of public conveyances, inns, and places of public amusement.

I am of the opinion that such discrimination practised by corporations and individuals in the exercise of their public or quasi-public functions is a badge of servitude the imposition of which Congress may prevent under its power, by appropriate legislation to enforce the Thirteenth Amendment; and, consequently, without reference to its enlarged power under the Fourteenth Amendment, the act of March 1, 1875, is not, in my judgment, repugnant to the Constitution.

It remains now to consider these cases with references to the power Congress has possessed since the adoption of the Fourteenth Amendment. . . .

Before the adoption of the recent amendments, it had become, as we have seen, the established doctrine of this court that negroes, whose ancestors had been imported and sold as slaves, could not become citizens of a State, or even of the United States, with the rights and privileges guaranteed to citizens by the national Constitution; further, that one might have all the rights and privileges of a citizen of a State without being a citizen in the sense in which that word was used in the national Constitution, and without being entitled to the privileges and immunities of citizens of the several States. Still, further, between the adoption of the Thirteenth Amendment and the proposal by Congress of the Fourteenth Amendment, on June 16, 1866, the statute books of several of the States, as we have seen, had become loaded down with enactments which, under the guise of Apprentice, Vagrant, and Contract regulations, sought to keep the colored race in a condition, practically, of servitude. It was openly announced that whatever might be the rights which persons of that race had, as freemen, under the guarantees of the national Constitution, they could not become citizens of a State, with the privileges belonging to citizens, except by the consent of such State; consequently, that their civil rights, as citizens of the State, depended entirely upon State legislation. To meet this new peril to the black race, that the purpose of the nation might not be doubted or defeated, and by way of further enlargement of the power of Congress, the Fourteenth Amendment was proposed for adoption . . .

The assumption that this amendment consists wholly of prohibitions upon State laws and State proceedings in hostility to its provisions, is unauthorized by its language. The first clause of the first section—"All persons born or naturalized in the United States, and subject to the jurisdiction thereof, are citizens of the United States, and of the State wherein they reside"—is of a distinctly affirmative character. In its application to the colored race, previously liberated, it created and granted, as well citizenship of the United States, as citizenship of the State in which they respectively resided. It introduced all of that race, whose ancestors had been imported and sold as slaves, at once, into the political community known as the "People of the United States." They became, instantly, citizens of the United States, *and* of their respective States. Further, they were brought, by this supreme act of the nation, within the direct operation of that provision of the Constitution which declares that "the citizens of each State shall be entitled to all privileges and immunities of citizens in the several States." Art. 4, § 2.

The citizenship thus acquired, by that race, in virtue of any affirmative grant from the nation, may be protected, not alone by the judicial branch of the government, but by congressional legislation of a primary direct character; this, because the power of Congress is not restricted to the enforcement of prohibitions upon State laws or State action. It is, in terms distinct and positive, to enforce "the *provisions* of *this article*" of amendment; not simply those of a prohibitive character, but the provisions—*all* of the provisions—affirmative and prohibitive, of the amendment. It is, therefore, a grave misconception to suppose that the fifth section of the amendment has reference exclusively to express prohibitions upon State laws or State action. If any right was created by that amendment, the grant of power, through appropriate legislation, to enforce its provisions, authorizes Congress, by means of legislation, operating throughout the entire Union, to guard, secure, and protect that right.

It is, therefore, an essential inquiry what, if any, right, privilege or immunity was given, by the nation, to colored persons, when they were made citizens of the State in which they reside? Did the constitutional grant of State citizenship to that race, of its own force, invest them with any rights, privileges and immunities whatever? That they became entitled, upon the adoption of the Fourteenth Amendment, "to all privileges and immunities of citizens in the several States," within the meaning of section 2 of article 4 of the Constitution, no one, I suppose, will for a moment question. What are the privileges and immunities to which, by that clause of the Constitution, they became entitled? To this it may be answered . . . that they are those which are fundamental in citizenship in a free republican government, such as are "common to the citizens in the latter States under their constitutions and laws by virtue of their being citizens." Of that provision it has been said, with the approval of this court, that no other one in the Constitution has tended so strongly to constitute the citizens of the United States one people. . . .

Equal Treatment

Although this court has wisely forborne any attempt, by a comprehensive definition, to indicate all of the privileges and immunities to which the citizen of a State is entitled, of right, when within the jurisdiction of other States, I hazard nothing, in view of former adjudications, in saying that no State can sustain her denial to colored citizens of other States, while within her limits, of privileges or immunities, fundamental in republican citizenship, upon the ground that she accords such privileges and immunities only to her white citizens and withholds them from her colored citizens. The colored citizens of other States, within the jurisdiction of that State, could claim, in virtue of section 2 of article 4 of the Constitution, every privilege and immunity which that State secures to her white citizens. Otherwise, it would be in the power of any State, by discriminating class legislation against its own citizens of a particular race or color, to withhold from citizens of other States, belonging to that proscribed race, when within her limits, privileges and immunities of the character regarded by all courts as fundamental in citizenship; and that, too, when the constitutional guaranty is that the citizens of each State shall be entitled to "all privileges and immunities of citizens of the several States." No State may, by discrimination against a portion of its own citizens of a particular race, in respect of privileges and immunities fundamental in citizenship, impair the constitutional right of citizens of other States, of whatever race, to enjoy in that State all such privileges and immunities as are there accorded to her most favored citizens. A colored citizen of Ohio or Indiana, while in the jurisdiction of Tennessee, is entitled to enjoy any privilege or immunity, fundamental in citizenship, which is given to citizens of the white race in the latter State. It is not to be supposed that any one will controvert this proposition.

But what was secured to colored citizens of the United States—as between them and their respective States—by the national grant to them of State citizenship? With what rights, privileges, or immunities did this grant invest them? There is one, if there be no other—exemption from race discrimination in respect of any civil

Prepare for Bloodshed

Henry McNeal Turner, a bishop of the African Methodist Episcopal Church, bitterly denounced both the judgment of the Court and those blacks who recommended a wait-and-see attitude toward the results of the decision. In a November 6, 1883, open letter published by the Memphis Appeal, *Turner took to task one of these cautious black leaders.*

First—That decision [of the Supreme Court] unsettles the civil status of the negro in this country which was virtually settled in 1872, when every Democrat and Republican in the United States voted for his rights and drove the negro question out of politics.

Second—That decision will either put the negro back into national politics, where his status will be either fought over again, or drive him out of the country, or result in his extermination. Mark my word, there will be bloodshed enough over that decision to drown every member of the Supreme Court in less than two years. Just wait and see.

Third—It absolves the allegiance of the negro to the United States. If the government that freed him cannot protect his freedom, then . . . he does not stand face to face with its laws and institutions, and the negro hereafter who will enlist in the armies of the government, or swear to defend the United States Constitution ought to be hung by the neck.

Fourth—The argument that the States have the right to fix his civil status is a farce. . . . This decision sends us back to the States to get our Civil rights, for the white people of the respective States to decide whether we shall be treated as people or dogs. All right, Mr. United States, as one I will go. As long as that decision is the law of the land and I am a rebel to this nation. I shall, however be loyal to Georgia and beyond her I shall owe or pay no allegiance. . . .

Now I ask, shall we sit still and be conservative, hold our peace and submit to this degradation? I hope, sir, you will not say yes. You cannot afford to do it. No, not as a member of the negro race. If the decision is correct, the United States constitution is a dirty rag, a cheat, a libel, and ought to be spit upon by every negro in the land. More, if the decision is correct and is accepted by the country, then prepare to return to Africa, or get ready for extermination.

right belonging to citizens of the white race in the same State. That, surely, is their constitutional privilege when within the jurisdiction of other States. And such must be their constitutional right, in their own State, unless the recent amendments be splendid baubles, thrown out to delude those who deserved fair and generous treatment at the hands of the nation. Citizenship in this country necessarily imports at least equality of civil rights among citizens of every race in the same State. It is fundamental in American citizenship that, in respect of such rights, there shall be

251

no discrimination by the State, or its officers, or by individuals or corporations exercising public functions or authority, against any citizen because of his race or previous condition of servitude. . . .

It can scarcely be claimed that exemption from race discrimination, in respect of civil rights, against those to whom State citizenship was granted by the nation, is any less, for the colored race, a new constitutional right, derived from and secured by the national Constitution, than is exemption from such discrimination in the exercise of the elective franchise. It cannot be that the latter is an attribute of national citizenship, while the other is not essential in national citizenship, or fundamental in State citizenship.

If, then, exemption from discrimination, in respect of civil rights, is a new constitutional right, secured by the grant of State citizenship to colored citizens of the United States—and I do not see how this can now be questioned—why may not the nation, by means of its own legislation of a primary direct character, guard, protect and enforce that right? It is a right and privilege which the nation conferred. It did not come from the States in which those colored citizens reside. It has been the established doctrine of this court during all its history, accepted as essential to the national supremacy, that Congress, in the absence of a positive delegation of power to the State legislatures, may, by its own legislation, enforce and protect any right derived from or created by the national Constitution. . . .

Public Duties

In every material sense applicable to the practical enforcement of the Fourteenth Amendment, railroad corporations, keepers of inns, and managers of places of public amusement are agents or instrumentalities of the State, because they are charged with duties to the public, and are amenable, in respect of their duties and functions, to governmental regulation. It seems to me that, within the principle settled in *Ex parte Virginia*, a denial, by these instrumentalities of the State, to the citizen, because of his race, of that equality of civil rights secured to him by law, is a denial by the State, within the meaning of the Fourteenth Amendment. If it be not, then that race is left, in respect of the civil rights in question, practically at the mercy of corporations and individuals wielding power under the States.

But the court says that Congress did not, in the act of 1866, assume, under the authority given by the Thirteenth Amendment, to adjust what may be called the social rights of men and races in the community. I agree that government has nothing to do with social, as distinguished from technically legal, rights of individuals. No government ever has brought, or ever can bring, its people into social intercourse against their wishes. Whether one person will permit or maintain social relations with another is a matter with which government has no concern. I agree that if one citizen chooses not to hold social intercourse with another, he is not and cannot be made amenable to the law for his conduct in that regard; for even upon grounds of race, no legal right of a citizen is violated by the refusal of others to maintain merely social relations with him., What I affirm is that no State, nor the officers of any State, nor any corporation or individual wielding power under State authority for the public benefit or the public convenience, can, consistently either with the freedom established by the fundamental law, or with that equality of civil rights which now belongs to every citizen, discriminate against freemen or citizens, in those rights, because of their race, or because they once labored under the disabilities of slavery imposed upon them as a race. The rights which Congress, by the act of 1865, endeavored to secure and protect are legal, not social rights. The right, for instance, of a colored citizen to use the accommodations of a public highway, upon the same terms as are permitted to white citizens, is no more a social right than his right, under the law, to use the public streets of a city or a town, or a turnpike road, or a public market, or a post office, of his right to sit in a public building with others, of whatever race, for the purpose of hearing the political questions of the day discussed. Scarcely a day passes without our seeing in this court-room citizens of the white and black races sitting side by side, watching the progress of our business. It would never occur to any one that the presence of a colored citizen in a court-house, or court-room, was an invasion of the social rights of white persons who may frequent such places. And yet, such a suggestion would be quite as sound in law—I say it with all respect—as is the suggestion that the claim of a colored citizen to use, upon the same terms as is permitted to white citizens, the accommodations of public highways, or public inns, or places of public amusement, established under the license of the law, is an invasion of the social rights of the white race. . . .

My brethren say, that when a man has emerged from slavery, and by the aid of beneficent legislation has shaken off the inseparable concomitants of that state, there must be some stage in the progress of his elevation when he takes the rank of a mere citizen, and ceases to be the special favorite of the laws, and when his rights as a citizen, or a man, are to be protected in the ordinary modes by which other men's rights are protected. It is, I submit, scarcely just to say that the colored race has been the special favorite of the laws. The statute of 1875, now adjudged to be unconstitutional, is for the benefit of citizens of every race and color. What the nation, through Congress, has sought to accomplish in reference to that race, is—what had already been done in every

State of the Union for the white race—to secure and protect rights belonging to them as freemen and citizens; nothing more. It was not deemed enough "to help the feeble up, but to support him after." The one underlying purpose of congressional legislation has been to enable the black race to take the rank of mere citizens. The difficulty has been to compel a recognition of the legal right of the black race to take the rank of citizens, and to secure the enjoyment of privileges belonging, under the law, to them as a component part of the people for whose welfare and happiness government is ordained. At every step, in this direction, the nation has been confronted with class tyranny, which a contemporary English historian says is, of all tyrannies, the most intolerable, "for it is ubiquitous in its operation, and weighs, perhaps, most heavily on those whose obscurity or distance would withdraw them from the notice of a single despot." To-day, it is the colored race which is denied, by corporations and individuals wielding public authority, rights fundamental in their freedom and citizenship. At some future time, it may be that some other race will fall under the ban of race discrimination. If the constitutional amendments be enforced, according to the intent with which, as I conceive, they were adopted, there cannot be, in this republic, any class of human beings in practical subjection to another class, with power in the latter to dole out to the former just such privileges as they may choose to grant. The supreme law of the land has decreed that no authority shall be exercised in this country upon the basis of discrimination, in respect of civil rights, against freemen and citizens because of their race, color, or previous condition of servitude. To that decree—for the due enforcement of which, by appropriate legislation, Congress has been invested with express power—every one must bow, whatever may have been, or whatever now are, his individual views as to the wisdom or policy, either of the recent changes in the fundamental law, or of the legislation which has been enacted to give them effect.

For the reasons stated I feel constrained to withhold my assent to the opinion of the court.

CHAPTER 6

Historians Debate Reconstruction

Chapter Preface

As evidenced throughout this volume, the participants in the debates during Reconstruction frequently stood at extremes on the issues, and their positions were often influenced by regional bias, personal prejudices, and race. Likewise, the tenor of the historical study of the Reconstruction era has typically varied from one extreme to another, repeating the sectarian divisions that existed during Reconstruction. The way in which historians' interpretations of Reconstruction have changed over the decades clearly illustrates the influence that contemporary attitudes can have on our understanding of historical events.

For the first fifty years of the twentieth century, the prevailing view of Reconstruction (advanced by both northern and southern scholars) closely followed the traditional southern perception of the era as a repressive and tragic mistake. This historical interpretation was established in the early 1900s by Professor William A. Dunning of Columbia University in New York and his colleagues. According to the Dunning School, the vindictive Radical Republicans crushed the helpless white Southerners under military occupation while carpetbaggers plundered the South and ignorant black politicians made a mockery of the laws. However, the Dunning School historians concluded, white Southerners eventually organized to bring justice to bear—by peaceful means whenever possible—and regained control of the South.

The prevalent racial prejudices of the early twentieth century undoubtedly influenced this view of Reconstruction. The tone of historian E. Merton Coulter's 1947 book *The South During Reconstruction* is indicative of the Dunning School writers:

> The desire for Negro suffrage did not originate with the freedmen—others opened Pandora's box out of which this evil flew. . . . When once he had [the vote], its power over him grew fast and worked further against the peace and contentment he needed. It made him vain and idle and put into his head dangerous desires, impossible of fulfillment.

Opposition to the dominant interpretation of Reconstruction did occasionally appear, most notably from black scholars. In his 1948 essay "Whither Reconstruction Historiography," historian John Hope Franklin wrote a scathing critique of *The South During Reconstruction* in which he reproached Coulter for "describ[ing] many phases of Negro life in sweeping and unsupported generalities that do not stand up under careful examination." W. E. B. Du Bois's 1935 book *Black Reconstruction* was one of the earliest comprehensive historical studies that presented an alternative assessment of Reconstruction. Such divergences from the Dunning school of thought, while mostly ignored by the prominent historians of the day, served as forerunners for the next wave of Reconstruction scholarship.

It was not until the 1950s that the Revisionist interpretation of Reconstruction gained dominance in the field of history. In the Revisionists' view, Reconstruction was tragic only in the sense that its progressive reforms were so soon destroyed by racist white Southerners. Radical Republicans had not been motivated by cruelty or greed after all, but actually had been idealists devoted to equal rights; the violence of white supremacists had simply been too much for the reformers and southern blacks to withstand. Regardless, the Revisionists argued, the civil rights amendments and legislation passed during Reconstruction could rightly be considered the true victory of Radical Reconstruction.

Revisionist theory arose in part from advances in historiographical research methods and new standards in scholarship, but it also reflected new attitudes brought about by the civil rights movement that was gaining strength in the 1950s and 1960s. Indeed, Revisionists often looked at the Reconstruction era to find explanations for the events they were experiencing in their own time. For example, Harold M. Hyman wrote in his 1967 book *The Radical Republicans and Reconstruction,*

> Intransigence on the part of Southern whites in the 1960's with respect to demands by Negroes for a proper share in the promise of American life appears to be intimately linked to tightly cherished misconceptions concerning the roles that Negroes supposedly played during Reconstruction. . . . [T]he rising aspirations of the Negroes in the 1960's are mocked by demeaning depictions of black men of the 1860's and 1870's.

By amending the Dunning School's negative portrayal of Reconstruction, many Revisionists hoped to increase understanding of the motives behind the civil rights movement of the twentieth century—motives that, they felt, were strikingly similar to those of blacks and Radical Republicans during the Reconstruction era.

The most recent trend in Reconstruction historiography is the Postrevisionist reaction to the optimistic scholarship of the mid-century. While they agree with much of the Revisionist interpretation, Postrevisionists argue that the accomplishments of Reconstruction were not as far-reaching as they could have been and that many Radical Republicans were not truly concerned with civil rights. In the viewpoints that follow, historian William R. Brock expresses a classically Revisionist assessment of the Radical Republicans and their intentions, while historian C. Vann Woodward presents an early Postrevisionist evaluation.

VIEWPOINT 1

"The generalities of the Radical ideology [of racial equality] . . . could not stand pressure. The weapons bent and broke in the hands of those who used them."

Reconstruction Failed Because Republican Reforms Were Too Radical for American Society

William R. Brock (1916-)

A professor emeritus of American history, William R. Brock taught at Cambridge University in England and the University of Glasgow in Scotland. He has written numerous articles and books on the U.S. Civil War and Reconstruction eras, including *Conflict and Transformation in the United States* and *An American Crisis: Congress and Reconstruction*, from which the following viewpoint is excerpted.

Brock argues that a central factor in the failure of reconstruction was that Radical Republican ideals of racial equality were not shared by the majority of American society. Legislation that championed the innate equality of the races invariably met resistance, Brock asserts, particularly because not even the Republicans themselves agreed on exactly how equality should be defined or which rights were inalienable. Brock contends that Republicans were more successful when they framed their proposed policies in terms not of racial ideology but of partisan politics—for example, supporting black suffrage in order to create a strong Republican voting bloc in the South. Although Brock writes that the relentless idealism of the Republicans was a crucial weakness of Radical Reconstruction, he acknowledges that this idealism provided the foundation for the civil rights movement of the twentieth century.

It is comparatively easy to explain the waning of Radicalism in terms of personal failure, evaporating enthusiasm, the urgent demands of business, and the tendency of all political organizations to fall into the hands of professionals. It is easy also to see how the challenge of the new age, with its manifest problems of the relationship between private business and public authority, had a divisive effect upon the Radicals . . . while drawing together the main body of Republicans around the citadel of American capitalism. But the break-up of Radicalism may also reflect more profound weaknesses in the position which it maintained.

It has been argued that much of the Radical success was explained by the pressures from below which drove cautious politicians even further than they had intended, and that this pressure must be explained in ideological terms and not as the product of mere interest groups. The ideology had expressed in abstract but attractive terms certain propositions about man in society which, for a moment in time, seemed to epitomise the aspirations of the Northern people. Racial equality, equal rights and the use of national authority to secure both were living ideas in the Reconstruction era. . . . For the first time these concepts were cast in the form of a political programme which could be achieved; but their success depended upon the response which they aroused from the Northern people. After Reconstruction the ideas persisted but failed to rouse the same enthusiasm; their formal acceptance was a very different thing from the popular emotion which could push them forward despite the usual obstacles to policies which disturb complacency and refuse to let men rest in peace. The question remains whether the slackening of the pressure behind the Radical ideology should be explained by rival distractions and changing interests or by a weakness in the ideology itself. Examination will show that the generalities of the Radical ideology—so attractive at first sight—could not stand pressure. The weapons bent and broke in the hands of those who used them.

An Ideology of Equality

A belief in racial equality has never won universal assent and to the majority of men in the mid-nineteenth century it seemed to be condemned both by experience and by science. The literal equality between men of obviously different physiological characteristics was an abolitionist invention and it rested upon emotional conviction rather than upon rational proof; the comparison between intelligent negroes and retarded poor whites proved little because the civilization of a few blacks did not redeem the mass from docile ignorance and the degradation of some whites did not detract from the high standards of the majority. The abolitionist argument was based largely upon pure *a priori* statements or upon experience with fugitive slaves: a mass of argument could be produced against the one, while the defiance of the occasional runaway did not prove that the mass of his fellows were not fitted by nature for a subordinate position. The behaviour of the negro was obviously different from that of the whites and, though those who knew him best granted him some admirable traits, they would also maintain that he was sadly deficient in the capacity for industry, thrift, self-reliance, enterprise, sexual restraint and the whole galaxy of virtues esteemed by nineteenth-century civilization. The abolitionist argument that the negro appeared 'inferior' because he had lived in slavery for generations failed to carry weight because no free negro society could be found to prove the proposition. Moreover there was an added complication in the mixed ancestry of so many of those who, like Frederick Douglass, were quoted as evidence of innate negro intelligence. This is not the place to enter upon the tangled problem of racial characteristics; it is sufficient to state that in the later nineteenth century racial equality was a hypothesis which was generally rejected. It was not accepted in the North any more than it was in the South and even abolitionists were anxious to disclaim any intention of forcing social contacts between the races and all shied away from the dread subject of racial amalgamation. An initial weakness of the Radical ideology was therefore its dependence upon a concept which was not self-evident, lacked scientific proof, and offended popular susceptibilities.

The usual weakness of equalitarian theory lies in demonstrating that people ought to be treated as equals in spite of natural inequalities, and this difficulty is acute when dealing with people of different races. While it is possible to argue, among men of the same race, that it is necessary to treat men as though they were equal, it is far harder to do so in the face of popular prejudice that men of a different race are marked at birth as 'inferior.' The conventional Republican argument was that men were unequal in capabilities but equal in rights, and in the American context this proposition rested mainly upon an appeal to the preamble of the Declaration of Independence; but the assertions of the Declaration were not 'self-evident' to most white Americans when applied to negroes. Moreover there were some particular difficulties in equalitarian theory when applied to a mass of people, concentrated in a single region, and occupying from time out of mind a subordinate position in society. Equality demands protection of the weak against the strong and positive law to afford it; but it usually involves the assumption that given certain legal rights the due process of law will enable men to maintain their equality. With the negroes this assumption could not be made: what was required was protection, maintained by enforceable law, at every point where the power of the dominant race was likely to impinge upon the weaker. With tradition, economic power, prejudice, social custom and, in most Southern districts, numbers all entrenched on one side, protection could not be provided merely by changing the law and leaving its administration to the local authorities and courts. The concept of negro equality demanded interference with the processes of local government on a scale never before contemplated in America or in any other nation. Would the Northern majority be prepared to exert continuously this kind of pressure and provide this kind of protection? In the answer to this question lay the second great weakness of the Radical ideology.

An Artificial Equality

Further difficulties lay in the complexities which sheltered behind the simple word 'equality.' Whatever the moral arguments the negro was not, and could not be in the immediate future, an equal to the white man in economic life, in competition for the scarce education facilities of the South, or in winning public office. Racial equality would have to be an artificial creation imposed upon Southern society; the negro would have to have guarantees which were not given to the white man, and the quest for equality would demand unequal incidence of the law. No other minority required special legislation to ensure equal status in the courts, or the care of a Federal bureau, or the use of force to protect the right to vote. Negro equality implied that something must be taken from the whites, and this was explicit in two features of Radical policy: confiscation and disqualification. [Congressman Thaddeus] Stevens never wavered in his belief that negro democracy must have an economic basis in negro landownership; confiscation and redistribution were therefore cardinal points in his programme. Yet the most passionate advocates of equality could not persuade the Republican majority to embark upon such a disturbance of property. Negro democracy would also be a sham if the former ruling class retained its grasp upon local and national office, and disqualification was necessary. This policy succeeded because it was supported by Northern fear of restored Southern domination at Washington, but it proved to be the most vulnerable and perhaps the least wise aspect of Reconstruction. Both confiscation and disqualification demonstrate the formidable difficulties which attend the imposition of equality upon a society in which it did not exist, and in which the beneficiaries of equalitar-

Reconstruction Was Not a Failure

Eric Foner, a professor of history at Columbia University, is the author of numerous books, including Reconstruction: America's Unfinished Revolution. *In the following excerpt from his* American Heritage *article "The New View of Reconstruction," Foner contends that the civil rights reforms of Radical Reconstruction were so extraordinary for the time that, despite later setbacks, reconstruction was a remarkable success.*

The United States was not the only nation to experience emancipation in the nineteenth century. Neither plantation slavery nor abolition was unique to the United States. But Reconstruction was. In a comparative perspective Radical Reconstruction stands as a remarkable experiment, the only effort of a society experiencing abolition to bring the former slaves within the umbrella of equal citizenship. Because the Radicals did not achieve everything they wanted, historians have lately tended to play down the stunning departure represented by black suffrage and officeholding. Former slaves, most fewer than two years removed from bondage, debated the fundamental questions of the polity: What is a republican form of government? Should the state provide equal education for all? How could political equality be reconciled with a society in which property was so unequally distributed? There was something inspiring in the way such men met the challenge of Reconstruction. . . .

Few modern scholars believe the Reconstruction governments established in the South in 1867 and 1868 fulfilled the aspirations of their humble constituents. While their achievements in such realms as education, civil rights, and the economic rebuilding of the South are now widely appreciated, historians today believe they failed to affect either the economic plight of the emancipated slave or the ongoing transformation of independent white farmers into cotton tenants. Yet their opponents did perceive the Reconstruction governments in precisely this way—as representatives of a revolution that had put the bottom rail, both racial and economic, on top. . . .

The ultimate outcome underscores the uniqueness of Reconstruction itself. Alone among the societies that abolished slavery in the nineteenth century, the United States, for a moment, offered the freedmen a measure of political control over their own destinies. However brief its sway, Reconstruction allowed scope for a remarkable political and social mobilization of the black community. It opened doors of opportunity that could never be completely closed.

ian policy were too weak, socially and economically, to stand upon their own feet. The price of equality was revolutionary change, vigilance and constant pressure, and who would pay the price when enthusiasm grew cold and the suspicion grew that the negroes were not yet ready to exercise rights which could not be secured without the coercion of their fellow citizens.

It is in this context that the work of [Congressman] John A. Bingham assumes great significance. In his fight for the civil rights clause of the Fourteenth Amendment he cut equal rights free from negro protection and made them national. The later perversion of this clause to protect the rights of corporations tended to obscure the significance of a measure which protected all citizens and all persons under the jurisdiction of the States, but once the importance of nationalized right was recognized the Fourteenth Amendment grew in stature. Conversely the Fifteenth Amendment was weak from the outset because it linked suffrage with race; it was a law for negro enfranchisement and could be enforced only so long as some people had an interest in doing so. If the Fifteenth Amendment had declared in unequivocal terms that all males over the age of twenty-one who were citizens of the United States had the right to vote it might have been recognised as a cornerstone of democracy and attracted popular support. As it was the Fifteenth Amendment enacted "impartial" suffrage which meant that the States could impose any qualification they chose provided that it was not based on race; this meant that the white majority of the nation had no particular interest in its enforcement.

Three Definitions

Beyond the major problem of equality by enforcement lay the vast and ramifying difficulty of definition. Was equality indivisible or if divisible which aspects were essential? The three classic definitions of equality—*in* the eyes of God, *under* the law, and *of* opportunity—each carried different implications. Equality in the eyes of God might well be an excuse for inequality on earth: Dives and Lazarus had both lived under the judgment of God, both received their deserts after death, and their inequality on earth was dramatic but irrelevant to their condition in eternity. Equality in the eyes of God implied some limitation upon the principle of subordination for it had been an essential part of the abolitionist case that the children of God should not be treated as less than human beings, but it provided no definition of the place of man in society. Many pious Northerners saw no inconsistency between Christian conviction and racial discrimination, and the brotherhood of man in Christ was no barrier to the belief that equality on earth was no part of God's purpose. It was therefore necessary to supplement the Christian concept of equality in eternity with the purely secular arguments for equality on earth.

Equality under the law had deep roots in the Anglo-Saxon tradition but in its mother country [England] it had not proved incompatible with aristocratic privilege, an established Church, denial of suffrage to the masses, and the exploitation of low paid labour. The guarantee of equal status in the courts was a great and important addition to the rights of negroes, but it would not of itself create a political and social revolution. Beyond the formal guarantee of equality under the law lay the intractable question of who should administer the law. The legal rights of negroes might be recognized in Southern courts but they were likely to be strictly interpreted; one could be confident that the white Southern judge would administer the law scrupulously, but between the negro and equal justice stood the white Southern jury. Equality under the law was a grand sweeping theory, without which no other form of secular equality was possible, but it did not erase the notion that the negro was an inferior man to whom only a grudging recognition was extended. It might be argued that, once the groundwork of legal equality had been laid, the progress towards equality in other fields would follow, yet one might doubt the certainty of this hypothesis. It was only in 1867 that the British Parliament was to decide after centuries of equality under the law that the agricultural labourer was entitled to a vote, and millions of simple Englishmen still went unlettered to their graves.

Equality of opportunity seemed to be a more positive demand. If the racial barrier could be removed from access to education, occupation and public office the negro would have the right to compete on equal terms with the whites in most of the fields to which his aspiration might lead him. Yet equality of opportunity implied inequality of achievement and in the South its immediate result might be the confirmation of white supremacy. If the negro was to be given a real chance of equal achievement he must be given positive aids which were not given to the white man, and one was brought back once more to the basic problem of equalitarian theory: that positive government was required to correct habitual inequality. This led on to the political difficulty that, in the climate of nineteenth-century opinion, sustained and purposeful government intervention was unpopular and improbable. The comparatively modest aims of the Freedmen's Bureau aroused intense hostility in the South and many doubts in the North; any further attempt to translate the commitment to equality into governmental responsibilities might wreck the whole structure of Reconstruction, yet without this the purpose of equalitarian Radicalism could not be achieved.

Many Republicans contended that it was unnecessary to embark upon the troubled sea of racial equality if one could stop in the safe haven of guaranteed rights. The negro was a man, and as a man he had certain inalienable rights; if these could be secured the vexed question of equality could be deferred or perhaps dismissed. This theory of inalienable right had better prospects than any theory of equality. American tradition had long accepted as its cornerstone the idea of man as an atom in society, entitled to do all that was within his power provided that it did not impinge upon the rights of others. But American tradition had usually failed to recognize the fact that rights were not 'inalienable', that the exercise of legal rights depended upon the consent of the majority, or that some rights of some men could always be denied by the sovereign power of the people. In Reconstruction Americans were brought face to face with the problem of free men whose 'rights' were denied by the local majority and could be secured only by external coercion. Moreover the whole attitude of Americans towards rights had been governed by their implicit acceptance of the idea of checks and balances. The rights of the people were a check upon the enlargement of authority, and to give some rights to some people at the expense of others had been damned by association with the idea of privilege. What was the intrinsic difference between rights conferred upon a chartered monopoly and rights conferred upon a weak minority? This conundrum had always been implicit in American political discourse but Reconstruction made it explicit. . . .

The Radical solution to the dilemma of rights which were natural but which could only be secured by artificial means was negro suffrage. With the vote the negro would be equipped to protect his own rights, and there were Jeffersonian echoes in the idea that the cultivator of the soil would not only defend his personal rights but also act as a repository for political virtue. The voting negro would protect himself against injustice and the Union against its enemies, but this concept of suffrage as a protective device proved inadequate when Reconstruction governments were compelled to assume the tasks of modern administration in a region where the best government had always been that which governed least. So long as the vote was merely protective the ignorance of the negro was not a relevant argument because a poor man could understand what had to be defended as well as the best educated; but when negro suffrage became the basis for an economic and social revolution guided by positive government it was relevant to ask whether the former slave was yet equal to his responsibilities.

The Radicals argued the case for the negro suffrage in the context of nineteenth-century liberal thought, and they can hardly be blamed for not having transcended the ideas of their age. Moreover they were inhibited by the political circumstances in which they had to operate. It was hard enough to convince Northern public opinion that negro suffrage was safe and just without complicating the question. In the summer of 1866 a Radical member of the Reconstruction Committee told Congress that 'we may as well state it plainly and fairly, so that there shall be no misunderstanding on the subject. It was our opinion that three fourths of the States of this Union (that is of the loyal States) could not be induced to vote to grant the right of suffrage, even in any degree or under any restriction, to the colored race.' Between this time and the passage of the Fifteenth Amendment a remarkable change took place in public opinion, but in order to foster it the Radicals were forced to rely less and less upon appeals to abstract justice and more and more upon the utility of the negro vote to the party and to the Union. This stress led them to pass lightly over the tasks which negro democracy might be called upon to perform, and to treat their votes merely as a counterweight in the political balance of the nation.

Radicals themselves hesitated at times over the problem of the vote. Was it one of the inalienable rights, or was it, as everyone else said, a political right which could be granted or withheld at the discretion of the political sovereign? Among the conservative Republicans, and particularly amongst the better educated, there was genuine hesitation about mass democracy, and if they turned one eye towards the negroes of the South they turned the other to the foreign-born city vote which formed the electoral basis of Boss [William] Tweed's New York ring. Reformers could join hands with the merely fearful in urging the case for universal literacy tests, and old Know-Nothings [members of the 1850s anti-immigrant party] could make common cause with new Republicans against universal suffrage. Yet literacy tests which would exclude the mass of the Southern negro people, and could be manipulated by the ruling State authorities, were useless as a political solution in the South, and Radicals were pushed from their early caution on the suffrage question to an outright avowal of belief in universal suffrage.

Northern Abandonment

Paradoxically some of the Radical arguments for negro suffrage tended to rebound. The idea that the vote would enable the negro to protect himself provided an excuse for non-intervention, and for the belief that the Southern question could now be treated as a local question. In 1880 James G. Blaine, writing in the *North American Review*, justified the grant of negro suffrage by saying that 'had the franchise not been bestowed upon the negro as his shield and weapon for defense, the demand upon the General Government to interfere for his protection, would have been constant, irritating and embarrassing. Great complaint has been made for years past of the Government's interference, simply to secure to the colored citizen his constitutional right. But this intervention has been trifling compared to that which would have been required if we had not given suffrage to the negro.' It was thus easy to infer that having instituted negro suffrage as an automatic regulator of the Southern political mechanism Northerners could turn their eyes away from what actually went on in the South. To be fair one should add that when Blaine wrote the extensive disenfranchisement of the negroes had not taken place, and that in some districts he could vote freely provided that he voted for the Democratic ticket.

It is not suggested that equal participation by the negro in Southern politics would have been automatically secured if the Radicals had succeeded in establishing the suffrage as an 'inalienable right,' but an unequivocal statement that all adult males had the right to vote would have been easier to enforce and more difficult to evade. Nor is it suggested that universal suffrage would have done anything to solve the vexed and unexamined question of what the negro was to do with his vote. What is suggested is that the Fifteenth Amendment was a weak compromise which failed to achieve the Radical aims and, in the long run, helped to discredit that freedom of State action which moderates wished to preserve. Under the Reconstruction Acts all 'loyal' males had voted; the Fifteenth Amendment allowed States to retreat from that position while the belief that the suffrage was secured on equitable terms allowed the Northern majority to relax pressure at the point where it was most needed. The keystone of the Radical arch proved too weak to hold up the edifice. In a sense negro suffrage was premature—though it could have been written into the law at no other time—but this was only in part the result of negro immaturity. Beneath the surface of the suffrage question lay larger problems of the role of government in a democratic State and these American society as a whole was unwilling or unready to contemplate. By 1880 *The Nation*, which had earlier given somewhat lukewarm support to negro suffrage while insisting that it should be impartial and not universal, was emphasizing that the *quality* of voters should be the primary consideration. For the intelligentsia who had, for the most part, thrown their influence behind Radical Republicanism, the great national problem was no longer the protection of negro rights but the defense of public morality, social respectability and economic orthodoxy against demagogues, bosses, agitators, agrarian Radicals, and mass ignorance. . . .

The arguments which have been presented in the preceding pages have attempted to show why the ideology of Radical Republicanism, which appeared so powerful during the crisis of Reconstruction, failed to gather that momentum which could have carried it forward in the years which followed. It is of course exceedingly improbable that the Radicals of the Reconstruction period could have conceived their problems in any other way or that they could have gone on to produce the ideas and institutions which would have corrected the weaknesses in their edifice. Radicalism shared the weaknesses of all liberal bourgeois movements of the nineteenth century, and it would have required a far more profound revolution in thought and action to make them view their situation through the eyes of twentieth-century liberals. In their equalitarian sentiments, in their realization that individual rights might be incompatible with local self-government, and in their attitude towards national power they were prophets of the future; yet they remained children of their age and were bound by its assumptions and inhibitions. And even if their vision occasionally transcended these limitations they were unlikely to persuade the majority of their countrymen that the revolution which they had initiated ought to proceed to further innovation. The failure of Radicalism is thus a part of the wider failure of bourgeois liberalism to solve the problems of the new age which was dawning; but having said this it is important to remember that if the Radicals shared in the weaknesses of their age they also had some achievements which were exceptional.

Achievements of Reconstruction

First among civilized nations the United States had met the problems of a bi-racial society, and first among civilized nations they had committed themselves to the proposition that in such a society human beings must have equal rights. If the definition of 'rights' was confused the idea that they must be recognized was clear. The civil rights clause of the Fourteenth Amendment was in many ways unsatisfactory, but it contained explosive material which could shatter the lines of racial discrimination. The United States had committed themselves to the statement that suffrage should be colour-blind, and if the phrasing of the Fifteenth Amendment invited evasion the principle which it enunciated would outlive attempts to defeat it. Americans may well differ upon the wisdom of these equalitarian ideas, but it is impossible to deny their importance for the future. The Fourteenth and Fifteenth Amendments could have been enacted only during the period of Reconstruction, and without them the subsequent history of the United States would have been very different. . . .

The authors of Reconstruction policy did not intend that it should perpetuate racial antagonism in Southern society, discredit colour-blind democracy, and provide further ammunition for Southern attacks upon the North. They were not disunionists, as Andrew Johnson called them, but they believed that the old Union, containing elements which could not combine, must be reconstructed. They hoped that the preamble to the Declaration of Independence should become the new formula for national existence, and they hoped to endow the national government with the power to ensure this result. These ideas were not negligible, absurd or unworthy. Their presentation was marred by a bitterness which was the legacy of war but was sometimes redeemed by the idealistic impulses which war had released. They left a record of failure in the South and permanent alterations in the law of a great nation. They faced intractable problems which still vex the modern world and they anticipated many of the assumptions with which men now tackle these problems. There was tragedy in the crisis of Reconstruction, but the tragic element transcends the particular circumstances of the post-war era and belongs to the whole condition of modern man.

VIEWPOINT 2

*On the issue of Negro equality the [Republican] party
remained divided, hesitant, and unsure of its purpose."*

Reconstruction Failed Because Republicans Were Not Committed to Racial Equality

C. Vann Woodward (1908-)

A native Southerner originally from Arkansas, C. Vann Woodward is one of the most prominent historians of the South and of race relations in the United States. He has published extensively, including *The Strange Career of Jim Crow, Reunion and Reaction: The Compromise of 1877 and the End of Reconstruction,* and *Mary Chesnut's Civil War,* for which he won the 1982 Pulitzer Prize for history. Woodward taught at a number of universities, including Columbia and Yale; now retired, he frequently writes for the *New York Review of Books,* the *New York Times Book Review,* and the *New Republic.*

The following viewpoint is excerpted from "Seeds of Failure in Radical Race Policy," a paper first presented in 1965 at the Reconstruction Conference at the University of Illinois. Woodward argues that, although the Republicans promoted themselves throughout Reconstruction as the party of racial equality, they actually were divided on the issue of race, and only a small number of Republicans were wholly supportive of full racial equality. Examining the racial biases of average northern constituencies during Reconstruction, Woodward concludes that most Republicans, whether themselves racist or not, represented people who supported segregation and white supremacy. Unpopular policies of civil rights reforms hurt Republicans in elections, he maintains, and caused many politicians to moderate their stances on racial equality. Woodward contends that the Republican Party sacrificed ideals of racial reform to the expediencies of partisan politics, thereby ensuring the failure of reconstruction.

The Republican leaders were quite aware in 1865 that the issue of Negro status and rights was closely connected with the two other great issues of Reconstruction—who should reconstruct the South and who should govern the country. But while they were agreed on the two latter issues, they were not agreed on the first. They were increasingly conscious that in order to reconstruct the South along the lines they planned they would require the support and the votes of the freedmen. And it was apparent to some that once the reconstructed states were restored to the Union the Republicans would need the votes of the freedmen to retain control over the national government. While they could agree on this much, they were far from agreeing on the status, the rights, the equality, or the future of the Negro.

The fact was that the constituency on which the Republican congressmen relied in the North lived in a race-conscious, segregated society devoted to the doctrine of white supremacy and Negro inferiority. "In virtually every phase of existence," writes Leon Litwack with regard to the North in 1860, "Negroes found themselves systematically separated from whites. They were either excluded from railway cars, omnibuses, stagecoaches, and steamboats or assigned to special 'Jim Crow' sections; they sat, when permitted, in secluded and remote corners of theatres and lecture halls; they could not enter most hotels, restaurants, and resorts, except as servants; they prayed in 'Negro pews' in the white churches. . . . Moreover, they were often educated in segregated schools, punished in segregated prisons, nursed in segregated hospitals, and buried in segregated cemeteries." Ninety-three per cent of the 225,000 northern Negroes in 1860 lived in states that denied them the ballot, and 7 per cent lived in the five New England states that permitted them to vote. Ohio and New York had discriminatory qualifications that practically eliminated Negro voting. In many northern states discriminatory laws excluded Negroes from interracial marriage, from militia service, from the jury box, and from the witness stand when whites were involved. Ohio denied them poor relief, and most states of the old Northwest had laws carrying penalties against Negroes settling in those states. Everywhere in the free states the Negro met with barriers to job opportunities, and in most places he encountered severe limitations to the protection of his life, liberty, and property.

One political consequence of these racial attitudes was that the major parties vied with each other in their professions of devotion to the dogma of white supremacy. Republicans were especially sensitive on the point because of their antislavery associations. Many of them, like Senator Lyman Trumbull of Illinois, the close friend of Lincoln, found no difficulty in reconciling antislavery with anti-Negro views. "We, the Republican party," said Senator Trumbull in 1858, "are the white man's party. We are for free white men, and for making white labor respectable and honorable, which it can never be when negro slave labor is brought into competition with it." Horace Greeley the following year regretted that it was "the controlling idea" of some of his fellow Republicans "to prove themselves 'the white man's party,' or else all the mean, low, ignorant, drunken, brutish whites will go against them from horror of 'negro equality.'" Greeley called such people "the one-horse politicians," but he could hardly apply that name to Lyman Trumbull, nor for that matter to William H. Seward, who in 1860 described the American Negro as "a foreign and feeble element like the Indians, incapable of assimilation"; nor to Senator Henry Wilson of Massachusetts, who firmly disavowed any belief "in the mental or the intellectual equality of the African race with this proud and domineering white race of ours." Trumbull, Seward, and Wilson were the front rank of Republican leadership and they spoke the mind of the Middle West, the Middle Atlantic states, and New England. . . .

Fear of Invasion

As the war for union began to take on the character of a war for freedom, northern attitudes toward the Negro paradoxically began to harden rather than soften. This hardening process was especially prominent in the northwestern or middle western states where the old fear of Negro invasion was intensified by apprehensions that once the millions of slaves below the Ohio River were freed they would push northward—this time by the thousands and tens of thousands, perhaps in mass exodus, instead of in driblets of one or two who came furtively as fugitive slaves. The prospect of Negro immigration, Negro neighbors, and Negro competition filled the whites with alarm, and their spokesmen voiced their fears with great candor. "There is," Lyman Trumbull told the Senate, in April, 1862, "a very great aversion in the West—I know it to be so in my state—against having free negroes come among us. Our people want nothing to do with the negro." And about the same time John Sherman, who was to give his name to the Radical

272

Reconstruction Act five years later, told Congress that in Ohio "we do not like negroes. We do not disguise our dislike. As my friend from Indiana [Congressman Joseph A. Wright] said yesterday, the whole people of the northwestern states are, for reasons whether correct or not, opposed to having many negroes among them and the principle or prejudice has been engrafted in the legislation of nearly all the northwestern States."

So powerful was this anti-Negro feeling that it almost over-whelmed antislavery feeling and seriously imperiled the passage of various confiscation and emancipation laws designed to free the slave. To combat the opposition Republican leaders such as George W. Julian of Indiana, Albert G. Riddle of Ohio, and Salmon P. Chase advanced the theory that emancipation would actually solve northern race problems. Instead of starting a mass migration of freedmen northward, they argued, the abolition of slavery would not only put a stop to the entry of fugitive slaves but would drain the northern Negroes back to the South. Once slavery were ended, the Negro would flee northern race prejudice and return to his natural environment and the congenial climate of the South.

One tentative answer of the Republican party to the northern fear of Negro invasion, however, was deportation of the freed-men and colonization abroad. The scheme ran into opposition from some Republicans, especially in New England, on the ground that it was inhumane as well as impractical. But with the powerful backing of President Lincoln and the support of west-ern Republicans Congress overcame the opposition. Lincoln was committed to colonization not only as a solution to the race prob-lem but as a means of allaying northern opposition to emancipa-tion and fears of Negro exodus. . . .

During the last two years of the war northern states began to modify or repeal some of their anti-Negro and discriminatory laws. But the party that emerged triumphant from the crusade to save the Union and free the slave was not in the best political and moral position to expand the rights and assure the equality of the freedman. There undoubtedly *did* emerge eventually an organiza-tion determined to overthrow Andrew Johnson's states' rights, white-supremacy policies and to take over the control of the South. But that was a different matter. On the issue of Negro equality the party remained divided, hesitant, and unsure of its purpose. The historic commitment to equality it eventually made was lacking in clarity, ambivalent in purpose, and capable of nu-merous interpretations. Needless to say, its meaning has been de-bated from that day to this.

The northern electorate the Republicans faced in seeking sup-port for their program of Reconstruction had undergone no con-

273

version in its wartime racial prejudices and dogmas. As George W. Julian, who deplored the fact himself, told his colleagues in the House in 1866, "the real trouble is that *we hate the negro*. It is not his ignorance that offends us, but his color."

Racism in the North

In the years immediately following the war every northern state in which the electorate or the legislature was given the opportunity to express its views on issues involving the political rights of the Negro reaffirmed its earlier and conservative stand. This included the states that reconsidered—and reaffirmed—their laws excluding Negroes from the polls. Five states with laws barring Negro testimony in court against whites repealed them, and a few acted against school segregation. Throughout these years, however, the North remained fundamentally what it was before—a society organized upon assumptions of racial privilege and segregation. As Senator Henry Wilson of Massachusetts told his colleagues in 1867, "There is not today a square mile in the United States where the advocacy of the equal rights and privileges of those colored men has not been in the past and is not now unpopular." Whether the senator was entirely accurate in his estimate of white opinion or not, he faithfully reflected the political constraints and assumptions under which his party operated as they cautiously and hesitantly framed legislation for Negro civil and political rights—a program they knew had to be made acceptable to the electorate that Senator Wilson described.

This is not to suggest that there was not widespread and sincere concern in the North for the terrible condition of the freedmen in the South. There can be no doubt that many northern people were deeply moved by the reports of atrocities, peonage, brutality, lynchings, riots, and injustices that filled the press. Indignation was especially strong over the Black Codes adopted by some of the Johnsonian state legislatures, for they blatantly advertised the intention of some southerners to substitute a degrading peonage for slavery and make a mockery of the moral fruits of northern victory. What is sometimes overlooked in analyzing northern response to the Negro's plight is the continued apprehension over the threat of a massive Negro invasion of the North. The panicky fear that this might be precipitated by emancipation had been allayed in 1862 by the promises of President Lincoln and other Republican spokesmen that once slavery were abolished the freedmen would cheerfully settle down to remain in the South, that northern Negroes would be drawn back to the South, and that deportation and colonization abroad would take care of any threat of northern invasion that remained. But not only had experiments with deportation come to grief, but southern white persecution and abuse combined with the ugly Black Codes had produced new and powerful incentives for a Negro exodus while removal of the shackles of slavery cleared the way for emigration.

The response of the Republican Congress to this situation was the Civil Rights Act of 1866, later incorporated into the Fourteenth Amendment. Undoubtedly part of the motivation for this legislation was a humanitarian concern for the protection of the Negro in the South, but another part of the motivation was concerned with the protection of the white man in the North. Senator Roscoe Conkling of New York, a member of the Joint Committee of Fifteen who helped draft the Civil Rights provisions, was quite explicit on this point. "Four years ago," he said in the campaign of 1866, "mobs were raised, passions were roused, votes were given, upon the idea that emancipated negroes were to burst in hordes upon the North. We then said, give them liberty and rights at the South, and they will stay there and never come into a cold climate to die. We say so still, and we want them let alone, and that is one thing that this part of the amendment is for."

Another prominent member of the Joint Committee who had a right to speak authoritatively of the meaning of its racial policy was George Boutwell of Massachusetts. Addressing his colleagues in 1866 Boutwell said:

> I bid the people, the working people of the North, the men who are struggling for subsistence, to beware of the day when the southern freedmen shall swarm over the borders in quest of those rights which should be secured to them in their native states. A just policy on our part leaves the black man in the South where he will soon become prosperous and happy. An unjust policy [in the South] forces him from home and into those states where his rights will be protected, to the injury of the black man and the white man both of the North and the South. Justice and expediency are united in indissoluble bonds, and the men of the North cannot be unjust to the former slaves without themselves suffering the bitter penalty of transgression.

The "bitter penalty" to which Boutwell referred was not the pangs of a Puritan conscience. It was an invasion of southern Negroes. "Justice and expediency" were, in the words of a more famous statesman [Daniel Webster] of Massachusetts, "one and inseparable."

The author and sponsor of the Civil Rights Act of 1866 was Senator Lyman Trumbull, the same man who had in 1858 described the Republicans as "the white man's party," and in 1862 had declared that "our people want nothing to do with the negro." He had nevertheless fought for the Freedman's Bureau and civil rights in the South. Trumbull's bill was passed and after Johnson's veto was repassed by an overwhelming majority. Limited in application, the Civil Rights Act did not confer political rights or the franchise on the freedmen.

The Fourteenth Amendment, which followed, was also equivocal on racial questions and freedmen's rights. Rejecting Senator [Charles] Sumner's plea for a guarantee of Negro suffrage, Congress left that decision up to the southern states. It also left northern states free to continue the disfranchisement of Negroes, but it exempted them from the penalties inflicted on the southern states for the same decision. The real concern of the franchise provisions of the Fourteenth Amendment was not with justice to the Negro but with justice to the North. The rebel states stood to gain some twelve seats in the House if all Negroes were counted as a basis of representation and to have about eighteen fewer seats if none were counted. The amendment fixed apportionment of representation according to enfranchisement.

There was a great deal of justice and sound wisdom in the amendment, and not only in the first section conferring citizenship and protecting rights, but in the other three sections as well. No sensible person could contend that the rebel states should be rewarded and the loyal states penalized in apportionment of representation by the abolition of slavery and the counting of voteless freedmen. That simply made no sense. Nor were there many in the North at least who could object to the temporary disqualification for office and ballot of such southern officeholders of the old regime as were described in the third section. The fourth section asserting the validity of the national debt and voiding the Confederate debts was obviously necessary. . . .

A Sorry Performance

After two years of stalling, of endless committee work and compromise, the First Reconstruction Act was finally adopted in the eleventh hour of the expiring Thirty-ninth Congress [on March 2, 1867]. Only after this momentous bill was passed was it realized that it had been drastically changed at the last moment by amendments that had not been referred to or considered by committees and that had been adopted without debate in the House and virtually without debate in the Senate. In a panicky spirit of urgency men who were ordinarily clearheaded yielded their better judgment to the demand for anything-is-better-than-nothing. Few of them liked what they got and fewer still understood the implications and the meaning of what they had done. Even John Sherman, who gave his name to the bill, was so badly confused and misled on its effect that he underestimated by some 90 per cent the number who would be disqualified from office and disfranchised. And this was one of the key provisions of the bill. It was, on the whole, a sorry performance and was far from doing justice to the intelligence and statesmanship and responsi-

276

bility of the men who shaped and passed the measure.

One thing was at least clear, despite the charges of the southern enemies and the claims of the northern friends of the act to the contrary. It was not primarily devised for the protection of Negro rights and the provision of Negro equality. Its primary purpose, however awkwardly and poorly implemented, was to put the southern states under the control of men loyal to the Union or men the Republicans thought they could trust to control those states for their purposes. So far as the Negro's future was concerned, the votes of the Congress that adopted the Reconstruction Act speak for themselves. Those votes had turned down [Thaddeus] Stevens' proposal to assure an economic foundation for Negro equality and Sumner's resolutions to give the Negro equal opportunity in schools and in homesteads and full civil rights. As for the Negro franchise, its provisions, like those for civil rights, were limited. The Negro franchise was devised for the passage of the Fourteenth Amendment and setting up the new southern state constitutions. But disfranchisement by educational and property qualifications was left an option, and escape from the whole scheme was left open by permitting the choice of military rule. No guarantee of proportional representation for the Negro population was contemplated and no assurance was provided for Negro officeholding.

A sudden shift from defiance to acquiescence took place in the South with the passage of the Reconstruction Act of March 2, 1867. How deep the change ran it would be hard to say. The evidence of it comes largely from public announcements of the press and conservative leaders, and on the negative side from the silence of the voices of defiance. The mood of submission and acquiescence was experimental, tentative, and precarious at best. It cannot be said to have predominated longer than seven months, from spring to autumn of 1867. That brief period was crucial for the future of the South and the Negro in the long agony of Reconstruction.

Southerners watched intently the forthcoming state elections in the North in October. They were expected to reflect northern reactions to radical Reconstruction and especially to the issue of Negro suffrage. There was much earnest speculation in the South. "It may be," said the Charleston *Mercury*, "that Congress but represents the feelings of its constituents, that it is but the moderate mouthpiece of incensed Northern opinion. It may be that measures harsher than any . . . that confiscation, incarceration, banishment may brood over us in turn! But all these things will not change our earnest belief—that *there will be a revulsion of popular feeling in the North.*"

Hopes were aroused first by the elections in Connecticut on April 1, less than a month after the passage of the Reconstruction

Racism Overpowered Idealism

In this extract from his book Retreat from Reconstruction, *Professor William Gillette of Rutgers University argues that northern dedication to racial equality was largely lip service. When Radical Reconstructionists failed to achieve their overly idealistic goals, Gillette concludes, they rapidly lost the support of their northern constituencies.*

The essential elements of retreat from reconstruction were to be found in the very achievement of reconstruction reform. . . . Most northerners during reconstruction were not pro-Negro but pro-Republican. Indeed, the hatred and fear of the Negro were only temporarily mitigated and subordinated by a greater fear: that of the Democrats' success and southern supremacy. During reconstruction, equal rights were mentioned in party platforms, laws, constitutions, and declarations of principle, but they hardly existed in fact. Racist or separatist customs remained stronger than so-called color-blind laws. And Republicans readily reassured whites that the "imaginary horrors of social equality" were merely Democratic propaganda, for as the Washington *National Republican* explained, the party wanted only "equality before the law, nor more nor less." Such changes as existed were concerned more with the forms, even the fictions, of freedom than with its sources and uses. As a consequence, reconstruction was sometimes paternal, but almost never brotherly.

When it did not produce all the results that had been intended— the conversion overnight of recently freed slaves into established citizens, the elimination of prejudice and violence, the establishment of peace, fair play, and good government—defection began. High morale and firm belief gave way precipitously to defeatism, cynicism, and laissez-faire, which only indicated how formidable, indeed intractable, were the obstacles that had to be grappled with and how ephemeral those idealistic impulses had been.

Act. The Democrats won in almost all quarters. The radical [New York] *Independent* taunted the North for hypocrisy. "Republicans in all the great states, North and West, are in a false position on this question," it said. "In Congress they are for impartial suffrage; at home they are against it." In only six states outside the South were Negroes permitted to vote, and in none with appreciable Negro population. The *Independent* thought that "it ought to bring a blush to every white cheek in the loyal North to reflect that the political equality of American citizens is likely to be sooner achieved in Mississippi than in Illinois—sooner on the plantation of Jefferson Davis than around the grave of Abraham Lincoln!" Election returns in October seemed to confirm this. Republican majorities were reduced throughout the North. In the New England states and in Nebraska and Iowa they were sharply reduced, and in New York, New Jersey, and Maryland the party of Reconstruction went down to defeat. Democrats scored striking victories in Pennsylvania and Ohio. In Ohio Republicans narrowly elected the governor by 8,000 votes but overwhelmed a Negro suffrage amendment by 40,000. In every state where the voters expressed themselves on the Negro suffrage issue they turned it down. . . .

Hypocrisy

The standard southern reply to northern demands [for black suffrage] was the endlessly reiterated charge of hypocrisy. Northern radicals, as a Memphis conservative put it, were "seeking to fasten what they themselves repudiate with loathing upon the unfortunate people of the South." And he pointed to the succession of northern states that had voted on and defeated Negro suffrage. A Raleigh editor ridiculed Republicans of the Pennsylvania legislature who voted 29 to 13 against the franchise for Negroes. "This is a direct confession, by Northern Radicals," he added, "that they refuse to grant in Pennsylvania the *'justice'* they would enforce on the South. . . . And this is Radical meanness and hypocrisy—this their love for the negro.

There was little in the Republican presidential campaign of 1868 to confute the southern charge of hypocrisy. The Chicago platform of May on which General [Ulysses S.] Grant was nominated contained as its second section this formulation of the double standard of racial morality: "The guaranty by Congress of equal suffrage to all loyal men at the South was demanded by every consideration of public safety, of gratitude, and of justice, and must be maintained; while the question of suffrage in all the loyal [i.e., northern] States properly belongs to the people of those States." Thus Negro *dis*franchisement was assured in the North along with enfranchisement in the South. No direct mention of the Negro was made in the platform, nor was there mention of schools or homesteads for freedmen. Neither Grant nor his running mate Schuyler Colfax was known for any personal commitment to Negro rights, and Republican campaign speeches in the North generally avoided the issue of Negro suffrage.

Congress acted to readmit seven of the reconstructed states to the Union in time for them to vote in the presidential election and contribute to the Republican majority. In attaching conditions to readmission, however, Congress deliberately refrained from specifying state laws protecting Negroes against discrimination in jury duty, officeholding, education, intermarriage, and a wide range of political and civil rights. By a vote of 30 to 5 the Senate defeated a bill attaching to the admission of Arkansas the condition that "no person on account of race or color shall be excluded from the benefits of education, or be deprived of an equal share of the moneys or other funds created or used by public authority to promote education. . . ."

Not until the election of 1868 was safely behind them did the Republicans come forward with proposals of national action on Negro suffrage that were to result in the Fifteenth Amendment. They were extremely sensitive to northern opposition to enfranchisement. By 1869 only seven northern states had voluntarily acted to permit the Negro to vote [five states granted black suffrage before the Civil War], and no state with a substantial Negro population outside the South had done so. Except for Minnesota and Iowa, which had only a handful of Negroes, Nebraska, which entered the Union with Negro suffrage as a congressional requirement, and Wisconsin by decision of her Supreme Court, every postwar effort to enfranchise the Negro in northern states had gone down to defeat.

As a consequence moderates and conservatives among Republicans took over and dominated the framing of the Fifteenth Amendment and very strongly left their imprint on the measure. . . . The issue lay between the moderates and the radicals. The former wanted a limited, negative amendment that would not confer suffrage on the freedmen, would not guarantee the franchise and take positive steps to protect it, but would merely prohibit its denial on the grounds of race and previous condition. The radicals demanded positive and firm guarantees, federal protection, and national control of suffrage. They would take away state control, North as well as South. They fully anticipated and warned of all the elaborate devices that states might resort to—and eventually did resort to—in order to disfranchise the Negro without violating the proposed amendment. These included such methods—later made famous—as the literacy and property tests, the understanding clause, the poll tax, as well as elaborate and difficult registration tricks and handicaps. But safeguards against them were all rejected by the moderates. Only four votes could be mustered for a bill to guarantee equal suffrage to all states, North as well as South. "This [Fifteenth] amendment," said its moderate proponent Oliver P. Morton, "leaves the whole power in the State as it exists, now, except that colored men shall not be disfranchised for the three reasons of race, color, or previous condition of slavery." And he added significantly, "They may, perhaps, require property or educational tests." Such tests were already in existence in Massachusetts and other northern states, and the debate made it perfectly apparent what might be expected to happen later in the South.

It was little wonder that southern Republicans, already faced with aggression against Negro voters and terribly apprehensive about the future, were intensely disappointed and unhappy about the shape the debate was taking. One of their keenest disappointments was the rejection of a clause prohibiting denial or abridgment of the right of officeholding on the ground of race. It is also not surprising that southern white conservatives, in view of these developments, were on the whole fairly relaxed about the proposed Fifteenth Amendment. The shrewder of them in fact began to wonder if the whole thing were concerned mainly, not with the Reconstruction of the South, but with maneuvers of internal politics in the northern states. After all, the Negroes were already fully enfranchised and voting regularly and solidly in all the southern states.

Motivating Factors

Were there other motives behind the Fifteenth Amendment? The evidence is somewhat inferential, but a recent study has drawn attention to the significance of the closely divided vote in such states as Indiana, Ohio, Connecticut, New York, and Pennsylvania. The Negro population of these states was small, of course, but so closely was the white electorate in them divided between the two major parties that a small Negro vote could often make the difference between victory and defeat. It was assumed, of course, that this potential Negro vote would be reliably Republican. Enfranchisement by state action had been defeated in those states, and federal action seemed the only way. There is no doubt that there was idealistic support for Negro enfranchisement, especially among antislavery people in the North. But it was not the antislavery idealists who shaped the Fifteenth Amendment and guided it through Congress. The effective leaders of legislative action were moderates with practical political considerations in mind—particularly that thin margin of difference in partisan voting strength in certain northern states. They had their way, and they relentlessly voted down all measures of the sort the idealists such as Senator Sumner were demanding. For successful adoption the amendment required ratification by twenty-eight states. Ratification would therefore have been impossible without support from the southern states, and an essential part of that had to come by requiring ratification as a condition of readmission of Virginia, and perhaps of Mississippi and Georgia as well.

The Fifteenth Amendment has often been read as evidence of renewed notice to the South of the North's firmness of purpose, as proof of its determination not to be cheated of its idealistic war aims, as a solemn rededication to those aims. Read more carefully, however, the Fifteenth Amendment reveals more deviousness than clarity of purpose, more partisan needs than idealistic aims, more timidity than boldness.

Signals of faltering purpose in the North such as the Fifteenth Amendment and state elections in 1867 were not lost on the South. They were carefully weighed for their implications for the strategy of resistance. The movement of counter Reconstruction was already well under way by the time the amendment was ratified in March, 1870, and in that year it took on new life in several quarters. Fundamentally it was a terroristic campaign of underground organizations, the Ku Klux Klan and several similar ones, for the intimidation of Republican voters and officials, the overthrow of their power, and the destruction of their organization. Terrorists used violence of all kinds, including murder by mob, by drowning, by torch; they whipped, they tortured, they maimed, they mutilated. It became perfectly clear that federal intervention of a determined sort was the only means of suppressing the movement and protecting the freedmen in their civil and political rights.

To meet this situation Congress passed the Enforcement Act of May 30, 1870, and followed it with the Second Enforcement Act and the Ku Klux Klan Act of 1871. These acts on the face of it would seem to have provided full and adequate machinery for the enforcement of the Fifteenth Amendment and the protection of the Negro and white Republican voters. They authorized the President to call out the Army and Navy and suspend the writ of habeas corpus; they empowered federal troops to implement court orders; and they reserved to the federal courts exclusive jurisdiction in all suffrage cases. The enforcement acts have gone down in history with the stereotypes "infamous" and "tyranical" tagged to them. As a matter of fact they were consistent with tradition and with democratic principle. Surviving remnants of them were invoked to authorize federal intervention at Little Rock in 1957 and at Oxford, Mississippi, in 1962. They are echoed in the Civil Rights Acts of 1957 and 1960, and they are surpassed in the powers conferred by the Civil Rights Act of 1964 and the Voting Rights Act of 1965.

Surely this impressive display of federal power and determination backed by gleaming steel and judicial majesty might be assumed to have been enough to bring the South to its senses and dispel forever the fantasies of southern intransigents. And in fact historians have in the main endorsed the assumption that the power of the Klan was broken by the impact of the so-called Force bills.

The truth is that while the Klan was nominally dissolved the campaign of violence, terror, and intimidation went forward save temporarily in places where federal power was displayed and so long as it was sustained. For all the efforts of the Department of Justice the deterioration of the freedman's status and the curtailment and denial of his suffrage continued steadily and rapidly. Federal enforcement officials met with impediments of all sorts. A close study of their efforts reveals that "In virtually every Southern state . . . federal deputy marshals, supervisors of elections, or soldiers were arrested by local law enforcement officers on charges ranging from false arrest or assault and battery to murder."

The obvious course for the avoidance of local passions was to remove cases to federal courts for trial, as provided under a section of the First Enforcement Act. But in practice this turned out to be "exceedingly difficult." And the effort to find juries that would convict proved often to be all but impossible, however carefully they were chosen, and with whatever admixture of color. The most overwhelming evidence of guilt proved unavailing at times. Key witnesses under intimidation simply refused to testify, and those that did were known to meet with terrible reprisals. The law authorized the organization of the *posse comitatus* and the use of troops to protect juries and witnesses. But in practice the local recruits were reluctant or unreliable, and federal troops were few and remote and slow to come, and the request for them was wrapped in endless red tape and bureaucratic frustration.

Cutting Corners

All these impediments to justice might have been overcome had sufficient money been made available by Congress. And right at this crucial point once again the northern will and purpose flagged and failed the cause they professed to sustain. It is quite clear where the blame lies. Under the new laws the cost of maintaining courts in the most affected districts of the South soared tremendously, quadrupled in some. Yet Congress starved the courts from the start, providing only about 1,000,000 dollars a year—far less than was required. The Attorney General had to cut corners, urge economy, and in 1873 instruct district attorneys to prosecute no case "unless the public interest imperatively demands it." An antiquated judicial structure proved wholly inadequate to handle the extra burden and clear their dockets. "If it takes a court over one month to try five offenders," asked the Attorney General concerning 420 indictments in South Carolina, "how long will it take to try four hundred, already indicted, and many hundreds more who deserve to be indicted?" He thought it "obvious that the attempt to bring to justice even a small portion of the guilty in that state must fail" under the circumstances. Quite apart from the inadequacy and inefficiency of the judicial structure, it is of significance that a majority of the Department of Justice officers in the South at this time, despite the carpetbagger infusion, were southern-born. A study by Everette Swinney concludes that "Some marshals and district attorneys were either sensitive to Southern public opinion or in substantial agreement with it.". . .

There is also sufficient evidence in existence to raise a question about how much the Enforcement Acts were intended for application in the policing of elections in the South all along, as against their possible application in other quarters of the Union. As it turned out, nearly half of the cost of policing was applied to elections of New York City, where Democratic bosses gave the opposition much trouble. Actually the bulk of federal expenditures under the Enforcement Acts was made in the North, which leads one student [Robert A. Horn] to conclude that their primary object from the start was not the distraught South under Reconstruction, but the urban strongholds of the Democrats in the North. Once again, as with the purposes behind the Fifteenth Amendment, one is left to wonder how much radical Reconstruction was really concerned with the South and how much with the party needs of the Republicans in the North.

Finally, to take a longer view, it is only fair to allow that if ambiguous and partisan motives in the writing and enforcement of Reconstruction laws proved to be the seeds of failure in American race policy for earlier generations, those same laws and constitutional amendments eventually acquired a wholly different significance for the race policy of a later generation. The laws outlasted the ambiguities of their origins.

For Discussion

Chapter One

1. What reasons does Abraham Lincoln give to support his argument that reconstruction is an executive function? Does the fact that his proclamation is a wartime measure influence his reasoning? Use information from the viewpoint to support your answer.
2. Why do you suppose Lincoln leaves open the possibility that other plans for reconstruction might be acceptable? Judging from Henry Winter Davis's manifesto, what is Davis's opinion about Lincoln's intent not to be held to only one plan of reconstruction?
3. Suppose the initial secession of the southern states had not been followed by a civil war. Might this have changed the argument of the Joint Committee on Reconstruction that the South had been a separate nation? Explain.
4. In what ways does Andrew Johnson interpret the Constitution to support his contention that the Union was never dissolved? Judging from Abraham Lincoln's proclamation, do you think he would have agreed with Johnson? Why or why not?
5. Both Ulysses S. Grant and Carl Schurz report the attitudes of southern whites toward the recently freed slaves. On what points do they agree? Which parts of their reports are based on fact, and which parts on opinion?

Chapter Two

1. What reasons does Andrew Johnson give for withholding automatic citizenship for the freed slaves? Do you think that Lyman Trumbull effectively counters Johnson's argument? Why or why not?
2. Do you agree with Trumbull that, by vetoing a bill that was supported by a two-thirds majority in Congress, Johnson violated the spirit of the Constitution? Why or why not?
3. How does John A. Bingham's proposed Fourteenth Amendment differ from the version that was ratified (see appendix)? Which version gives more power to the central government, and which gives more to the states? Do you think Andrew J. Rogers approved of the changes to the amendment? Cite examples from his viewpoint to explain why or why not?
4. Does Charles Sumner convincingly prove his contention that Andrew Johnson is "the impersonation of the tyrannical slave power"? Explain.
5. How does Sumner's rhetorical style differ from that of James Grimes? Of the two, which would you say bases his argument more on appeals to emotion, and which on facts? Whose speech do you find more convincing? Explain.

Chapter Three

1. What distinctions does William Manning Lowe make between carpet-baggers and northern migrants to the South who are not carpetbag-gers? Do you think Oliver Morton would agree with these definitions? Why or why not?
2. Do you think that the migration of a large number of U.S. citizens from one state or region to another could result today in tensions sim-ilar to those during Reconstruction? Why or why not?
3. John Brown Gordon places much of the blame for the rise of white supremacy groups on the severity of Radical Reconstruction. Do you think that these organizations would have arisen had moderate recon-struction policies prevailed? Why or why not?
4. The Federal Grand Jury states that it found that many men who pub-licly deplored the Klan were actually high-ranked members. Does the knowledge that John Brown Gordon was a Klansman affect your as-sessment of his opinions? Explain.
5. Joseph Gurney Cannon cites the claim of Southerners that violence is their response to carpetbag rule. Taking into consideration the previ-ous viewpoints in this chapter, do you feel that this claim is valid? Why or why not?
6. Do you agree with Henry Lillie Pierce's contention that the Enforce-ment Bill was introduced primarily for party reasons? Are his argu-ments convincing? Explain.

Chapter Four

1. Do Benjamin M. Boyer and Frederick Douglass express any racial or ethnic prejudices in their viewpoints concerning black suffrage? If so, do these prejudices help or hinder their arguments?
2. Thaddeus Stevens believed that distributing land to the freed slaves was more important than giving them the vote. How do you think Frederick Douglass would respond to this argument? If Stevens's plan had been implemented, what effect do you think it would have had on the outcome of Reconstruction?
3. According to Burwell C. Ritter, the original white owners of southern land have a stronger claim to it than the freed slaves who worked the land. Which group do you believe most warranted the disputed land, and why?
4. Describe the stylistic differences between the viewpoints of Henry McNeal Turner and James S. Pike. How might their respective careers as a minister and as a journalist have influenced their styles? Which do you find more effective?
5. How might Pike respond to Turner's assertion that white politicians cannot represent black constituencies any more effectively than black politicians? Is Pike wholly critical of black politicians? Explain.
6. In what ways do Henry Davis McHenry and James T. Rapier differ in their definitions of equal rights that are enforceable by the Civil Rights Act? Which forms of racial discrimination, if any, do they agree cannot be affected by law?

Chapter Five

1. What reasons does John Mercer Langston give for asserting that the Compromise of 1877 will not "prove injurious" to blacks? Do you think Langston held the same views eight years later, at the time George Washington Cable wrote his article? Explain.
2. Cable's criticism of Reconstruction is written as a white Southerner to white Southerners. Do you think his argument is effective as such? Why or why not?
3. On what points of the Exodus do Frederick Douglass and Richard Theodore Greener agree? On which do they disagree? Whose argument do you find more convincing, and why?
4. Does the fact that Frederick Douglass himself migrated to the North make his argument less credible? What distinction might Douglass make between his plight as a runaway slave and that of the Exodusters?
5. Compare the views of Joseph P. Bradley with those of Henry Davis McHenry in Chapter Four. How do their arguments against the Civil Rights Act differ? Whose argument is stronger, and why?
6. Can you tell from their viewpoints whether Joseph P. Bradley and John Marshall Harlan hold any racial or ethnic prejudices? Why or why not? Which do you think had more bearing on their decisions—prejudice or interpretations of constitutional law? Explain.

Chapter Six

1. How does William R. Brock's evaluation of the Radical Republicans differ from that of C. Vann Woodward? Which viewpoints in this book could Brock use to support his argument? Which could Woodward cite as evidence for his views?
2. Historians still debate the outcome and impact of Reconstruction. On which results of Reconstruction do William R. Brock and C. Vann Woodward agree, if any?

General Questions

1. Which common themes are prevalent in the viewpoints defending segregation? Are any of these arguments still commonly used today, and if so, which ones? Which have lost their power to convince?
2. Based on the viewpoints in this book, do you think Reconstruction was a success in any aspects? Explain. What is your general assessment of the outcome of Reconstruction?

Chronology

January 1, 1863	President Abraham Lincoln signs the Emancipation Proclamation.
December 8, 1863	Lincoln announces his Proclamation of Amnesty, which delineates his Ten Percent Plan for reconstruction.
July 2, 1864	Congress passes the Wade-Davis Bill, which is designed to give Congress control over reconstruction. Lincoln pocket-vetoes the bill two days later.
November 8, 1864	President Lincoln is reelected to a second term.
January 16, 1865	General William T. Sherman issues Special Field Order Number 15, which sets aside portions of southern land for the exclusive settlement of the freed slaves.
January 31, 1865	Congress approves the Thirteenth Amendment by a vote of 119-56.
March 3, 1865	The Bureau for Refugees, Freedmen, and Abandoned Lands, known as the Freedmen's Bureau, is established by an act of Congress.
April 9, 1865	Confederate general Robert E. Lee surrenders to Union general Ulysses S. Grant at Appomattox Courthouse.
April 11, 1865	President Lincoln delivers his last public address, in which he endorses limited black suffrage.
April 14, 1865	Lincoln is shot by John Wilkes Booth: he dies the next day. Three hours after Lincoln's death, Vice President Andrew Johnson takes the presidential oath of office.
May 29, 1865	President Johnson announces his reconstruction policy, which grants pardons to former Rebels who pledge loyalty to the Union.
July 1865	General Oliver Howard, commissioner of the Freedmen's Bureau, issues Circular 13 instructing bureau agents to set aside forty-acre tracts of land for the freedmen.
September 1865	Johnson instructs Howard to rescind Circular 13. In October, Howard announces to black settlers that their land will be returned to the original white owners.
November 24, 1865	Mississippi becomes the first state to enact a Black Code. Most of the other southern states shortly follow suit.

December 18, 1865	The Thirteenth Amendment is ratified.
April 9, 1866	Overriding a presidential veto, Congress passes the Civil Rights Act of 1866.
May 1-3, 1866	A major race riot erupts in Memphis, Tennessee; forty-six blacks and two white Unionists are killed.
June 13, 1866	Congress approves the Fourteenth Amendment.
July 24, 1866	Congress readmits Tennessee to the Union.
July 30, 1866	A race riot breaks out in New Orleans. Thirty-four blacks and three white Radicals are among the forty casualties.
November 1866	Republicans sweep the congressional elections, providing them with the majority needed to consistently override presidential vetoes.
March 2, 1867	Congress enacts two bills over Johnson's veto: the First Reconstruction Act, which divides the former Confederacy into five military districts, and the Tenure of Office Act, which prohibits the president from dismissing a cabinet officer without the Senate's consent.
March 23, 1867	The Second Reconstruction Act is passed by Congress over a presidential veto.
July 19, 1867	Congress passes the Third Reconstruction Act over a presidential veto.
August 12, 1867	President Johnson suspends War Secretary Edwin Stanton and asks the Senate to agree to his dismissal under the terms of the Tenure of Office Act.
November 5, 1867	In Montgomery, Alabama, the first reconstruction state constitutional convention begins. During the following months, all of the former Confederate states hold conventions.
January 13, 1868	The Senate declines to remove Stanton from his cabinet office.
February 21, 1868	Johnson dismisses Stanton, who refuses to leave and barricades himself in his office.
February 24, 1868	The House of Representatives votes 126-47 to impeach President Johnson.
March 11, 1868	Congress passes the Fourth Reconstruction Act.
March 13, 1868	Johnson's impeachment trial begins.
May 28, 1868	The Senate acquits President Johnson of high crimes and misdemeanors.
June 22-25, 1868	Congress readmits Alabama, Arkansas, North Carolina, South Carolina, Louisiana, Florida, and Georgia to the Union.
July 21, 1868	The Fourteenth Amendment is ratified.
September 1868	After Georgia's state government removes its black members, Congress returns Georgia to military rule.

November 3, 1868	General Ulysses S. Grant is elected president.
February 26, 1869	Congress approves the Fifteenth Amendment.
January 20, 1870	Hiram R. Revels of Mississippi is elected as the first black U.S. senator.
January 26, 1870	Congress readmits Virginia to the Union.
February 23, 1870	Mississippi is readmitted to the Union.
March 30, 1870	The Fifteenth Amendment is ratified. In the following months, several southern states pass poll-tax laws that are designed to reduce the effectiveness of the Fifteenth Amendment by restricting black voters.
	Texas is readmitted to the Union.
May 31, 1870	Congress passes the First Enforcement Act in an effort to deal with increasing violence and civil rights violations in the South.
July 15, 1870	Congress readmits Georgia to the Union for the second time.
October 25, 1870	In Eutaw, Alabama, whites fire into a Republican campaign rally, killing four blacks and wounding fifty.
February 28, 1871	Congress passes the Second Enforcement Act.
March 4, 1871	The first black representatives to the U.S. Congress take their seats. They are Joseph H. Rainey, Robert DeLarge, Robert Brown Elliot, Benjamin S. Turner, and Josiah T. Walls.
March 6-7, 1871	In Meridian, Mississippi, a white Republican judge and more than thirty blacks are killed during a race riot.
April 20, 1871	Congress passes the Third Enforcement Act, also called the Ku Klux Klan Act.
October 17, 1871	President Grant sends federal troops to South Carolina to put down the Ku Klux Klan.
May 22, 1872	Congress passes the Amnesty Act, which removes political disabilities from all but approximately five hundred of the most prominent former Confederates.
June 10, 1872	The Freedmen's Bureau Act is allowed to expire, and the bureau is dissolved.
November 5, 1872	In a landslide victory, President Grant is elected to a second term.
December 9, 1872	P.B.S. Pinchback of Louisiana becomes the first black governor in America when Louisiana's sitting governor is suspended due to impeachment proceedings.
April 13, 1873	On Easter Sunday, more than sixty blacks are killed by armed whites in Colfax, Louisiana.

April 14, 1873	In the Slaughterhouse Cases, the U.S. Supreme Court rules that the Fourteenth Amendment protects only those rights that derive from federal—not state—citizenship.
September 18, 1873	The failure of a major banking firm triggers the Panic of 1873, an economic depression that persists for five years.
November 4, 1874	Democrats sweep the congressional elections and gain a majority in the House of Representatives.
December 7, 1874	On December 7 and the following days, bands of armed whites kill an estimated three hundred blacks in Vicksburg, Mississippi.
January 5, 1875	President Grant dispatches federal troops to Vicksburg, Mississippi.
February 3, 1875	Blanche K. Bruce is elected to the U.S. Senate, bringing black representation in Congress to its peak of eight.
March 1, 1875	Congress passes the Civil Rights Act of 1875, which outlaws segregation.
March 1875	Congress fails to pass a Fourth Enforcement Bill before adjourning.
September 4-6, 1875	Thirty blacks and three whites are killed in a race riot in Clinton, Mississippi.
March 27, 1876	In *U.S. v. Cruikshank*, the U.S. Supreme Court overturns convictions under the Enforcement Acts of 1870, ruling that the federal government can only prohibit civil rights violations by the states, not by private individuals.
July 8, 1876	A race riot in Hamburg, South Carolina, results in the deaths of seven blacks.
September 20, 1876	A race riot erupts in Ellenton, South Carolina; several whites and approximately one hundred blacks are killed.
October 16, 1876	Six whites and one black die in a race riot in Cainhoy, South Carolina.
October 26, 1876	Grant sends federal troops to intervene in South Carolina.
November 7, 1876	The presidential election results in a dispute over who won.
February 26, 1877	The Compromise of 1877 secures Republican Rutherford B. Hayes's claim to the presidency in exchange for the return of home rule to the South.
April 24, 1877	Hayes withdraws the last federal troops from the South.
February 1879	The Exodus Movement begins.

October 15, 1883	The Supreme Court declares the Civil Rights Act of 1875 unconstitutional, opening the way for the passage of numerous "Jim Crow" laws.
February 8, 1894	Congress repeals the Second Enforcement Act, thereby giving the states direct control over elections and enabling the southern states to virtually disfranchise blacks without federal interference.
May 18, 1896	In *Plessy* v. *Ferguson*, the Supreme Court upholds the principle of "separate but equal" racial segregation.

Annotated Bibliography

Historical Studies

Martin Abbott, *The Freedmen's Bureau in South Carolina, 1865-1872*. Chapel Hill: University of North Carolina Press, 1967. A state history of the organization entrusted with providing emergency relief and education for southern blacks during the transition from slavery to freedom.

Richard H. Abbott, *The Republican Party and the South, 1855-1877: The First Southern Strategy*. Chapel Hill: University of North Carolina Press, 1986. A history of the efforts of the Republican Party to expand into the postwar South, even as the party stressed black rights.

Michael Les Benedict, *A Compromise of Principle: Congressional Republicans and Reconstruction, 1863-1869*. New York: Norton, 1974. Examines the divisions within the Republican Party over Reconstruction issues and concludes that the true Radicals were generally in the minority.

Michael Les Benedict, *The Impeachment and Trial of Andrew Johnson*. New York: Norton, 1973. Evenhanded account of the only impeachment trial of a president in American history, which concludes that there were legitimate constitutional grounds for voting to convict Andrew Johnson.

Lerone Bennett, *Black Power, U.S.A.: The Human Side of Reconstruction, 1867-1877*. Chicago: Johnson Publishing, 1967. Includes memorable portraits of black politicians and activists and the positive contributions they made during Reconstruction.

George Bentley, *A History of the Freedmen's Bureau*. Philadelphia: University of Pennsylvania Press, 1955. An administrative and political history of the Freedmen's Bureau from its inception in 1865 to its demise in 1872.

Claude G. Bowers, *The Tragic Era: The Revolution After Lincoln*. Cambridge, MA: Houghton Mifflin, 1929. A dramatic, if not exactly evenhanded, account of Reconstruction that emphasizes northern corruption and resurrects the political career of President Andrew Johnson.

William R. Brock, *An American Crisis: Congress and Reconstruction, 1865-1867*. New York: St. Martin's Press, 1963. A British historian looks at American Reconstruction and wonders how a substantial majority of Republicans could be found to support "extremist" reconstruction policies.

Ronald E. Butchart, *Northern Schools, Southern Blacks, and Reconstruction: Freedmen's Education, 1862-1875.* Westport, CT: Greenwood Press, 1980. This study of northern missionaries in the South highlights the conflicting personalities and ideologies within this movement and accuses most missionaries of preaching black docility to white Southerners.

Dan Carter, *When the War Was Over: The Failure of Self-Reconstruction in the South, 1865-1867.* Baton Rouge: Louisiana State University Press, 1985. A history of postwar southern politics, economics, and society in the context of an effort to determine what went wrong with presidential reconstruction.

LaWanda Cox and John H. Cox, *Politics, Principle, and Prejudice, 1865-1866: Dilemma of Reconstruction America.* Glencoe, IL: Free Press, 1963. This thorough examination of presidential reconstruction focuses on Andrew Johnson's racial attitudes and political maneuvering.

Richard N. Current, *Those Terrible Carpetbaggers.* New York: Oxford University Press, 1988. A revisionist biographical study of ten of the most important carpetbaggers.

Richard O. Curry, ed., *Radicalism, Racism, and Party Realignment: The Border States During Reconstruction.* Baltimore: Johns Hopkins University Press, 1969. Historical essays by noted scholars on political realignment and economic reforms in the border states.

David H. Donald, *The Politics of Reconstruction, 1863-1867.* Baton Rouge: Louisiana State University Press, 1965. Examines the voting records of northern Republicans and concludes that the desire to be reelected was the primary factor in determining whether or not one was a Radical Republican on reconstruction issues.

Edmund Drago, *Black Politicians and Reconstruction in Georgia: A Splendid Failure.* Baton Rouge: Louisiana State University Press, 1982. This in-depth evaluation of black political leadership determines that the black elite in Georgia lacked sufficient skills and self-confidence for achieving lasting political success.

W. E. B. Du Bois, *Black Reconstruction in America: 1860-1880.* New York: Russell & Russell, 1935. An impassioned account of the contributions southern blacks made to political reform and social justice during Reconstruction.

William Dunning, *Reconstruction, Political and Economic, 1865-1877.* New York: Harper, 1907. For its time, a pioneering survey of Reconstruction that was highly critical of Radical rule.

Roger Fischer, *The Segregation Struggle in Louisiana, 1862-1877.* Urbana: University of Illinois Press, 1974. A study focusing on the elite "free persons of color" in New Orleans who provided the leadership in the fight against the segregation of schools and public accommodations.

Eric Foner, *Reconstruction: America's Unfinished Revolution, 1863-1877.* New York: Harper & Row, 1988. The best recent general history of this very important era in American history.

Edward Gambill, *Conservative Ordeal: Northern Democrats and Reconstruction, 1865-1868*. Ames: Iowa State University Press, 1981. Political history of a Democratic Party that was unable to shed its wartime labels of treason and defeatism, even as it succeeded in blocking elements of Radical Republicanism.

William Gillette, *Retreat from Reconstruction, 1869-1879*. Baton Rouge: Louisiana State University Press, 1979. Attributes the failure of Reconstruction to the power of the Democrats, administrative inefficiencies in Washington, racism, and a lack of commitment on the part of northern Republicans.

Thomas Holt, *Black over White: Negro Political Leadership in South Carolina During Reconstruction*. Urbana: University of Illinois Press, 1977. A study of South Carolina's black elected officials, the divisions among them, their battles with the white governors who controlled patronage, and their ultimate failure.

Harold M. Hyman, *A More Perfect Union: The Impact of the Civil War and Reconstruction on the Constitution*. New York: Knopf, 1973. Explores the effect of the Civil War and Reconstruction on the Constitution and vice versa.

Harold M. Hyman, ed. *New Frontiers of the American Reconstitution*. Urbana: University of Illinois Press, 1966. A series of interpretive essays on Reconstruction from a conference of leading historians of the period.

Gerald D. Jaynes, *Branches Without Roots: Genesis of the Black Working Class in the American South, 1862-1882*. New York: Oxford University Press, 1986. A history of the process by which southern planters and black laborers looked to the sharecropping system as a solution to their varying economic problems.

Robert Kaczorowski, *The Politics of Judicial Interpretations: The Federal Courts, Department of Justice and Civil Rights, 1866-1876*. Dobbs Ferry, NY: Oceana Publications, 1985. Examination of a revolutionary era in the history of the American Constitution when federal courts and the Justice Department fought against politically and racially motivated terrorism in the South.

Peter Kolchin, *First Freedom: The Responses of Alabama's Blacks to Emancipation and Reconstruction*. Westport, CT: Greenwood Press, 1972. A study of black migration, labor, family, religion, social structure, and awakening political consciousness in the first half-decade of Reconstruction.

J. Morgan Kousser and James M. McPherson, eds., *Region, Race, and Reconstruction: Essays in Honor of C. Vann Woodward*. New York: Oxford University Press, 1982. A wide-ranging series of essays on important aspects of Reconstruction history.

Peggy Lamson, *The Glorious Failure: Black Congressman Robert Brown Elliott and the Reconstruction in South Carolina*. New York: Norton, 1973. A sympathetic portrait of a black politician who had to work in an atmosphere of increasing white hostility.

Leon Litwack, *Been in the Storm So Long: The Aftermath of Slavery*. New

York: Knopf, 1979. A monumental chronicle of the response of ex-slaves to freedom, whether that freedom was achieved by Union troops or by independent action on the part of the former slaves.

Peyton McCrary, *Abraham Lincoln and Reconstruction: The Louisiana Experiment*. Princeton, NJ: Princeton University Press, 1978. A study of Lincoln's policy of reconstruction in action in northern-occupied Louisiana before the end of the Civil War.

William McFeely, *Yankee Stepfather: General O. O. Howard and the Freedmen*. New Haven, CT: Yale University Press, 1968. This indictment of the Freedmen's Bureau argues that the bureau was a liability to ex-slaves because General Howard permitted it to be used by President Andrew Johnson to placate southern whites.

Eric McKitrick, *Andrew Johnson and Reconstruction*. Chicago: University of Chicago Press, 1960. A study of a president who proved to be equally inept at wielding presidential power and achieving North-South reconciliation.

James M. McPherson, *Ordeal by Fire: The Civil War and Reconstruction*. New York: Knopf, 1982. A very readable, evenhanded general history of the entire tumultuous period of the Civil War and Reconstruction.

James M. McPherson, *The Struggle for Equality: Abolitionists and the Negro in the Civil War and Reconstruction*. Princeton, NJ: Princeton University Press, 1964. A study of major and minor figures as they debated emancipation and what should be their work following emancipation.

William F. Messner, *Freedmen and the Ideology of Free Labor: Louisiana 1862-1865*. Lafayette: University of Southwestern Louisiana, 1978. A history of the work of Union military officials who managed race relations at a time when blacks in Louisiana were no longer willing to be enslaved but were not yet free.

James Mohr, ed., *Radical Republicans in the North: State Politics During Reconstruction*. Baltimore: Johns Hopkins University Press, 1976. Essays on the Radical Republicans and their dealings with the race issue, black civil rights, Republican factionalism, and the reemergence of nativism in the northern states.

David Montgomery, *Beyond Equality: Labor and the Radical Republicans, 1862-1872*. New York: Knopf, 1967. A history of the labor union movement and its impact on the Republican Party during the Civil War and Reconstruction.

Robert C. Morris, *Reading, 'Riting, and Reconstruction: The Education of Freedmen in the South, 1861-1870*. Chicago: University of Chicago Press, 1981. A survey of religious and benevolent associations and the educational tools they used in their efforts at educating the ex-slaves.

Daniel A. Novack, *The Wheel of Servitude: Black Forced Labor After Slavery*. Lexington: University Press of Kentucky, 1978. A brief survey of laws and court decisions regarding black involuntary servitude after the Civil War.

Walter T. K. Nugent, *Money and American Society, 1865-1880*. New York: Norton, 1968. An attempt to connect the "money question" to larger political and economic issues of the Reconstruction era by examining the debates over gold, silver, and greenbacks.

Otto Olsen, ed., *Reconstruction and Redemption in the South*. Baton Rouge: Louisiana State University Press, 1980. Essays that emphasize that Reconstruction failed because support for the Republican Party and its agenda was shaky in the South from the outset.

Claude Oubre, *Forty Acres and a Mule: The Freedmen's Bureau and Black Landownership*. Baton Rouge: Louisiana State University Press, 1978. A history of black landownership and the operations of the Freedmen's Bureau and the Homestead Act in various southern states.

Nell Irvin Painter, *Exodusters: Black Migration to Kansas After Reconstruction*. New York: Knopf, 1977. A study of the causes as well as the results of the Exodus movement.

Michael Perman, *Reunion Without Compromise: The South and Reconstruction, 1865-1868*. New York: Cambridge University Press, 1973. An analysis of the strategy and tactics of the anti-secessionist white moderates who took control of many southern governments after 1865.

Michael Perman, *The Road to Redemption: Southern Politics 1869-1879*. Chapel Hill: University of North Carolina Press, 1984. An impressive political history that traces the rise of the white "redeemers" and the demise of Reconstruction.

Keith I. Polakoff, *The Politics of Inertia: The Election of 1876 and the End of Reconstruction*. Baton Rouge: Louisiana State University Press, 1973. A narrative history of party politics during an era of decentralized political parties, of the Hayes-Tilden presidential contest, and of the complicated constitutional crisis that followed it.

Lawrence N. Powell, *New Masters: Northern Planters During the Civil War and Reconstruction*. New Haven, CT: Yale University Press, 1980. Expansive study of 524 Yankee cotton planters in six states of the Lower South and their efforts to get rich at the expense of the defeated southern whites and the black freedmen.

Howard Rabinowitz, *Race Relations in the Urban South, 1865-1890*. New York: Oxford University Press, 1978. Examines changes in race relations from the piecemeal postwar ventures in integration to the pervasive post-Reconstruction efforts to construct a segregated society in the urban South.

George Rable, *But There Was No Peace: The Role of Violence in the Politics of Reconstruction*. Athens: University of Georgia Press, 1984. A history of the inexorable movement from individual acts of violence to organized political violence during Reconstruction.

Peter Rachleff, *Black Labor in the South: Richmond, Virginia, 1865-1890*. Philadelphia: Temple University Press, 1984. A detailed history of the organized political and labor activities of blacks as well as of the attempts at interracial worker alliances in the former capital of the

Confederacy.

Roger L. Ransom and Richard Sutch, *One Kind of Freedom: The Economic Consequences of Emancipation*. New York: Cambridge University Press, 1977. A study of the evolution of southern agriculture from the slave system to the sharecropping system that also denied blacks their full freedom and opportunities or economic rewards.

James L. Roark, *Masters Without Slaves: Southern Planters in the Civil War and Reconstruction*. New York: Norton, 1977. Examines the process by which masters ceased to be masters and assesses their coming to terms with their new status through an analysis of the records of some 160 planter families.

Willie Lee Rose, *Rehearsal for Reconstruction: The Port Royal Experiment*. Indianapolis: Bobbs-Merrill, 1964. A fascinating account of a wartime experiment in land reform in the Sea Islands of South Carolina.

James E. Sefton, *Andrew Johnson and the Uses of Constitutional Power*. Boston: Little, Brown, 1980. An examination of Johnson's presidency that views the president less as an incorrigible racist than as a prisoner of his principles, his politics, and his often difficult personality.

James E. Sefton, *The United States Army and Reconstruction, 1865-1877*. Baton Rouge: Louisiana State University Press, 1967. A history of an occupying army as it tried to keep order and enforce black civil rights via the constitutional amendments of the Reconstruction era.

Terry L. Seip, *The South Returns to Congress: Men, Economic Measures and Intersectional Relationships, 1868-1879*. Baton Rouge: Louisiana State University Press, 1983. A quantitative analysis of the 251 Republicans and Democrats who represented the South without always being able to control the fate of the South during Reconstruction.

Jerrell H. Shofner, *Nor Is It Over Yet: Florida in the Era of Reconstruction, 1863-1877*. Gainesville: University Press of Florida, 1974. A proradical history of Reconstruction in Florida that looks beyond "evil" carpetbaggers and scalawags to find genuine idealism but also discovers that black Floridians made few lasting gains.

Gene Smith, *High Crimes and Misdemeanors*. New York: William Morrow, 1977. A popular history of the impeachment and trial of President Andrew Johnson.

Kenneth Stampp, *The Era of Reconstruction, 1865-1877*. New York: Knopf, 1965. A still serviceable overview of the important issues, problems, personalities, and debates of Reconstruction.

Mark Summers, *Railroads, Reconstruction, and the Gospel of Prosperity: Aid Under the Radical Republicans, 1865-1877*. Princeton, NJ: Princeton University Press, 1984. A history of the essentially futile attempt made by Radical Republicans to build a New South and a biracial Republican Party through federal aid to railroad construction in the post–Civil War South.

Hans L. Trefousse, *Impeachment of a President: Andrew Johnson, the Blacks, and Reconstruction.* Knoxville: University of Tennessee Press, 1975. A revisionist history of the political impeachment of a president who stood in the way of the Radical Republican agenda.

Hans L. Trefousse, *The Radical Republicans: Lincoln's Vanguard for Racial Justice.* New York: Knopf, 1969. A study of those radicals who helped found the Republican Party and kept the party committed to full emancipation and genuine racial justice.

Allen W. Trelease, *White Terror: The Ku Klux Klan Conspiracy and Southern Reconstruction.* New York: Harper & Row, 1971. This state-by-state history argues that the success of the Klan came from the willingness of white Southerners to close ranks behind it in support of white supremacy and as a counterrevolutionary reaction to the Republican Party.

William P. Vaughan, *Schools for All: The Blacks and Public Education in the South, 1865-1877.* Lexington: University Press of Kentucky, 1974. A study of the extensive efforts to use the schoolhouse to ensure that emancipation was achieved in more than name only.

Sarah W. Wiggins, *The Scalawag in Alabama Politics, 1865-1881.* University: University of Alabama Press, 1977. A history that discovers that most Alabama scalawags were educated and propertied political opportunists rather than inexperienced small farmers from the northern counties of the state.

Joel Williamson, *After Slavery: The Negro in South Carolina During Reconstruction, 1861-1877.* Chapel Hill: University of North Carolina Press, 1965. For its time, a revisionist history that argues that South Carolina blacks made significant economic and political progress on their own until the Democrats returned to power in the state.

Forrest G. Wood, *Black Scare: The Racist Response to Emancipation and Reconstruction.* Berkeley: University of California Press, 1968. An examination of racist ideologies and their impact on various political and economic issues during what the author believes was the first white backlash in American history.

C. Vann Woodward, *Reunion and Reaction: The Compromise of 1877 and the End of Reconstruction.* Garden City, NY: Doubleday, 1956. A dramatic account of deal making in Washington that kept the presidency in Republican hands but ensured that the Republican Party would no longer be the protector of blacks in the South.

Primary Sources and Document Collections

Sidney Andrews, *The South Since the War.* Boston: Ticknor and Fields, 1866. Observations of a northern reporter who traveled through the post-war South in 1865.

Herbert Aptheker, ed., *A Documentary History of the Negro People in the United States.* Vol. 2. New York: Citadel Press, 1951. Thorough anthology that examines the effects of Reconstruction on northern as well as southern blacks.

Ira Berlin et al., eds., *Freedom: A Documentary History of Emancipation, 1861-1867*. New York: Cambridge University Press, 1982- . Ongoing, extensive documentary survey of emancipation and the transition to freedom.

Powell Clayton, *Aftermath of the Civil War in Arkansas*. New York: Neale Publishing, 1915. The reminiscences of a Union officer who remained in Arkansas after the war, became the governor of Arkansas (1868-1871, and fought to expose the Ku Klux Klan in his state.

LaWanda Cox and John H. Cox, eds., *Reconstruction, the Negro, and the New South*. Columbia: University of South Carolina Press, 1973. A collection of primary sources concentrating on those Reconstruction issues that concerned the freed slaves.

Richard N. Current, ed., *Reconstruction, 1865-1877*. Englewood Cliffs, NJ: Prentice-Hall, 1965. A comprehensive sourcebook of primary documents that presents all sides of the controversies surrounding Reconstruction.

Walter L. Fleming, *Documentary History of Reconstruction*. 2 vols. Gloucester, MA: Peter Smith, 1960. Reprint of the 1906 and 1907 volumes. This somewhat dated but still useful source contains many documents not found in more recent compilations.

Harold Hyman, ed., *The Radical Republicans and Reconstruction, 1861-1870*. Indianapolis: Bobbs-Merrill, 1967. A collection of important primary source material relating to the major issues of Reconstruction.

William L. Katz, ed., *Two Black Teachers During the Civil War*. New York: Arno Press, 1969. Reprints of documents concerning Mary S. Peake and Charlotte Forten, two black women from the North who taught in southern freedmen's schools at the start of Reconstruction.

Edward King, *The Great South*. Hartford, CT: American Publishing, 1875. Essays of a northern journalist who toured the South during Reconstruction.

Annjennette Sophie McFarlin, ed., *Black Congressional Reconstruction Orators and their Orations, 1869-1879*. Metuchen, NJ: Scarecrow Press, 1976. Seventeen black politicians of the Reconstruction era are highlighted in this anthology of speeches.

Edward McPerson, *The Political History of the United States of America During the Period of Reconstruction*. 2nd ed. New York: Negro Universities Press, 1969. Reprint of the 1875 collection of political documents concerning Reconstruction.

John Hammond Moore, ed., *The Juhl Letters to the Charleston Courier: A View of the South, 1865-1871*. Athens: University of Georgia Press, 1974. Julius J. Fleming's collected articles provide a white Southerner's view of events during Reconstruction.

Charles Nordhoff, *The Cotton States in the Spring and Summer of 1875*. New York: Burt Franklin, 1876. State-by-state examination of how the South fared under Radical Reconstruction.

James S. Pike, *The Prostrate State: South Carolina Under Negro Government*.

New York: D. Appleton, 1874. A highly partisan account of South Carolina's state government during Reconstruction that condemns northern reformers and black politicians alike.

The Reconstruction Amendments' Debates: The Legislative History and Contemporary Debates in Congress on the Thirteenth, Fourteenth and Fifteenth Amendments. Richmond: The Virginia Commission on Constitutional Government, 1967. An exhaustive collection of congressional debates and documents regarding the creation of the Reconstruction amendments.

Dorothy Sterling, ed., *The Trouble They Seen: Black People Tell the Story of Reconstruction.* Garden City, NY: Doubleday, 1976. A collection of black testimony on Reconstruction.

Dorothy Sterling, ed., *We Are Your Sisters: Black Women in the Nineteenth Century.* New York: Norton, 1984. This collection of primary sources captures the reaction of northern and southern black women to freedom, reconstruction, and the Exodus movement.

Brenda Stevenson, ed., *The Journals of Charlotte Forten Grimké.* New York: Oxford University Press, 1988. Emancipation and Reconstruction from the viewpoint of a free-born black woman.

Emma Lou Thornbrough, ed., *Black Reconstructionists.* Englewood Cliffs, NJ: Prentice-Hall, 1972. This anthology of primary sources contains documents by black reconstructionists as well as whites' responses.

Albion W. Tourgée, *A Fool's Errand.* New York: Fords, Howard, and Hulbert, 1879. In this autobiographical novel, the author relates his experiences as a carpetbagger in North Carolina.

Hans L. Trefousse, ed., *Background for Radical Reconstruction.* Boston: Little, Brown, 1970. Contains testimony from the hearings of the Joint Committee on Reconstruction, the elect Committee on the Memphis riots and massacres, and the Select Committee on the New Orleans riots.

John Wallace, *Carpet-Bag Rule in Florida.* Jacksonville, FL: Da Costa Publishing, 1888. Firsthand account of the experiences of a former slave and ex-Union soldier during Reconstruction in Florida.

T. Harry Williams, ed., *Hayes: The Diary of a President, 1875-1881.* New York: D. McKay, 1964. The diary of Rutherford B. Hayes provides a firsthand account of the Compromise of 1877 and the end of Reconstruction.

Harvey Wish, ed., *Reconstruction in the South, 1865-1877.* New York: Farrar, Straus, 1964. A general anthology of sources from both the North and the South.

Carter G. Woodson, ed., *Negro Orators and Their Orations.* New York: Russell & Russell, 1969. Contains speeches given by black politicians, ministers, and community leaders of the Reconstruction era.

Appendix

The Reconstruction Amendments to the U.S. Constitution

Amendment XIII

SECTION 1. Neither slavery nor involuntary servitude, except as a punishment for crime whereof the party shall have been duly convicted, shall exist within the United States, or any place subject to their jurisdiction.

SECTION 2. Congress shall have power to enforce this article by appropriate legislation.

Amendment XIV

SECTION 1. All persons born or naturalized in the United States, and subject to the jurisdiction thereof, are citizens of the United States and of the State wherein they reside. No State shall make or enforce any law which shall abridge the privileges or immunities of citizens of the United States; nor shall any State deprive any person of life, liberty, or property, without due process of law; nor deny to any person within its jurisdiction the equal protection of the laws.

SECTION 2. Representatives shall be apportioned among the several States according to their respective numbers, counting the whole number of persons in each State, excluding Indians not taxed. But when the right to vote at any election for the choice of electors for President and Vice President of the United States, representatives in Congress, the executive and judicial officers of a State, or the members of the legislature thereof, is denied to any of the male inhabitants of such State, being twenty-one years of age, and citizens of the United States, or in any way abridged, except for participating in rebellion, or other crime, the basis of representation therein shall be reduced in the proportion which the number of such male citizens shall bear to the whole number of male citizens twenty-one years of age in such State.

SECTION 3. No person shall be senator or representative in Congress, or elector of President and Vice President, or hold any office, civil or military, under the United States, or under any State, who having previously taken an oath, as a member of Congress, or as an officer of the United States, or as a member of any State legislature, or as an executive or judicial officer of any State, to support the Constitution of the United States, shall have engaged in insurrection or rebellion against the same, or given aid or comfort to the enemies thereof. But Congress may by a vote of two thirds of each House, remove such disability.

SECTION 4. The validity of the public debt of the United States, authorized by law, including debts incurred for payment of pensions and bounties for services in suppressing insurrection or rebellion, shall not be questioned. But neither the United States nor any State shall assume or pay any debt or obligation incurred in aid of insurrection or rebellion against the United States, or any claim for the loss or emancipation of any slave; but all such debts, obligations, and claims shall be held illegal and void.

SECTION 5. The Congress shall have the power to enforce, by appropriate legislation, the provisions of this article.

Amendment XV

SECTION 1. The right of the citizens of the United States to vote shall not be denied or abridged by the United States or by any State on account of race, color, or previous condition of servitude.

SECTION 2. The Congress shall have power to enforce this article by appropriate legislation.

Index